MznLnx

Missing Links Exam Preps

Exam Prep for

Economics Today: The Micro View

Miller, Edition

The MznLnx Exam Prep is your link from the texbook and lecture to your exams.
The MznLnx Exam Preps are unauthorized and comprehensive reviews of your textbooks.

All material provided by MznLnx and Rico Publications (c) 2010
Textbook publishers and textbook authors do not particpate in or contribute to these reviews.

MznLnx

Rico
Publications

Exam Prep for Economics Today: The Micro View
Edition
Miller

Publisher: Raymond Houge
Assistant Editor: Michael Rouger
Text and Cover Designer: Lisa Buckner
Marketing Manager: Sara Swagger
Project Manager, Editorial Production: Jerry Emerson
Art Director: Vernon Lowerui

Product Manager: Dave Mason
Editorial Assitant: Rachel Guzmanji
Pedagogy: Debra Long
Cover Image: Jim Reed/Getty Images
Text and Cover Printer: City Printing, Inc.
Compositor: Media Mix, Inc.

(c) 2010 Rico Publications
ALL RIGHTS RESERVED. No part of this work
covered by the copyright may be reproduced or
used in any form or by an means--graphic, electronic,
or mechanical, including photocopying, recording,
taping, Web distribution, information storage, and
retrieval systems, or in any other manner--without the
written permission of the publisher.

Printed in the United States
ISBN:

For more information about our products, contact us at:
Dave.Mason@RicoPublications.com

For permission to use material from this text or
product, submit a request online to:
Dave.Mason@RicoPublications.com

Contents

CHAPTER 1
The Nature of Economics — 1

CHAPTER 2
Scarcity and the World of Trade-Offs — 9

CHAPTER 3
Demand and Supply — 16

CHAPTER 4
Extensions of Demand and Supply Analysis — 24

CHAPTER 5
The Public Sector and Public Choice — 29

CHAPTER 6
Taxes, Transfers, and Public Spending — 43

CHAPTER 7
Consumer Choice — 49

CHAPTER 8
Demand and Supply Elasticity — 55

CHAPTER 9
Rents, Profits, and the Financial Environment of Business — 60

CHAPTER 10
The Firm: Cost and Output Determination — 71

CHAPTER 11
Perfect Competition — 78

CHAPTER 12
Monopoly — 85

CHAPTER 13
Monopolistic Competition — 93

CHAPTER 14
Oligopoly and Strategic Behavior — 99

CHAPTER 15
Regulation and Antitrust Policy in a Globalized Economy — 108

CHAPTER 16
The Labor Market: Demand, Supply, and Outsourcing — 118

CHAPTER 17
Union and Labor Market Monopoly Power — 126

CHAPTER 18
Income, Poverty, and Health Care — 135

CHAPTER 19
Environmental Economics — 145

CHAPTER 20
Comparative Advantage and the Open Economy — 148

Contents (Cont.)

CHAPTER 21
  Exchange Rates and the Balance of Payments   155
ANSWER KEY   164

TO THE STUDENT

COMPREHENSIVE

The *MznLnx* Exam Prep series is designed to help you pass your exams. Editors at MznLnx review your textbooks and then prepare these practice exams to help you master the textbook material. Unlike study guides, workbooks, and practice tests provided by the texbook publisher and textbook authors, *MznLnx* gives you **all** of the material in each chapter in exam form, not just samples, so you can be sure to nail your exam.

MECHANICAL

The MznLnx Exam Prep series creates exams that will help you learn the subject matter as well as test you on your understanding. Each question is designed to help you master the concept. Just working through the exams, you gain an understanding of the subject--its a simple mechanical process that produces success.

INTEGRATED STUDY GUIDE AND REVIEW

MznLnx is not just a set of exams designed to test you, its also a comprehensive review of the subject content. Each exam question is also a review of the concept, making sure that you will get the answer correct without having to go to other sources of material. You learn as you go! Its the easiest way to pass an exam.

HUMOR

Studying can be tedious and dry. MznLnx's instructional design includes moderate humor within the exam questions on occassion, to break the tedium and revitalize the brain

Chapter 1. The Nature of Economics 1

1. The _____ is the audit, evaluation, and investigative arm of the United States Congress. It is located in the Legislative branch of the United States government.

The _____ was established as the General Accounting Office by the Budget and Accounting Act of 1921 (Pub.L.

   a. 130-30 fund
   b. 100-year flood
   c. Government Accountability Office
   d. 1921 recession

2. _____, in law and economics, is a form of risk management primarily used to hedge against the risk of a contingent loss. _____ is defined as the equitable transfer of the risk of a loss, from one entity to another, in exchange for a premium, and can be thought of as a guaranteed small loss to prevent a large, possibly devastating loss. An insurer is a company selling the _____; an insured or policyholder is the person or entity buying the _____.
   a. Insurance
   b. AD-IA Model
   c. ACCRA Cost of Living Index
   d. ACEA agreement

3. _____ is a specific term used in companies' financial reporting from the company-whole point of view. Because that use excludes the effects of changing ownership interest, an economic measure of _____ is necessary for financial analysis from the shareholders' point of view

_____ is defined by the Financial Accounting Standards Board, or FASB, as e;the change in equity [net assets] of a business enterprise during a period from transactions and other events and circumstances from nonowner sources. It includes all changes in equity during a period except those resulting from investments by owners and distributions to owners.e;

_____ is the sum of net income and other items that must bypass the income statement because they have not been realized, including items like an unrealized holding gain or loss from available for sale securities and foreign currency translation gains or losses.

   a. Real income
   b. Net national income
   c. Windfall gain
   d. Comprehensive income

4. A _____ is an object whose consumption increases the utility of the consumer, for which the quantity demanded exceeds the quantity supplied at zero price. _____s are usually modeled as having diminishing marginal utility. The first individual purchase has high utility; the second has less.
   a. Composite good
   b. Merit good
   c. Pie method
   d. Good

5. In economic models, the _____ time frame assumes no fixed factors of production. Firms can enter or leave the marketplace, and the cost (and availability) of land, labor, raw materials, and capital goods can be assumed to vary. In contrast, in the short-run time frame, certain factors are assumed to be fixed, because there is not sufficient time for them to change.
   a. Price/performance ratio
   b. Diseconomies of scale
   c. Productivity world
   d. Long-run

Chapter 1. The Nature of Economics

6. _____ is a common market structure where many competing producers sell products that are differentiated from one another (ie. the products are substitutes, but are not exactly alike.) Many markets are monopolistically competitive, common examples include the markets for restaurants, cereal, clothing, shoes and service industries in large cities.
   a. Mathematical economics
   b. Perfect competition
   c. Financial crisis
   d. Monopolistic competition

7. A _____ or labor union is an organization of workers who have banded together to achieve common goals in key areas and working conditions. The _____, through its leadership, bargains with the employer on behalf of union members (rank and file members) and negotiates labor contracts (Collective bargaining) with employers. This may include the negotiation of wages, work rules, complaint procedures, rules governing hiring, firing and promotion of workers, benefits, workplace safety and policies.
   a. Case-Shiller Home Price Indices
   b. Trade union
   c. Consumer goods
   d. Guaranteed investment contracts

8. A _____ refers to any type debt instrument, such as a loan, bond, mortgage that does not have a fixed rate of interest over the life of the instrument. Such debt typically uses an index or other base rate for establishing the interest rate for each relevant period. One of the most common rates to use as the basis for applying interest rates is the London Inter-bank Offered Rate, or LIBOR
   a. Disposal tax effect
   b. Moneylender
   c. Money market
   d. Floating interest rate

9. The United States federal _____ is a refundable tax credit. For tax year 2008, a claimant with one qualifying child can receive a maximum credit of $2,917. For two or more qualifying children, the maximum credit is $4,824.
   a. Earned Income Tax Credit
   b. AD-IA Model
   c. ACCRA Cost of Living Index
   d. ACEA agreement

10. The _____ is an international organization that oversees the global financial system by following the macroeconomic policies of its member countries, in particular those with an impact on exchange rates and the balance of payments. It is an organization formed to stabilize international exchange rates and facilitate development. It also offers financial and technical assistance to its members, making it an international lender of last resort.
    a. International Monetary Fund
    b. Office of Thrift Supervision
    c. ACEA agreement
    d. ACCRA Cost of Living Index

11. An _____ is a tax levied on the financial income of people, corporations, or other legal entities. Various _____ systems exist, with varying degrees of tax incidence. Income taxation can be progressive, proportional, or regressive.
    a. AD-IA Model
    b. ACCRA Cost of Living Index
    c. Income Tax
    d. ACEA agreement

12. To _____ is to impose a financial charge or other levy upon a taxpayer by a state or the functional equivalent of a state.

    _____es are also imposed by many subnational entities. _____es consist of direct _____ or indirect _____, and may be paid in money or as its labour equivalent (often but not always unpaid.)

a. 130-30 fund
b. Tax
c. 100-year flood
d. 1921 recession

13. The term _____ describes two different concepts:

- The first is a recognition of partial payment already made towards taxes due.
- The second is a state benefit paid to workers through the tax system, which has the effect of increasing (rather than reducing) net income.

Within the Australian, Canadian, United Kingdom, and United States tax systems, a _____ is a recognition of partial payment already made towards taxes due. A similar concept exists (fr:Avoir fiscal) in the French tax system. This situation arises, for example, when standard rate tax has been deducted at source , but the tax-payer is subject to further taxation at a higher rate. It also applies in dividend imputation systems.

a. 1921 recession
b. 100-year flood
c. 130-30 fund
d. Tax Credit

14. _____s is the social science that studies the production, distribution, and consumption of goods and services. The term _____s comes from the Ancient Greek οἰκονομία from οἶκος (oikos, 'house') + νόμος (nomos, 'custom' or 'law'), hence 'rules of the house(hold)'. Current _____ models developed out of the broader field of political economy in the late 19th century, owing to a desire to use an empirical approach more akin to the physical sciences.

a. Opportunity cost
b. Economic
c. Energy economics
d. Inflation

15. In economics and sociology, an _____ is any factor (financial or non-financial) that enables or motivates a particular course of action, or counts as a reason for preferring one choice to the alternatives. It is an expectation that encourages people to behave in a certain way. Since human beings are purposeful creatures, the study of _____ structures is central to the study of all economic activity (both in terms of individual decision-making and in terms of co-operation and competition within a larger institutional structure.)

a. Isocost
b. Economic reform
c. Incentive
d. Epstein-Zin preferences

16. _____ was a survey conducted by the U.S. Department of Justice to gauge the prevalence of alcohol and illegal drug use among prior arrestees. It was a reformulation of the prior Drug Use Forecasting (DUF) program, focused on five drugs in particular: cocaine, marijuana, methamphetamine, opiates, and PCP.

Participants were randomly selected from arrest records in major metropolitan areas; because no personally identifying information is taken from each record chosen, the resulting data can be correlated to arrest rates, but not to the total population of persons charged.

a. ACEA agreement
b. Arrestee Drug Abuse Monitoring
c. AD-IA Model
d. ACCRA Cost of Living Index

17. In finance, a _____ is a debt security, in which the authorized issuer owes the holders a debt and, depending on the terms of the _____, is obliged to pay interest (the coupon) and/or to repay the principal at a later date, termed maturity. A _____ is a formal contract to repay borrowed money with interest at fixed intervals.

Thus a _____ is like a loan: the issuer is the borrower (debtor), the holder is the lender (creditor), and the coupon is the interest.

- a. Callable
- b. Zero-coupon
- c. Bond
- d. Prize Bond

18. A security is a fungible, negotiable instrument representing financial value. _____ are broadly categorized into debt _____; equity _____, e.g., common stocks; and derivative (finance) contracts such as forwards, futures, options and swaps. The company or other entity issuing the security is called the issuer.

- a. Red herring prospectus
- b. Settlement risk
- c. Pass-Through Certificates
- d. Securities

19. The U.S. _____ is an independent agency of the United States government which holds primary responsibility for enforcing the federal securities laws and regulating the securities industry, the nation's stock and options exchanges, and other electronic securities markets. The SEC was created by section 4 of the Securities Exchange Act of 1934 (now codified as 15 U.S.C. § 78d and commonly referred to as the 1934 Act.)

- a. 1921 recession
- b. Securities and Exchange Commission
- c. 100-year flood
- d. 130-30 fund

20. _____ was a Scottish moral philosopher and a pioneer of political economy. One of the key figures of the Scottish Enlightenment, Smith is the author of The Theory of Moral Sentiments and An Inquiry into the Nature and Causes of the Wealth of Nations. The latter, usually abbreviated as The Wealth of Nations, is considered his magnum opus and the first modern work of economics.

- a. Alan Greenspan
- b. Adolph Fischer
- c. Adolf Hitler
- d. Adam Smith

21. An Inquiry into the Nature and Causes of the _____ is the magnum opus of the Scottish economist Adam Smith. It is a clearly written account of economics at the dawn of the Industrial Revolution, as well as a rhetorical piece written for the generally educated individual of the 18th century - advocating a free market economy as more productive and more beneficial to society.

The work is credited as a watershed in history and economics due to its comprehensive, largely accurate characterization of economic mechanisms that survive in modern economics; and also for its effective use of rhetorical technique, including structuring the work to contrast real world examples of free and fettered markets.

- a. The Rise and Fall of the Great Powers
- b. Wealth of Nations
- c. Black Book of Communism
- d. The Bell Curve

22. _____ is a branch of economics that deals with the performance, structure, and behavior of a national or regional economy as a whole. Along with microeconomics, _____ is one of the two most general fields in economics. It is the study of the behavior and decision-making of entire economies.

- a. New Trade Theory
- b. Nominal value
- c. Tobit model
- d. Macroeconomics

23. _____ is a branch of economics that studies how individuals, households and firms and some states make decisions to allocate limited resources, typically in markets where goods or services are being bought and sold. _____ examines how these decisions and behaviours affect the supply and demand for goods and services, which determines prices; and how prices, in turn, determine the supply and demand of goods and services.

Whereas macroeconomics involves the 'sum total of economic activity, dealing with the issues of growth, inflation and unemployment, and with national economic policies relating to these issues' and the effects of government actions on them.

   a. Recession
   b. New Keynesian economics
   c. Countercyclical
   d. Microeconomics

24. In ethical philosophy, _____ is the principle that an action is rational if and only if it maximizes one's self-interest. The view is a normative form of egoism. However, it is different from other forms of egoism, such as ethical egoism and psychological egoism.

   a. Rational egoism
   b. Adam Smith
   c. Adolph Fischer
   d. Adolf Hitler

25. In economics, a model is a theoretical construct that represents economic processes by a set of variables and a set of logical and/or quantitative relationships between them. The _____ is a simplified framework designed to illustrate complex processes, often but not always using mathematical techniques. Frequently, _____s use structural parameters.

   a. AD-IA Model
   b. ACCRA Cost of Living Index
   c. ACEA agreement
   d. Economic model

26. _____ is the a method of technical and economic research of the systems for purpose to optimize a parity between system's consumer functions or properties and expenses to achieve those functions or properties.

This methodology for continuous perfection of production, industrial technologies, organizational structures was developed by Juryj Sobolev in 1948 at the 'Perm telephone factory'

- 1948 Juryj Sobolev - the first success in application of a method analysis at the 'Perm telephone factory'.
- 1949 - the first application for the invention as result of use of the new method.

Today in economically developed countries practically each enterprise or the company use methodology of the kind of functional-cost analysis as a practice of the quality management, most full satisfying to principles of standards of series ISO 9000.

- Interest of consumer not in products itself, but the advantage which it will receive from its usage.
- The consumer aspires to reduce his expenses
- Functions needed by consumer can be executed in the various ways, and, hence, with various efficiency and expenses. Among possible alternatives of realization of functions exist such in which the parity of quality and the price is the optimal for the consumer.

The goal of _____ is achievement of the highest consumer satisfaction of production at simultaneous decrease in all kinds of industrial expenses Classical _____ has three English synonyms - Value Engineering, Value Management, Value Analysis.

   a. Monopoly wage   b. Willingness to pay
   c. Function cost analysis   d. Staple financing

27. Cä"terä«s paribus is a Latin phrase, literally translated as 'with other things the same.' It is commonly rendered in English as 'all other things being equal.' A prediction, or a statement about causal or logical connections between two states of affairs, is qualified by _____ in order to acknowledge, and to rule out, the possibility of other factors which could override the relationship between the antecedent and the consequent.

A _____ assumption is often fundamental to the predictive purpose of scientific inquiry. In order to formulate scientific laws, it is usually necessary to rule out factors which interfere with examining a specific causal relationship.

   a. Friedman-Savage utility function   b. Capital outflow
   c. Ceteris paribus   d. Dematerialization

28. In finance, the _____s between two currencies specifies how much one currency is worth in terms of the other. It is the value of a foreign natione;s currency in terms of the home natione;s currency. For example an _____ of 102 Japanese yen to the United States dollar means that JPY 102 is worth the same as USD 1.

   a. ACEA agreement   b. Interbank market
   c. ACCRA Cost of Living Index   d. Exchange rate

29. To tax is to impose a financial charge or other levy upon a taxpayer by a state or the functional equivalent of a state.

_____ are also imposed by many subnational entities. _____ consist of direct tax or indirect tax, and may be paid in money or as its labour equivalent (often but not always unpaid.)

   a. 130-30 fund   b. 1921 recession
   c. 100-year flood   d. Taxes

30. In economics and especially in the theory of competition, _____ are obstacles in the path of a firm that make it difficult to enter a given market.

_____ are the source of a firm's pricing power - the ability of a firm to raise prices without losing all its customers.

The term refers to hindrances that an individual may face while trying to gain entrance into a profession or trade.

   a. Social dumping   b. Group boycott
   c. Barriers to entry   d. Limit price

Chapter 1. The Nature of Economics

31. The terms '_____' and 'independent variable' are used in similar but subtly different ways in mathematics and statistics as part of the standard terminology in those subjects. They are used to distinguish between two types of quantities being considered, separating them into those available at the start of a process and those being created by it, where the latter (_____s) are dependent on the former (independent variables.)

In traditional calculus, a function is defined as a relation between two terms called variables because their values vary.

   a. 1921 recession
   b. 130-30 fund
   c. 100-year flood
   d. Dependent variable

32. In economics, _____ is how a natione;s total economy is distributed among its population. ._____ has always been a central concern of economic theory and economic policy. Classical economists such as Adam Smith, Thomas Malthus and David Ricardo were mainly concerned with factor _____, that is, the distribution of income between the main factors of production, land, labour and capital.
   a. Equipment trust certificate
   b. Income distribution
   c. Authorised capital
   d. Eco commerce

33. The terms 'dependent variable' and '_____' are used in similar but subtly different ways in mathematics and statistics as part of the standard terminology in those subjects. They are used to distinguish between two types of quantities being considered, separating them into those available at the start of a process and those being created by it, where the latter (dependent variables) are dependent on the former (_____s.)

The _____ is typically the variable being manipulated or changed and the dependent variable is the observed result of the _____ being manipulated.

   a. ACEA agreement
   b. AD-IA Model
   c. Independent variable
   d. ACCRA Cost of Living Index

34. An inverse or negative relationship is a mathematical relationship in which one variable, say y, decreases as another, say x, increases. For a linear (straight-line) relation, this can be expressed as y = a-bx, where -b is a constant value less than zero and a is a constant. For example, there is an _____ between education and unemployment -- that is, as education increases, the rate of unemployment decreases.
   a. Inverse relationship
   b. AD-IA Model
   c. ACCRA Cost of Living Index
   d. ACEA agreement

35. _____ is a broad label that refers to any individuals or households that use goods and services generated within the economy. The concept of a _____ is used in different contexts, so that the usage and significance of the term may vary.

Typically when business people and economists talk of _____s they are talking about person as _____, an aggregated commodity item with little individuality other than that expressed in the buy/not-buy decision.

a. 130-30 fund
b. 1921 recession
c. 100-year flood
d. Consumer

Chapter 2. Scarcity and the World of Trade-Offs

1. _____ describes a set of laws relating to domestic agriculture and imports of foreign agricultural products. Governments usually implement agricultural policies with the goal of achieving a specific outcome in the domestic agricultural product markets. Outcomes can involve, for example, a guaranteed supply level, price stability, product quality, product selection, land use or employment.
   - a. ACCRA Cost of Living Index
   - b. ACEA agreement
   - c. Agricultural Policy
   - d. Intercropping

2. A _____ refers to any type debt instrument, such as a loan, bond, mortgage that does not have a fixed rate of interest over the life of the instrument. Such debt typically uses an index or other base rate for establishing the interest rate for each relevant period. One of the most common rates to use as the basis for applying interest rates is the London Inter-bank Offered Rate, or LIBOR
   - a. Moneylender
   - b. Money market
   - c. Disposal tax effect
   - d. Floating interest rate

3. The United States federal _____ is a refundable tax credit. For tax year 2008, a claimant with one qualifying child can receive a maximum credit of $2,917. For two or more qualifying children, the maximum credit is $4,824.
   - a. Earned Income Tax Credit
   - b. ACCRA Cost of Living Index
   - c. AD-IA Model
   - d. ACEA agreement

4. An _____ is a tax levied on the financial income of people, corporations, or other legal entities. Various _____ systems exist, with varying degrees of tax incidence. Income taxation can be progressive, proportional, or regressive.
   - a. ACCRA Cost of Living Index
   - b. AD-IA Model
   - c. Income Tax
   - d. ACEA agreement

5. To _____ is to impose a financial charge or other levy upon a taxpayer by a state or the functional equivalent of a state.

   _____es are also imposed by many subnational entities. _____es consist of direct _____ or indirect _____, and may be paid in money or as its labour equivalent (often but not always unpaid.)

   - a. 130-30 fund
   - b. 100-year flood
   - c. 1921 recession
   - d. Tax

6. The term _____ describes two different concepts:

   - The first is a recognition of partial payment already made towards taxes due.
   - The second is a state benefit paid to workers through the tax system, which has the effect of increasing (rather than reducing) net income.

   Within the Australian, Canadian, United Kingdom, and United States tax systems, a _____ is a recognition of partial payment already made towards taxes due. A similar concept exists (fr:Avoir fiscal) in the French tax system. This situation arises, for example, when standard rate tax has been deducted at source , but the tax-payer is subject to further taxation at a higher rate. It also applies in dividend imputation systems.

   - a. 100-year flood
   - b. 130-30 fund
   - c. 1921 recession
   - d. Tax Credit

Chapter 2. Scarcity and the World of Trade-Offs

7. _____s is the social science that studies the production, distribution, and consumption of goods and services. The term _____s comes from the Ancient Greek οἰκονομία from οἶκος (oikos, 'house') + νόμος (nomos, 'custom' or 'law'), hence 'rules of the house(hold)'. Current _____ models developed out of the broader field of political economy in the late 19th century, owing to a desire to use an empirical approach more akin to the physical sciences.
   a. Opportunity cost
   b. Energy economics
   c. Economic
   d. Inflation

8. A _____ is an object whose consumption increases the utility of the consumer, for which the quantity demanded exceeds the quantity supplied at zero price. _____s are usually modeled as having diminishing marginal utility. The first individual purchase has high utility; the second has less.
   a. Pie method
   b. Merit good
   c. Composite good
   d. Good

9. _____ refers to the stock of skills and knowledge embodied in the ability to perform labor so as to produce economic value. It is the skills and knowledge gained by a worker through education and experience. Many early economic theories refer to it simply as labor, one of three factors of production, and consider it to be a fungible resource -- homogeneous and easily interchangeable. Other conceptions of labor dispense with these assumptions.
   a. Price theory
   b. Law of increasing costs
   c. General equilibrium
   d. Human capital

10. _____ is a slogan popularized by Karl Marx in his 1875 Critique of the Gotha Program. The phrase summarizes the principles that, under a communist system, every person should contribute to society to the best of his ability and consume from society in proportion to his needs, regardless of how much he has contributed. In the Marxist view, such an arrangement will be made possible by the abundance of goods and services that a developed communist society will produce; the idea is that there will be enough to satisfy everyone's needs.
    a. Proletarianization
    b. Reserve army of labour
    c. Temporal single-system interpretation
    d. From each according to his ability, to each according to his need

11. In general _____ refers to any non-human asset made by humans and then used in production. Often, it refers to economic capital in some ambiguous combination of infrastructural capital and natural capital. As these are combined in process-specific and firm-specific ways that neoclassical macroeconomics does not differentiate at its level of analysis, it is common to refer only to physical vs. human capital and seek so-called 'balanced growth' that develops both in tandem

    Such analyses, however, fails to make distinctions considered critical by many modern economists.

    a. Linkage principle
    b. Net domestic product
    c. Factor cost
    d. Physical capital

12. In economics, _____ refers to the ability of a person or a country to produce a particular good at a lower marginal cost and opportunity cost than another person or country. It is the ability to produce a product most efficiently given all the other products that could be produced. It can be contrasted with absolute advantage which refers to the ability of a person or a country to produce a particular good at a lower absolute cost than another.
    a. Triffin dilemma
    b. Gravity model of trade
    c. Hot money
    d. Comparative advantage

13. _____ is a broad label that refers to any individuals or households that use goods and services generated within the economy. The concept of a _____ is used in different contexts, so that the usage and significance of the term may vary.

Typically when business people and economists talk of _____s they are talking about person as _____, an aggregated commodity item with little individuality other than that expressed in the buy/not-buy decision.

   a. Consumer
   c. 100-year flood
   b. 130-30 fund
   d. 1921 recession

14. _____ or economic opportunity loss is the value of the next best alternative foregone as the result of making a decision. _____ analysis is an important part of a company's decision-making processes but is not treated as an actual cost in any financial statement. The next best thing that a person can engage in is referred to as the _____ of doing the best thing and ignoring the next best thing to be done.
   a. Economic ideology
   c. Industrial organization
   b. Economic
   d. Opportunity cost

15. _____ is the a method of technical and economic research of the systems for purpose to optimize a parity between system's consumer functions or properties and expenses to achieve those functions or properties.

This methodology for continuous perfection of production, industrial technologies, organizational structures was developed by Juryj Sobolev in 1948 at the 'Perm telephone factory'

- 1948 Juryj Sobolev - the first success in application of a method analysis at the 'Perm telephone factory' .
- 1949 - the first application for the invention as result of use of the new method.

Today in economically developed countries practically each enterprise or the company use methodology of the kind of functional-cost analysis as a practice of the quality management, most full satisfying to principles of standards of series ISO 9000.

- Interest of consumer not in products itself, but the advantage which it will receive from its usage.
- The consumer aspires to reduce his expenses
- Functions needed by consumer can be executed in the various ways, and, hence, with various efficiency and expenses. Among possible alternatives of realization of functions exist such in which the parity of quality and the price is the optimal for the consumer.

The goal of _____ is achievement of the highest consumer satisfaction of production at simultaneous decrease in all kinds of industrial expenses Classical _____ has three English synonyms - Value Engineering, Value Management, Value Analysis.

   a. Staple financing
   c. Willingness to pay
   b. Monopoly wage
   d. Function cost analysis

16. The U.S. _____ (EEOC) is a federal agency whose goal is ending employment discrimination. The _____ investigates discrimination complaints based on an individual's race, color, national origin, religion, sex, age, disability and retaliation for reporting and/or opposing a discriminatory practice. The Commission is also tasked with filing suits on behalf of alleged victim(s) of discrimination against employers and as an adjudicatory for claims of discrimination brought against federal agencies.
    a. AD-IA Model
    b. ACCRA Cost of Living Index
    c. ACEA agreement
    d. EEOC

17. In neoclassical economics and microeconomics, _____ describes the perfect being a market in which there are many small firms, all producing homogeneous goods. In the short term, such markets are productively inefficient as output will not occur where mc is equal to ac, but allocatively efficient, as output under _____ will always occur where mc is equal to mr, and therefore where mc equals ar. However, in the long term, such markets are both allocatively and productively efficient.
    a. General equilibrium
    b. Law of supply
    c. Co-operative economics
    d. Perfect competition

18. In calculus, a function f defined on a subset of the real numbers with real values is called _____, if for all x and y such that $x \geq y$ one has $f(x) \geq f(y)$, so f preserves the order. In layman's terms, the sign of the slope is always positive (the curve tending upwards) or zero (i.e., non-decreasing, or asymptotic, or depicted as a horizontal, flat line) Likewise, a function is called monotonically decreasing (non-increasing) if, whenever $x \geq y$, then $f(x) \geq f(y)$, so it reverses the order.
    a. 100-year flood
    b. 130-30 fund
    c. 1921 recession
    d. Monotonic

19. In economics, market concentration is a function of the number of firms and their respective shares of the total production (alternatively, total capacity or total reserves) in a market. Alternative terms are _____ and Seller concentration.

Market concentration is related to the concept of industrial concentration, which concerns the distribution of production within an industry, as opposed to a market.

    a. Industry concentration
    b. AD-IA Model
    c. ACCRA Cost of Living Index
    d. ACEA agreement

20. This concept is also known as the law of diminishing marginal returns, the _____, or the law of increasing opportunity cost.

The concept of diminishing returns can be traced back to the concerns of early economists such as Johann Heinrich von Thünen, Turgot, Thomas Malthus and David Ricardo.

Suppose that one kilogram of seed applied to a plot of land of a fixed size produces one ton of crop.

    a. Bennett Amendment
    b. Fair Labor Standards Act
    c. Law of increasing relative cost
    d. Lang Law

21. _____ is the increase in the amount of the goods and services produced by an economy over time. It is conventionally measured as the percent rate of increase in real gross domestic product, or real GDP. Growth is usually calculated in real terms, i.e. inflation-adjusted terms, in order to net out the effect of inflation on the price of the goods and services produced.
- a. ACEA agreement
- b. Economic growth
- c. AD-IA Model
- d. ACCRA Cost of Living Index

22. In microeconomics, _____ is quite simply the conversion of inputs into outputs. It is an economic process that uses resources to create a good or service that is suitable for exchange. This can include manufacturing, storing, shipping, and packaging.
- a. Solved
- b. MET
- c. Production
- d. Red Guards

23. In Marxian economics, _____ originally referred to the means of production. Individuals, organizations and governments use _____ in the production of other goods or commodities. _____ include factories, machinery, tools, equipment, and various buildings which are used to produce other products for consumption.
- a. Capital deepening
- b. Wealth inequality in the United States
- c. Capital intensive
- d. Capital goods

24. _____ is a common concept in economics, and gives rise to derived concepts such as consumer debt. Generally _____ is defined by opposition to production. But the precise definition can vary because different schools of economists define production quite differently.
- a. Foreclosure data providers
- b. Federal Reserve Bank Notes
- c. Consumption
- d. Cash or share options

25. A _____ is a situation that involves losing one quality or aspect of something in return for gaining another quality or aspect. It implies a decision to be made with full comprehension of both the upside and downside of a particular choice.

In economics the term is expressed as opportunity cost, referring the most preferred alternative given up.

- a. Whitemail
- b. Nonmarket
- c. Friedman-Savage utility function
- d. Trade-off

26. _____ was a survey conducted by the U.S. Department of Justice to gauge the prevalence of alcohol and illegal drug use among prior arrestees. It was a reformulation of the prior Drug Use Forecasting (DUF) program, focused on five drugs in particular: cocaine, marijuana, methamphetamine, opiates, and PCP.

Participants were randomly selected from arrest records in major metropolitan areas; because no personally identifying information is taken from each record chosen, the resulting data can be correlated to arrest rates, but not to the total population of persons charged.

- a. AD-IA Model
- b. ACCRA Cost of Living Index
- c. ACEA agreement
- d. Arrestee Drug Abuse Monitoring

Chapter 2. Scarcity and the World of Trade-Offs

27. In economics, _____ refers to the ability of a party to produce a good or service using fewer real resources than another entity producing the same good or service..A party has an _____ when using the same input as another party, it can produce a greater output. Since _____ is determined by a simple comparison of labor productivities, it is possible for a a party to have no _____ in anything. It can be contrasted with the concept of comparative advantage which refers to the ability to produce a particular good at a lower opportunity cost.
   a. ACCRA Cost of Living Index
   b. International economics
   c. Index number
   d. Absolute advantage

28. In finance, a _____ is a debt security, in which the authorized issuer owes the holders a debt and, depending on the terms of the _____, is obliged to pay interest (the coupon) and/or to repay the principal at a later date, termed maturity. A _____ is a formal contract to repay borrowed money with interest at fixed intervals.

Thus a _____ is like a loan: the issuer is the borrower (debtor), the holder is the lender (creditor), and the coupon is the interest.

   a. Zero-coupon
   b. Callable
   c. Prize Bond
   d. Bond

29. A security is a fungible, negotiable instrument representing financial value. _____ are broadly categorized into debt _____; equity _____, e.g., common stocks; and derivative (finance) contracts such as forwards, futures, options and swaps. The company or other entity issuing the security is called the issuer.
   a. Settlement risk
   b. Red herring prospectus
   c. Pass-Through Certificates
   d. Securities

30. The U.S. _____ is an independent agency of the United States government which holds primary responsibility for enforcing the federal securities laws and regulating the securities industry, the nation's stock and options exchanges, and other electronic securities markets. The SEC was created by section 4 of the Securities Exchange Act of 1934 (now codified as 15 U.S.C. § 78d and commonly referred to as the 1934 Act.)
   a. Securities and Exchange Commission
   b. 130-30 fund
   c. 100-year flood
   d. 1921 recession

31. _____ was a Scottish moral philosopher and a pioneer of political economy. One of the key figures of the Scottish Enlightenment, Smith is the author of The Theory of Moral Sentiments and An Inquiry into the Nature and Causes of the Wealth of Nations. The latter, usually abbreviated as The Wealth of Nations, is considered his magnum opus and the first modern work of economics.
   a. Adolph Fischer
   b. Adolf Hitler
   c. Alan Greenspan
   d. Adam Smith

32. An Inquiry into the Nature and Causes of the _____ is the magnum opus of the Scottish economist Adam Smith. It is a clearly written account of economics at the dawn of the Industrial Revolution, as well as a rhetorical piece written for the generally educated individual of the 18th century - advocating a free market economy as more productive and more beneficial to society.

The work is credited as a watershed in history and economics due to its comprehensive, largely accurate characterization of economic mechanisms that survive in modern economics; and also for its effective use of rhetorical technique, including structuring the work to contrast real world examples of free and fettered markets.

a. The Bell Curve
b. The Rise and Fall of the Great Powers
c. Black Book of Communism
d. Wealth of Nations

33. The _____ is an international organization that oversees the global financial system by following the macroeconomic policies of its member countries, in particular those with an impact on exchange rates and the balance of payments. It is an organization formed to stabilize international exchange rates and facilitate development. It also offers financial and technical assistance to its members, making it an international lender of last resort.
   a. ACEA agreement
   b. Office of Thrift Supervision
   c. ACCRA Cost of Living Index
   d. International Monetary Fund

34. _____ is a policy or ideology of violence intended to intimidate or cause terror for the purpose of 'exerting pressure on decision making by state bodies.' The term 'terror' is largely used to indicate clandestine, low-intensity violence that targets civilians and generates public fear. Thus 'terror' is distinct from asymmetric warfare, and violates the concept of a common law of war in which civilian life is regarded. The term '-ism' is used to indicate an ideology --typically one that claims its attacks are in the domain of a 'just war' concept, though most condemn such as crimes against humanity.
   a. 1921 recession
   b. 100-year flood
   c. 130-30 fund
   d. Terrorism

Chapter 3. Demand and Supply

1. _____ in economics and business is the result of an exchange and from that trade we assign a numerical monetary value to a good, service or asset. If Alice trades Bob 4 apples for an orange, the _____ of an orange is 4 apples. Inversely, the _____ of an apple is 1/4 oranges.
   - a. Price
   - b. Price book
   - c. Premium pricing
   - d. Price war

2. _____ is defined as the measure of responsiveness in the quantity demanded for a commodity as a result of change in price of the same commodity. It is a measure of how consumers react to a change in price. In other words, it is percentage change in quantity demanded as per the percentage change in price of the same commodity.
   - a. 130-30 fund
   - b. 1921 recession
   - c. 100-year flood
   - d. Price elasticity of demand

3. CÄ"terÄ«s paribus is a Latin phrase, literally translated as 'with other things the same.' It is commonly rendered in English as 'all other things being equal.' A prediction, or a statement about causal or logical connections between two states of affairs, is qualified by _____ in order to acknowledge, and to rule out, the possibility of other factors which could override the relationship between the antecedent and the consequent.

   A _____ assumption is often fundamental to the predictive purpose of scientific inquiry. In order to formulate scientific laws, it is usually necessary to rule out factors which interfere with examining a specific causal relationship.

   - a. Friedman-Savage utility function
   - b. Capital outflow
   - c. Dematerialization
   - d. Ceteris paribus

4. Economics:
   - _____, the desire to own something and the ability to pay for it
   - _____ curve, a graphic representation of a _____ schedule
   - _____ deposit, the money in checking accounts
   - _____ pull theory, the theory that inflation occurs when _____ for goods and services exceeds existing supplies
   - _____ schedule, a table that lists the quantity of a good a person will buy it each different price
   - _____ side economics, the school of economics at believes government spending and tax cuts open economy by raising _____

   - a. Production
   - b. Demand
   - c. McKesson ' Robbins scandal
   - d. Variability

5. In economics, _____ is the ratio of the percent change in one variable to the percent change in another variable. It is a tool for measuring the responsiveness of a function to changes in parameters in a relative way. Commonly analyzed are _____ of substitution, price and wealth.
   - a. ACCRA Cost of Living Index
   - b. Elasticity
   - c. Elasticity of demand
   - d. ACEA agreement

Chapter 3. Demand and Supply

6. Price _____ is defined as the measure of responsiveness in the quantity demanded for a commodity as a result of change in price of the same commodity. It is a measure of how consumers react to a change in price. In other words, it is percentage change in quantity demanded by the percentage change in price of the same commodity.
   a. Elasticity of demand
   b. ACCRA Cost of Living Index
   c. Elasticity
   d. ACEA agreement

7. In finance, the _____s between two currencies specifies how much one currency is worth in terms of the other. It is the value of a foreign natione;s currency in terms of the home natione;s currency. For example an _____ of 102 Japanese yen to the United States dollar means that JPY 102 is worth the same as USD 1.
   a. ACEA agreement
   b. ACCRA Cost of Living Index
   c. Interbank market
   d. Exchange rate

8. In economics, the _____ is an economic law that states that consumers buy more of a good when its price decreases and less when its price increases.

   There are certain goods which do not follow this law. These include Veblen and Giffen goods

   a. Georgism
   b. Financial crisis
   c. Market failure
   d. Law of demand

9. The _____ proposed by John L. Lewis in 1932, was a federation of unions that organized workers in industrial unions in the United States and Canada from 1935 to 1955. The Taft-Hartley Act of 1947 required union leaders to swear that they were not Communists. Many CIO leaders refused to obey that requirement, later found unconstitutional.
   a. Multinational corporation
   b. Chinese correction
   c. Foreign direct investment
   d. Congress of Industrial Organizations

10. _____ is a field of economics that studies the strategic behavior of firms, the structure of markets and their interactions. The study of _____ adds to the perfectly competitive model real-world frictions such as limited information, transaction cost, cost of adjusting prices, government actions, and barriers to entry by new firms into a market. It then considers how firms are organized and how they compete.
    a. Economic ideology
    b. Industrial Organization
    c. Economic
    d. Inflation

11. _____ is the price of a commodity such as a good or service in terms of another; ie, the ratio of two prices. A _____ may be expressed in terms of a ratio between any two prices or the ratio between the price of one particular good and a weighted average of all other goods available in the market. A _____ is an opportunity cost.
    a. Food cooperative
    b. False economy
    c. False shortage
    d. Relative price

12. In economics, a _____ is a table that lists the quantity of a good a person will buy it each different price See Demand curve.
    a. Rational irrationality
    b. Free contract
    c. Federal Reserve districts
    d. Demand schedule

Chapter 3. Demand and Supply

13. _____ are the inflation-indexed bonds issued by the U.S. Treasury. The principal is adjusted to the Consumer Price Index, the commonly used measure of inflation. The coupon rate is constant, but generates a different amount of interest when multiplied by the inflation-adjusted principal, thus protecting the holder against inflation.

   a. 1921 recession
   b. 100-year flood
   c. 130-30 fund
   d. Treasury Inflation-Protected Securities

14. The _____ is an international organization that oversees the global financial system by following the macroeconomic policies of its member countries, in particular those with an impact on exchange rates and the balance of payments. It is an organization formed to stabilize international exchange rates and facilitate development. It also offers financial and technical assistance to its members, making it an international lender of last resort.

   a. International Monetary Fund
   b. ACEA agreement
   c. ACCRA Cost of Living Index
   d. Office of Thrift Supervision

15. In economics, the _____ can be defined as the graph depicting the relationship between the price of a certain commodity, and the amount of it that consumers are willing and able to purchase at that given price. It is a graphic representation of a demand schedule. The _____ for all consumers together follows from the _____ of every individual consumer: the individual demands at each price are added together.

   a. Wage curve
   b. Cost curve
   c. Demand curve
   d. Kuznets curve

16. In algebra, a _____ is a function depending on n that associates a scalar, det(A), to an n×n square matrix A. The fundamental geometric meaning of a _____ is a scale factor for measure when A is regarded as a linear transformation. _____s are important both in calculus, where they enter the substitution rule for several variables, and in multilinear algebra.

   For a fixed nonnegative integer n, there is a unique _____ function for the n×n matrices over any commutative ring R. In particular, this function exists when R is the field of real or complex numbers.

   a. 130-30 fund
   b. 1921 recession
   c. 100-year flood
   d. Determinant

17. _____ is a broad label that refers to any individuals or households that use goods and services generated within the economy. The concept of a _____ is used in different contexts, so that the usage and significance of the term may vary.

   Typically when business people and economists talk of _____s they are talking about person as _____, an aggregated commodity item with little individuality other than that expressed in the buy/not-buy decision.

   a. 1921 recession
   b. Consumer
   c. 100-year flood
   d. 130-30 fund

18. In neoclassical economics and microeconomics, _____ describes the perfect being a market in which there are many small firms, all producing homogeneous goods. In the short term, such markets are productively inefficient as output will not occur where mc is equal to ac, but allocatively efficient, as output under _____ will always occur where mc is equal to mr, and therefore where mc equals ar. However, in the long term, such markets are both allocatively and productively efficient.
   a. General equilibrium
   b. Perfect competition
   c. Law of supply
   d. Co-operative economics

19. To _____ is to impose a financial charge or other levy upon a taxpayer by a state or the functional equivalent of a state.

_____es are also imposed by many subnational entities. _____es consist of direct _____ or indirect _____, and may be paid in money or as its labour equivalent (often but not always unpaid.)

   a. 1921 recession
   b. 130-30 fund
   c. 100-year flood
   d. Tax

20. To tax is to impose a financial charge or other levy upon a taxpayer by a state or the functional equivalent of a state.

_____ are also imposed by many subnational entities. _____ consist of direct tax or indirect tax, and may be paid in money or as its labour equivalent (often but not always unpaid.)

   a. 130-30 fund
   b. 1921 recession
   c. 100-year flood
   d. Taxes

21. In economics and especially in the theory of competition, _____ are obstacles in the path of a firm that make it difficult to enter a given market.

_____ are the source of a firm's pricing power - the ability of a firm to raise prices without losing all its customers.

The term refers to hindrances that an individual may face while trying to gain entrance into a profession or trade.

   a. Barriers to entry
   b. Group boycott
   c. Limit price
   d. Social dumping

22. A _____ is an object whose consumption increases the utility of the consumer, for which the quantity demanded exceeds the quantity supplied at zero price. _____s are usually modeled as having diminishing marginal utility. The first individual purchase has high utility; the second has less.
   a. Pie method
   b. Composite good
   c. Good
   d. Merit good

23. In economics, market concentration is a function of the number of firms and their respective shares of the total production (alternatively, total capacity or total reserves) in a market. Alternative terms are _____ and Seller concentration.

Market concentration is related to the concept of industrial concentration, which concerns the distribution of production within an industry, as opposed to a market.

  a. ACEA agreement
  b. AD-IA Model
  c. ACCRA Cost of Living Index
  d. Industry concentration

24. In consumer theory, an _____ is a good that decreases in demand when consumer income rises, unlike normal goods, for which the opposite is observed. It is a good that consumers demand increases when their income increases. Inferiority, in this sense, is an observable fact relating to affordability rather than a statement about the quality of the good.
  a. Information good
  b. Export-oriented
  c. Inferior good
  d. Independent goods

25. A _____ is the transfer of wealth from one party (such as a person or company) to another. A _____ is usually made in exchange for the provision of goods, services or both, or to fulfill a legal obligation.

The simplest and oldest form of _____ is barter, the exchange of one good or service for another.

  a. Payment
  b. Social gravity
  c. Going concern
  d. Soft count

26. In economics, a _____ is a redistribution of income in the market system. These payments are considered to be nonexhaustive because they do not directly absorb resources or create output. Examples of certain _____s include welfare (financial aid), social security, and government subsidies for certain businesses (firms.)
  a. 100-year flood
  b. 1921 recession
  c. 130-30 fund
  d. Transfer payment

27. _____ describes a set of laws relating to domestic agriculture and imports of foreign agricultural products. Governments usually implement agricultural policies with the goal of achieving a specific outcome in the domestic agricultural product markets. Outcomes can involve, for example, a guaranteed supply level, price stability, product quality, product selection, land use or employment.
  a. ACCRA Cost of Living Index
  b. ACEA agreement
  c. Intercropping
  d. Agricultural Policy

28. _____ is an equity (stock) exchange located at 11 Wall Street in lower Manhattan, New York, USA. It is the largest stock exchange in the world by dollar value of its listed companies' securities. As of October 2008, the combined capitalization of all domestic _____ listed companies was US$10.1 trillion.
  a. 100-year flood
  b. 130-30 fund
  c. New York Stock Exchange
  d. 1921 recession

29. In economics, the _____ is the tendency of suppliers to offer more of a good at a higher price. The relationship between price and quantity supplied is usually a positive relationship. A rise in price is associated with a rise in quantity supplied.
  a. Market failure
  b. Heterodox economics
  c. Mathematical economics
  d. Law of supply

30. _____ is a practice of protecting the environment, on individual, organisational or governmental level, for the benefit of the natural environment and (or) humans.

Due to the pressures of population and technology the biophysical environment is being degraded, sometimes permanently. This has been recognised and governments began placing restraints on activities that caused environmental degradation.

    a. ACCRA Cost of Living Index
    b. Environmental Protection
    c. AD-IA Model
    d. ACEA agreement

31. _____ or government expenditure is classified by economists into three main types. Government purchases of goods and services for current use are classed as government consumption. Government purchases of goods and services intended to create future benefits, such as infrastructure investment or research spending, are classed as government investment.
    a. 130-30 fund
    b. 1921 recession
    c. 100-year flood
    d. Government spending

32. In economics, _____ is how a natione;s total economy is distributed among its population. . _____ has always been a central concern of economic theory and economic policy. Classical economists such as Adam Smith, Thomas Malthus and David Ricardo were mainly concerned with factor _____, that is, the distribution of income between the main factors of production, land, labour and capital.
    a. Income distribution
    b. Authorised capital
    c. Eco commerce
    d. Equipment trust certificate

33. _____ is a common concept in economics, and gives rise to derived concepts such as consumer debt. Generally _____ is defined by opposition to production. But the precise definition can vary because different schools of economists define production quite differently.
    a. Foreclosure data providers
    b. Consumption
    c. Federal Reserve Bank Notes
    d. Cash or share options

34. The term '_____' refers to the concept of collecting information and attempting to spot a pattern in the information. In some fields of study, the term '_____' has more formally-defined meanings.

In project management _____ is a mathematical technique that uses historical results to predict future outcome.

    a. Coefficient of determination
    b. Trend analysis
    c. Probit model
    d. Quantile regression

35. The U.S. _____ is a federal agency whose goal is ending employment discrimination. The _____ investigates discrimination complaints based on an individual's race, color, national origin, religion, sex, age, disability and retaliation for reporting and/or opposing a discriminatory practice. The Commission is also tasked with filing suits on behalf of alleged victim(s) of discrimination against employers and as an adjudicatory for claims of discrimination brought against federal agencies.

Chapter 3. Demand and Supply

a. Equal Employment Opportunity Commission
b. ACCRA Cost of Living Index
c. AD-IA Model
d. ACEA agreement

36. In economics, _____ refers to either

1. a simplifying assumption made by the new classical school that markets always go to where the quantity supplied equals the quantity demanded; or
2. the process of getting there via price adjustment.

A _____ price is the price of a good or service at which quantity supplied is equal to quantity demanded. Also called the equilibrium price.

In simple terms, this means that markets tend to move towards prices which balance the quantity supplied and the quantity demanded, such that the market will eventually be cleared of all surpluses and shortages (excess supply and demand.) The first version assumes that this process occurs instantaneously.

a. Market data
b. Market portfolio
c. Market clearing
d. Noise trader

37. A _____ refers to any type debt instrument, such as a loan, bond, mortgage that does not have a fixed rate of interest over the life of the instrument. Such debt typically uses an index or other base rate for establishing the interest rate for each relevant period. One of the most common rates to use as the basis for applying interest rates is the London Inter-bank Offered Rate, or LIBOR
a. Moneylender
b. Floating interest rate
c. Money market
d. Disposal tax effect

38. The United States federal _____ is a refundable tax credit. For tax year 2008, a claimant with one qualifying child can receive a maximum credit of $2,917. For two or more qualifying children, the maximum credit is $4,824.
a. Earned Income Tax Credit
b. ACCRA Cost of Living Index
c. AD-IA Model
d. ACEA agreement

39. An _____ is a tax levied on the financial income of people, corporations, or other legal entities. Various _____ systems exist, with varying degrees of tax incidence. Income taxation can be progressive, proportional, or regressive.
a. Income Tax
b. ACCRA Cost of Living Index
c. AD-IA Model
d. ACEA agreement

40. The term _____ describes two different concepts:

- The first is a recognition of partial payment already made towards taxes due.
- The second is a state benefit paid to workers through the tax system, which has the effect of increasing (rather than reducing) net income.

Chapter 3. Demand and Supply

Within the Australian, Canadian, United Kingdom, and United States tax systems, a _____ is a recognition of partial payment already made towards taxes due. A similar concept exists (fr:Avoir fiscal) in the French tax system. This situation arises, for example, when standard rate tax has been deducted at source, but the tax-payer is subject to further taxation at a higher rate. It also applies in dividend imputation systems.

    a. 130-30 fund
    c. 100-year flood
    b. Tax Credit
    d. 1921 recession

41. _____s is the social science that studies the production, distribution, and consumption of goods and services. The term _____s comes from the Ancient Greek οἰκονομία from οἶκος (oikos, 'house') + νόμος (nomos, 'custom' or 'law'), hence 'rules of the house(hold)'. Current _____ models developed out of the broader field of political economy in the late 19th century, owing to a desire to use an empirical approach more akin to the physical sciences.
    a. Energy economics
    c. Inflation
    b. Opportunity cost
    d. Economic

Chapter 4. Extensions of Demand and Supply Analysis

1. In economics, the _____ of a good or of a service is the utility of the specific use to which an agent would put a given increase in that good or service, or of the specific use that would be abandoned in response to a given decrease. In other words, _____ is the utility of the marginal use -- which, on the assumption of economic rationality, would be the least urgent use of the good or service, from the best feasible combination of actions in which its use is included. Under the mainstream assumptions, the _____ of a good or service is the posited quantified change in utility obtained by increasing or by decreasing use of that good or service.
   - a. 1921 recession
   - b. 100-year flood
   - c. 130-30 fund
   - d. Marginal utility

2. In finance, the _____s between two currencies specifies how much one currency is worth in terms of the other. It is the value of a foreign natione;s currency in terms of the home natione;s currency. For example an _____ of 102 Japanese yen to the United States dollar means that JPY 102 is worth the same as USD 1.
   - a. Exchange rate
   - b. ACCRA Cost of Living Index
   - c. Interbank market
   - d. ACEA agreement

3. In economics, _____ is how a natione;s total economy is distributed among its population. . _____ has always been a central concern of economic theory and economic policy. Classical economists such as Adam Smith, Thomas Malthus and David Ricardo were mainly concerned with factor _____, that is, the distribution of income between the main factors of production, land, labour and capital.
   - a. Income distribution
   - b. Equipment trust certificate
   - c. Eco commerce
   - d. Authorised capital

4. A _____ is any systematic process enabling many market players to bid and ask: helping bidders and sellers interact and make deals. It is not just the price mechanism but the entire system of regulation, qualification, credentials, reputations and clearing that surrounds that mechanism and makes it operate in a social context.

   Because a _____ relies on the assumption that players are constantly involved and unequally enabled, a _____ is distinguished specifically from a voting system where candidates seek the support of voters on a less regular basis.
   - a. Price mechanism
   - b. Market system
   - c. Contestable market
   - d. Competitive equilibrium

5. To _____ is to impose a financial charge or other levy upon a taxpayer by a state or the functional equivalent of a state.

   _____es are also imposed by many subnational entities. _____es consist of direct _____ or indirect _____, and may be paid in money or as its labour equivalent (often but not always unpaid.)
   - a. 100-year flood
   - b. 130-30 fund
   - c. 1921 recession
   - d. Tax

6. To tax is to impose a financial charge or other levy upon a taxpayer by a state or the functional equivalent of a state.

   _____ are also imposed by many subnational entities. _____ consist of direct tax or indirect tax, and may be paid in money or as its labour equivalent (often but not always unpaid.)

a. 1921 recession	b. Taxes
c. 100-year flood	d. 130-30 fund

7. In economics, _____ is a measure of the relative satisfaction from consumption of various goods and services. Given this measure, one may speak meaningfully of increasing or decreasing _____, and thereby explain economic behavior in terms of attempts to increase one's _____. For illustrative purposes, changes in _____ are sometimes expressed in units called utils.

a. Utility	b. Ordinal utility
c. Utility function	d. Expected utility hypothesis

8. The U.S. _____ is a federal agency whose goal is ending employment discrimination. The _____ investigates discrimination complaints based on an individual's race, color, national origin, religion, sex, age, disability and retaliation for reporting and/or opposing a discriminatory practice. The Commission is also tasked with filing suits on behalf of alleged victim(s) of discrimination against employers and as an adjudicatory for claims of discrimination brought against federal agencies.

a. ACCRA Cost of Living Index	b. ACEA agreement
c. AD-IA Model	d. Equal Employment Opportunity Commission

9. _____ in economics and business is the result of an exchange and from that trade we assign a numerical monetary value to a good, service or asset. If Alice trades Bob 4 apples for an orange, the _____ of an orange is 4 apples. Inversely, the _____ of an apple is 1/4 oranges.

a. Price war	b. Price
c. Price book	d. Premium pricing

10. Competition law, known in the United States as _____ law, has three main elements:

- prohibiting agreements or practices that restrict free trading and competition between business entities. This includes in particular the repression of cartels.
- banning abusive behaviour by a firm dominating a market, or anti-competitive practices that tend to lead to such a dominant position. Practices controlled in this way may include predatory pricing, tying, price gouging, refusal to deal, and many others.
- supervising the mergers and acquisitions of large corporations, including some joint ventures. Transactions that are considered to threaten the competitive process can be prohibited altogether, or approved subject to 'remedies' such as an obligation to divest part of the merged business or to offer licences or access to facilities to enable other businesses to continue competing.

The substance and practice of competition law varies from jurisdiction to jurisdiction. Protecting the interests of consumers (consumer welfare) and ensuring that entrepreneurs have an opportunity to compete in the market economy are often treated as important objectives. Competition law is closely connected with law on deregulation of access to markets, state aids and subsidies, the privatisation of state owned assets and the establishment of independent sector regulators. In recent decades, competition law has been viewed as a way to provide better public services.

a. Antitrust	b. Intellectual property law
c. Anti-Inflation Act	d. United Kingdom competition law

11.

The _____ was the first United States Federal statute to limit cartels and monopolies. It falls under antitrust law.

The Act provides: 'Every contract, combination in the form of trust or otherwise, or conspiracy, in restraint of trade or commerce among the several States, or with foreign nations, is declared to be illegal'. The Act also provides: 'Every person who shall monopolize, or attempt to monopolize, or combine or conspire with any other person or persons, to monopolize any part of the trade or commerce among the several States, or with foreign nations, shall be deemed guilty of a felony [. . .]' The Act put responsibility upon government attorneys and district courts to pursue and investigate trusts, companies and organizations suspected of violating the Act. The Clayton Act extended the right to sue under the antitrust laws to 'any person who shall be injured in his business or property by reason of anything forbidden in the antitrust laws.' Under the Clayton Act, private parties may sue in U.S. district court and should they prevail, they may be awarded treble damages and the cost of suit, including reasonable attorney's fees.

- a. 1921 recession
- b. 130-30 fund
- c. Sherman Antitrust Act
- d. 100-year flood

12. _____ is the controlled distribution of resources and scarce goods or services. _____ controls the size of the ration, one's allotted portion of the resources being distributed on a particular day or at a particular time.

In economics, it is often common to use the word '_____' to refer to one of the roles that prices play in markets, while _____ is called 'non-price _____.' Using prices to ration means that those with the most money (or other assets) and who want a product the most are first to receive it.

- a. 100-year flood
- b. 1921 recession
- c. 130-30 fund
- d. Rationing

13. The underground economy or _____ is a market where all commerce is conducted without regard to taxation, law or regulations of trade. The term is also often known as the underdog, shadow economy, black economy, parallel economy or phantom trades.

In modern societies the underground economy covers a vast array of activities.

- a. Protectionism
- b. Market economy
- c. Social market economy
- d. Black market

14. A _____ is a government imposed limit on how high a price can be charged on a product. For a _____ to be effective, it must differ from the free market price. In the graph at right, the supply and demand curves intersect to determine the free-market quantity and price.

- a. Pricing
- b. Fire sale
- c. Product sabotage
- d. Price ceiling

Chapter 4. Extensions of Demand and Supply Analysis

15. Economic _____ is defined as an excess distribution to any factor in a production process above that which is required to induce the factor into the process or any excess above that which is necessary to keep the factor in its current use..

Classical Factor _____ is primarily concerned with the fee paid for the use of fixed (e.g. natural) resources. The classical definition is expressed as any excess payment above that required to induce or provide for production.

   a. 100-year flood
   c. 1921 recession
   b. Rent
   d. 130-30 fund

16. _____ refers to laws or ordinances that set price controls on the renting of residential housing. It functions as a price ceiling.

_____ exists in approximately 40 countries around the world.

   a. Tenant rights
   c. National Housing Conference
   b. 100-year flood
   d. Rent control

17. A _____ is a government- or group-imposed limit on how low a price can be charged for a product. In order for a _____ to be effective, it must be greater than the equilibrium price. An ineffective _____, below equilibrium price.

A _____ can be set below the free-market equilibrium price.

   a. Price floor
   c. Flat rate
   b. Price markdown
   d. Two-part tariff

18. _____ describes a set of laws relating to domestic agriculture and imports of foreign agricultural products. Governments usually implement agricultural policies with the goal of achieving a specific outcome in the domestic agricultural product markets. Outcomes can involve, for example, a guaranteed supply level, price stability, product quality, product selection, land use or employment.
   a. Agricultural Policy
   c. Intercropping
   b. ACEA agreement
   d. ACCRA Cost of Living Index

19. The _____ is an economic and political union of 27 member states, located primarily in Europe. It was established by the Treaty of Maastricht on 1 November 1993, upon the foundations of the pre-existing European Economic Community. With a population of almost 500 million, the _____ generates an estimated 30% share (US$18.4 trillion in 2008) of the nominal gross world product.
   a. European Court of Justice
   c. ACEA agreement
   b. ACCRA Cost of Living Index
   d. European Union

20. A _____ is the lowest hourly, daily or monthly wage that employers may legally pay to employees or workers. Equivalently, it is the lowest wage at which workers may sell their labor. Although _____ laws are in effect in a great many jurisdictions, there are differences of opinion about the benefits and drawbacks of a _____.

a. Microfoundations
b. Minimum wage
c. Permanent war economy
d. Marginal propensity to consume

21. In economics, a _____ may be either a subsidy or a price control, both with the intended effect of keeping the market price of a good higher than the competitive equilibrium level.

In the case of a price control, a _____ is the minimum legal price a seller may charge, typically placed above equilibrium. It is the support of certain price levels at or above market values by the government.

a. Marginal profit
b. Price support
c. Labor intensity
d. Payment schedule

22. The _____ is an international organization that oversees the global financial system by following the macroeconomic policies of its member countries, in particular those with an impact on exchange rates and the balance of payments. It is an organization formed to stabilize international exchange rates and facilitate development. It also offers financial and technical assistance to its members, making it an international lender of last resort.

a. ACEA agreement
b. ACCRA Cost of Living Index
c. Office of Thrift Supervision
d. International Monetary Fund

23. In economics, an _____ is any good (e.g. a commodity) or service brought into one country from another country in a legitimate fashion, typically for use in trade.It is a good that is brought in from another country for sale. _____ goods or services are provided to domestic consumers by foreign producers. An _____ in the receiving country is an export to the sending country.

a. Incoterms
b. Import
c. Economic integration
d. Import quota

24. An _____ is a type of protectionist trade restriction that sets a physical limit on the quantity of a good that can be imported into a country in a given period of time. Quotas, like other trade restrictions, are used to benefit the producers of a good in a domestic economy at the expense of all consumers of the good in that economy.

Critics say quotas often lead to corruption (bribes to get a quota allocation), smuggling (circumventing a quota), and higher prices for consumers.

a. Economic integration
b. International Monetary Systems
c. Agreement on Agriculture
d. Import quota

25. The _____ is a term used for industries primarily concerned with the design or manufacture of clothing as well as the distribution and use of textiles.

Prior to the manufacturing processes were mechanized, textiles were produced in the home, and excess sold for extra money. Most cloth was made from either wool, cotton, or flax, depending on the era and location.

a. 100-year flood
b. 130-30 fund
c. Textile industry
d. Textile manufacture during the Industrial Revolution

Chapter 5. The Public Sector and Public Choice

1. _____s is the social science that studies the production, distribution, and consumption of goods and services. The term _____s comes from the Ancient Greek οἰκονομία from οἶκος (oikos, 'house') + νόμος (nomos, 'custom' or 'law'), hence 'rules of the house(hold)'. Current _____ models developed out of the broader field of political economy in the late 19th century, owing to a desire to use an empirical approach more akin to the physical sciences.

   a. Economic
   b. Energy economics
   c. Opportunity cost
   d. Inflation

2. In finance, the _____s between two currencies specifies how much one currency is worth in terms of the other. It is the value of a foreign natione;s currency in terms of the home natione;s currency. For example an _____ of 102 Japanese yen to the United States dollar means that JPY 102 is worth the same as USD 1.

   a. ACEA agreement
   b. Interbank market
   c. Exchange rate
   d. ACCRA Cost of Living Index

3. An _____ is a tax levied on the financial income of people, corporations, or other legal entities. Various _____ systems exist, with varying degrees of tax incidence. Income taxation can be progressive, proportional, or regressive.

   a. AD-IA Model
   b. ACEA agreement
   c. ACCRA Cost of Living Index
   d. Income tax

4. In economics, a _____ exists when the production or use of goods and services by the market is not efficient. That is, there exists another outcome where all involved can be made better off. _____s can be viewed as scenarios where individuals' pursuit of pure self-interest leads to results that are not efficient - that can be improved upon from the societal point-of-view.

   a. General equilibrium
   b. Financial economics
   c. Fixed exchange rate
   d. Market failure

5. A _____ is any systematic process enabling many market players to bid and ask: helping bidders and sellers interact and make deals. It is not just the price mechanism but the entire system of regulation, qualification, credentials, reputations and clearing that surrounds that mechanism and makes it operate in a social context.

   Because a _____ relies on the assumption that players are constantly involved and unequally enabled, a _____ is distinguished specifically from a voting system where candidates seek the support of voters on a less regular basis.

   a. Competitive equilibrium
   b. Contestable market
   c. Price mechanism
   d. Market system

6. To _____ is to impose a financial charge or other levy upon a taxpayer by a state or the functional equivalent of a state.

   _____es are also imposed by many subnational entities. _____es consist of direct _____ or indirect _____, and may be paid in money or as its labour equivalent (often but not always unpaid.)

   a. 100-year flood
   b. 130-30 fund
   c. 1921 recession
   d. Tax

7. _____ are the income that is gained by governments because of taxation of the people.

Just as there are different types of tax, the form in which _____ is collected also differs; furthermore, the agency that collects the tax may not be part of central government, but may be an alternative third-party licenced to collect tax which they themselves will use. For example:

- In the UK, the DVLA collects road tax, which is then passed on the treasury.

_____s on purchases can come from two forms: 'tax' itself is a percentage of the price added to the purchase (such as sales tax in US states, or VAT in the UK), while 'duty' is a fixed amount added to the purchase price (such as is commonly found on cigarettes.) In order to calculate the total tax raised from these sales, we must work out the effective tax rate multiplied by the quantity supplied.

- a. Tax and spend
- b. Tax revenue
- c. Taxation as slavery
- d. Taxable wage

8. To tax is to impose a financial charge or other levy upon a taxpayer by a state or the functional equivalent of a state.

_____ are also imposed by many subnational entities. _____ consist of direct tax or indirect tax, and may be paid in money or as its labour equivalent (often but not always unpaid.)

- a. 1921 recession
- b. 130-30 fund
- c. 100-year flood
- d. Taxes

9. _____ is a broad label that refers to any individuals or households that use goods and services generated within the economy. The concept of a _____ is used in different contexts, so that the usage and significance of the term may vary.

Typically when business people and economists talk of _____s they are talking about person as _____, an aggregated commodity item with little individuality other than that expressed in the buy/not-buy decision.

- a. 130-30 fund
- b. 1921 recession
- c. 100-year flood
- d. Consumer

10. Many _____ are related to the environmental consequences of production and use

- Systemic risk describes the risks to the overall economy arising from the risks which the banking system takes. That the private costs of banking failure may be smaller than the social costs justifies banking regulations, although regulations could create a moral hazard.

- Anthropogenic climate change is attributed to greenhouse gas emissions from burning oil, gas, and coal. Global warming has been ranked as the #1 externality of all economic activity, in the magnitude of potential harms and yet remains unmitigated.

Chapter 5. The Public Sector and Public Choice

a. Total Economic Value
b. White certificates
c. Green certificate
d. Negative externalities

11. A _____ refers to any type debt instrument, such as a loan, bond, mortgage that does not have a fixed rate of interest over the life of the instrument. Such debt typically uses an index or other base rate for establishing the interest rate for each relevant period. One of the most common rates to use as the basis for applying interest rates is the London Inter-bank Offered Rate, or LIBOR
    a. Disposal tax effect
    b. Moneylender
    c. Floating interest rate
    d. Money market

12. The United States federal _____ is a refundable tax credit. For tax year 2008, a claimant with one qualifying child can receive a maximum credit of $2,917. For two or more qualifying children, the maximum credit is $4,824.
    a. Earned Income Tax Credit
    b. ACEA agreement
    c. ACCRA Cost of Living Index
    d. AD-IA Model

13. The term _____ describes two different concepts:

   - The first is a recognition of partial payment already made towards taxes due.
   - The second is a state benefit paid to workers through the tax system, which has the effect of increasing (rather than reducing) net income.

Within the Australian, Canadian, United Kingdom, and United States tax systems, a _____ is a recognition of partial payment already made towards taxes due. A similar concept exists (fr:Avoir fiscal) in the French tax system. This situation arises, for example, when standard rate tax has been deducted at source, but the tax-payer is subject to further taxation at a higher rate. It also applies in dividend imputation systems.

   a. 100-year flood
   b. Tax Credit
   c. 1921 recession
   d. 130-30 fund

14. In economics, an externality or spillover of an economic transaction is an impact on a party that is not directly involved in the transaction. In such a case, prices do not reflect the full costs or benefits in production or consumption of a product or service. A positive impact is called an _____, while a negative impact is called an external cost.
    a. ACCRA Cost of Living Index
    b. AD-IA Model
    c. External benefit
    d. ACEA agreement

15. The U.S. _____ (EEOC) is a federal agency whose goal is ending employment discrimination. The _____ investigates discrimination complaints based on an individual's race, color, national origin, religion, sex, age, disability and retaliation for reporting and/or opposing a discriminatory practice. The Commission is also tasked with filing suits on behalf of alleged victim(s) of discrimination against employers and as an adjudicatory for claims of discrimination brought against federal agencies.
    a. AD-IA Model
    b. ACCRA Cost of Living Index
    c. ACEA agreement
    d. EEOC

16. In economics, the _____ of a good or of a service is the utility of the specific use to which an agent would put a given increase in that good or service, or of the specific use that would be abandoned in response to a given decrease. In other words, _____ is the utility of the marginal use -- which, on the assumption of economic rationality, would be the least urgent use of the good or service, from the best feasible combination of actions in which its use is included. Under the mainstream assumptions, the _____ of a good or service is the posited quantified change in utility obtained by increasing or by decreasing use of that good or service.
   a. Marginal utility
   b. 130-30 fund
   c. 100-year flood
   d. 1921 recession

17. _____ is an equity (stock) exchange located at 11 Wall Street in lower Manhattan, New York, USA. It is the largest stock exchange in the world by dollar value of its listed companies' securities. As of October 2008, the combined capitalization of all domestic _____ listed companies was US$10.1 trillion.
   a. 1921 recession
   b. 130-30 fund
   c. New York Stock Exchange
   d. 100-year flood

18. In economics and especially in the theory of competition, _____ are obstacles in the path of a firm that make it difficult to enter a given market.

_____ are the source of a firm's pricing power - the ability of a firm to raise prices without losing all its customers.

The term refers to hindrances that an individual may face while trying to gain entrance into a profession or trade.

   a. Group boycott
   b. Social dumping
   c. Barriers to entry
   d. Limit price

19. In economics, an _____ or spillover of an economic transaction is an impact on a party that is not directly involved in the transaction. In such a case, prices do not reflect the full costs or benefits in production or consumption of a product or service. A positive impact is called an external benefit, while a negative impact is called an external cost.
   a. Environmental impact assessment
   b. Existence value
   c. Environmental tariff
   d. Externality

20. Under the system of feudalism, a _____, fief, feud, feoff often consisted of inheritable lands or revenue-producing property granted by a liege lord, generally to a vassal, in return for a form of allegiance, originally to give him the means to fulfill his military duties when called upon. However anything of value could be held in fief, such as an office, a right of exploitation (e.g., hunting, fishing) or any other type of revenue, rather than the land it comes from.

Originally, the feudal institution of vassalage did not imply the giving or receiving of landholdings (which were granted only as a reward for loyalty), but by the eighth century the giving of a landholding was becoming standard.

   a. Fiefdom
   b. 100-year flood
   c. 1921 recession
   d. 130-30 fund

Chapter 5. The Public Sector and Public Choice

21. In economics, _____ is a measure of the relative satisfaction from consumption of various goods and services. Given this measure, one may speak meaningfully of increasing or decreasing _____, and thereby explain economic behavior in terms of attempts to increase one's _____. For illustrative purposes, changes in _____ are sometimes expressed in units called utils.
    a. Utility function
    b. Expected utility hypothesis
    c. Ordinal utility
    d. Utility

22. In economics, _____ refers to the ability of a person or a country to produce a particular good at a lower marginal cost and opportunity cost than another person or country. It is the ability to produce a product most efficiently given all the other products that could be produced. It can be contrasted with absolute advantage which refers to the ability of a person or a country to produce a particular good at a lower absolute cost than another.
    a. Triffin dilemma
    b. Comparative advantage
    c. Hot money
    d. Gravity model of trade

23. A _____ is the exclusive authority to determine how a resource is used, whether that resource is owned by government or by individuals. All economic goods have a _____s attribute. This attribute has three broad components

    1. The right to use the good
    2. The right to earn income from the good
    3. The right to transfer the good to others

The concept of _____s as used by economists and legal scholars are related but distinct. The distinction is largely seen in the economists' focus on the ability of an individual or collective to control the use of the good.

    a. Post-sale restraint
    b. Property right
    c. Holder in due course
    d. High-reeve

24. _____ describes a set of laws relating to domestic agriculture and imports of foreign agricultural products. Governments usually implement agricultural policies with the goal of achieving a specific outcome in the domestic agricultural product markets. Outcomes can involve, for example, a guaranteed supply level, price stability, product quality, product selection, land use or employment.
    a. Intercropping
    b. ACCRA Cost of Living Index
    c. ACEA agreement
    d. Agricultural Policy

25. The _____ is an independent agency of the United States government, established in 1914 by the _____ Act. Its principal mission is the promotion of 'consumer protection' and the elimination and prevention of what regulators perceive to be harmfully 'anti-competitive' business practices, such as coercive monopoly.

The _____ Act was one of President Wilson's major acts against trusts.

    a. Federal Trade Commission
    b. 1921 recession
    c. 100-year flood
    d. 130-30 fund

26. In microeconomics, _____ is the extra revenue that an additional unit of product will bring. It is the additional income from selling one more unit of a good; sometimes equal to price. It can also be described as the change in total revenue/change in number of units sold.

a. Market demand schedule
b. Reservation price
c. Long term
d. Marginal revenue

27. _____ is a common market structure where many competing producers sell products that are differentiated from one another (ie. the products are substitutes, but are not exactly alike.) Many markets are monopolistically competitive, common examples include the markets for restaurants, cereal, clothing, shoes and service industries in large cities.
   a. Mathematical economics
   b. Monopolistic competition
   c. Financial crisis
   d. Perfect competition

28. In neoclassical economics and microeconomics, _____ describes the perfect being a market in which there are many small firms, all producing homogeneous goods. In the short term, such markets are productively inefficient as output will not occur where mc is equal to ac, but allocatively efficient, as output under _____ will always occur where mc is equal to mr, and therefore where mc equals ar. However, in the long term, such markets are both allocatively and productively efficient.
   a. General equilibrium
   b. Perfect competition
   c. Law of supply
   d. Co-operative economics

29. Competition law, known in the United States as _____ law, has three main elements:

   - prohibiting agreements or practices that restrict free trading and competition between business entities. This includes in particular the repression of cartels.
   - banning abusive behaviour by a firm dominating a market, or anti-competitive practices that tend to lead to such a dominant position. Practices controlled in this way may include predatory pricing, tying, price gouging, refusal to deal, and many others.
   - supervising the mergers and acquisitions of large corporations, including some joint ventures. Transactions that are considered to threaten the competitive process can be prohibited altogether, or approved subject to 'remedies' such as an obligation to divest part of the merged business or to offer licences or access to facilities to enable other businesses to continue competing.

The substance and practice of competition law varies from jurisdiction to jurisdiction. Protecting the interests of consumers (consumer welfare) and ensuring that entrepreneurs have an opportunity to compete in the market economy are often treated as important objectives. Competition law is closely connected with law on deregulation of access to markets, state aids and subsidies, the privatisation of state owned assets and the establishment of independent sector regulators. In recent decades, competition law has been viewed as a way to provide better public services.

   a. United Kingdom competition law
   b. Intellectual property law
   c. Anti-Inflation Act
   d. Antitrust

Chapter 5. The Public Sector and Public Choice

30. _____, known in the United States as antitrust law, has three main elements:

- prohibiting agreements or practices that restrict free trading and competition between business entities. This includes in particular the repression of cartels.
- banning abusive behaviour by a firm dominating a market, or anti-competitive practices that tend to lead to such a dominant position. Practices controlled in this way may include predatory pricing, tying, price gouging, refusal to deal, and many others.
- supervising the mergers and acquisitions of large corporations, including some joint ventures. Transactions that are considered to threaten the competitive process can be prohibited altogether, or approved subject to 'remedies' such as an obligation to divest part of the merged business or to offer licences or access to facilities to enable other businesses to continue competing.

The substance and practice of _____ varies from jurisdiction to jurisdiction. Protecting the interests of consumers (consumer welfare) and ensuring that entrepreneurs have an opportunity to compete in the market economy are often treated as important objectives. _____ is closely connected with law on deregulation of access to markets, state aids and subsidies, the privatisation of state owned assets and the establishment of independent sector regulators. In recent decades, _____ has been viewed as a way to provide better public services.

a. Fee simple
b. Due diligence
c. Competition law
d. Hostile work environment

31. _____ is a common concept in economics, and gives rise to derived concepts such as consumer debt. Generally _____ is defined by opposition to production. But the precise definition can vary because different schools of economists define production quite differently.

a. Foreclosure data providers
b. Consumption
c. Federal Reserve Bank Notes
d. Cash or share options

32. _____, officially the Islamic Republic of _____, is a landlocked country that is located approximately in the center of Asia. It is variously designated as geographically located within Central Asia, South Asia, and the Middle East. It is bordered by Pakistan in the south and east, Iran in the south and west, Turkmenistan, Uzbekistan and Tajikistan in the north, and China in the far northeast.

a. ACEA agreement
b. Afghanistan
c. ACCRA Cost of Living Index
d. AD-IA Model

33. _____ refers to an absence of excessive fluctuations in the macroeconomy. An economy with fairly constant output growth and low and stable inflation would be considered economically stable. An economy with frequent large recessions, a pronounced business cycle, very high or variable inflation, or frequent financial crises would be considered economically unstable.

a. Economic stability
b. Export subsidy
c. Income effect
d. Export-led growth

34. A _____ is an object whose consumption increases the utility of the consumer, for which the quantity demanded exceeds the quantity supplied at zero price. _____s are usually modeled as having diminishing marginal utility. The first individual purchase has high utility; the second has less.

Chapter 5. The Public Sector and Public Choice

a. Merit good
c. Pie method
b. Composite good
d. Good

35. The concept of a _____ introduced in economics introduced by Richard Musgrave (1957, 1959) is a commodity which is judged that an individual or society should have on the basis of some concept of need, rather than ability and willingness to pay. The term is, perhaps, less often used today than it was in the 1960s to 1980s but the concept still lies behind many economic actions by governments which are not performed specifically for financial reasons or by supporting incomes (eg via tax rebates.) Examples include the provision of food stamps to support nutrition, the delivery of health services to improve quality of life and reduce morbidity, subsidized housing and arguably education.
   a. Final good
   c. Merit good
   b. Private good
   d. Positional goods

36. Economics:

   - _____,the desire to own something and the ability to pay for it
   - _____ curve,a graphic representation of a _____ schedule
   - _____ deposit, the money in checking accounts
   - _____ pull theory,the theory that inflation occurs when _____ for goods and services exceeds existing supplies
   - _____ schedule,a table that lists the quantity of a good a person will buy it each different price
   - _____ side economics,the school of economics at believes government spending and tax cuts open economy by raising _____

   a. Production
   c. Variability
   b. McKesson ' Robbins scandal
   d. Demand

37. In economics, the _____ can be defined as the graph depicting the relationship between the price of a certain commodity, and the amount of it that consumers are willing and able to purchase at that given price. It is a graphic representation of a demand schedule. The _____ for all consumers together follows from the _____ of every individual consumer: the individual demands at each price are added together.
   a. Wage curve
   c. Demand curve
   b. Cost curve
   d. Kuznets curve

38. In economics, a _____ is a good or service whose consumption is considered unhealthy, degrading, or otherwise socially undesirable due to the perceived negative effects on the consumers themselves. It is over-consumed if left to market forces. Examples of _____ s include tobacco, alcoholic beverages, recreational drugs, gambling, junk food and prostitution.
   a. Durable good
   c. Credence good
   b. Search good
   d. Demerit good

39. In economics, _____ is the transfer of income, wealth or property from some individuals to others.

One premise of _____ is that money should be distributed to benefit the poorer members of society, and that the rich have an obligation to assist the poor, thus creating a more financially egalitarian society. Another argument is that the rich exploit the poor or otherwise gain unfair benefits.

Chapter 5. The Public Sector and Public Choice

a. 100-year flood
b. 1921 recession
c. 130-30 fund
d. Redistribution

40. A _____ is the transfer of wealth from one party (such as a person or company) to another. A _____ is usually made in exchange for the provision of goods, services or both, or to fulfill a legal obligation.

The simplest and oldest form of _____ is barter, the exchange of one good or service for another.

a. Social gravity
b. Going concern
c. Soft count
d. Payment

41. In economics, a _____ is a redistribution of income in the market system. These payments are considered to be nonexhaustive because they do not directly absorb resources or create output. Examples of certain _____s include welfare (financial aid), social security, and government subsidies for certain businesses (firms.)

a. 1921 recession
b. 130-30 fund
c. 100-year flood
d. Transfer payment

42. _____ are the divisions at which tax rates change in a progressive tax system (or an explicitly regressive tax system, although this is much rarer.) Essentially, they are the cutoff values for taxable income -- income past a certain point will be taxed at a higher rate.

a. Popiwek
b. Tax farming
c. Disposable income
d. Tax brackets

43. _____ or government expenditure is classified by economists into three main types. Government purchases of goods and services for current use are classed as government consumption. Government purchases of goods and services intended to create future benefits, such as infrastructure investment or research spending, are classed as government investment.

a. 1921 recession
b. 130-30 fund
c. Government spending
d. 100-year flood

44. _____ is the difference between a lower selling price and a higher purchase price, resulting in a financial loss for the seller. Pursuant to IRS TAX TIP 2009-35 'If your _____es exceed your capital gains, the excess can be deducted on your tax return, up to an annual limit of $3,000 ($1,500 if you are married filing separately.)' .

a. 130-30 fund
b. 1921 recession
c. 100-year flood
d. Capital loss

45. A mutual _____ or stockholder is an individual or company (including a corporation) that legally owns one or more shares of stock in a joint stock company. A company's _____s collectively own that company. Thus, the typical goal of such companies is to enhance _____ value.

a. Prime Standard
b. Relative valuation
c. Shareholder
d. Profit warning

46. _____ is a specific term used in companies' financial reporting from the company-whole point of view. Because that use excludes the effects of changing ownership interest, an economic measure of _____ is necessary for financial analysis from the shareholders' point of view

_____ is defined by the Financial Accounting Standards Board, or FASB, as e;the change in equity [net assets] of a business enterprise during a period from transactions and other events and circumstances from nonowner sources. It includes all changes in equity during a period except those resulting from investments by owners and distributions to owners.e;

_____ is the sum of net income and other items that must bypass the income statement because they have not been realized, including items like an unrealized holding gain or loss from available for sale securities and foreign currency translation gains or losses.

a. Comprehensive income
b. Windfall gain
c. Real income
d. Net national income

47. In economics, _____ is the analysis of the effect of a particular tax on the distribution of economic welfare. _____ is said to 'fall' upon the group that, at the end of the day, bears the burden of the tax. The key concept is that the _____ or tax burden does not depend on where the revenue is collected, but on the price elasticity of demand and price elasticity of supply.

a. 1921 recession
b. 130-30 fund
c. 100-year flood
d. Tax incidence

48. The _____ is the audit, evaluation, and investigative arm of the United States Congress. It is located in the Legislative branch of the United States government.

The _____ was established as the General Accounting Office by the Budget and Accounting Act of 1921 (Pub.L.

a. 100-year flood
b. 1921 recession
c. Government Accountability Office
d. 130-30 fund

49. _____ was a predominant American integrated oil producing, transporting, refining, and marketing company. Established in 1870 as an Ohio Corporation, it was the largest oil refiner in the world and operated as a major company trust and was one of the world's first and largest multinational corporations until it was broken up by the United States Supreme Court in 1911. John D. Rockefeller was a founder, chairman and major shareholder, and the company made him a billionaire and eventually the richest man in history.

a. 1921 recession
b. 130-30 fund
c. 100-year flood
d. Standard Oil

50. A variety of measures of _____ and output are used in economics to estimate total economic activity in a country or region, including gross domestic product (GDP), gross national product (GNP), and net _____

There are three main ways of calculating these numbers; the output approach, the income approach and the expenditure approach. In theory, the three must yield the same, because total expenditures on goods and services must equal the total income paid to the producers (Gnational income), and that must also equal the total value of the output of goods and services (GNP.)

a. Gross world product
c. Volume index
b. GNI per capita
d. National income

51. A _____ is a consumption tax charged at the point of purchase for certain goods and services. The tax is usually set as a percentage by the government charging the tax. There is usually a list of exemptions.
   a. 100-year flood
   c. 130-30 fund
   b. 1921 recession
   d. Sales tax

52. The term '_____' refers to the concept of collecting information and attempting to spot a pattern in the information. In some fields of study, the term '_____' has more formally-defined meanings.

In project management _____ is a mathematical technique that uses historical results to predict future outcome.
   a. Quantile regression
   c. Probit model
   b. Trend analysis
   d. Coefficient of determination

53. The _____ is an international organization that oversees the global financial system by following the macroeconomic policies of its member countries, in particular those with an impact on exchange rates and the balance of payments. It is an organization formed to stabilize international exchange rates and facilitate development. It also offers financial and technical assistance to its members, making it an international lender of last resort.
   a. Office of Thrift Supervision
   c. ACCRA Cost of Living Index
   b. International Monetary Fund
   d. ACEA agreement

54. A trade union or _____ is an organization of workers who have banded together to achieve common goals in key areas and working conditions. The trade union, through its leadership, bargains with the employer on behalf of union members (rank and file members) and negotiates labor contracts (Collective bargaining) with employers. This may include the negotiation of wages, work rules, complaint procedures, rules governing hiring, firing and promotion of workers, benefits, workplace safety and policies.
   a. Demand-side technologies
   c. Business valuation standards
   b. Basis of futures
   d. Labor union

55. A _____ is a group of people who share or are motivated by at least one common issue or interest, or work together on a specific project(s) to achieve a common objective. _____s are also characterised by attempts to share and exercise political and social power and to make decisions on a consensus-driven and egalitarian basis. _____s differ from cooperatives in that they are not necessarily focused upon an economic benefit or saving (but can be that as well.)
   a. 100-year flood
   c. 1921 recession
   b. 130-30 fund
   d. Collective

56. In economics and sociology, an _____ is any factor (financial or non-financial) that enables or motivates a particular course of action, or counts as a reason for preferring one choice to the alternatives. It is an expectation that encourages people to behave in a certain way. Since human beings are purposeful creatures, the study of _____ structures is central to the study of all economic activity (both in terms of individual decision-making and in terms of co-operation and competition within a larger institutional structure).

Chapter 5. The Public Sector and Public Choice

a. Incentive
b. Epstein-Zin preferences
c. Isocost
d. Economic reform

57. _____ is subcontracting a process, such as product design or manufacturing, to a third-party company. The decision to outsource is often made in the interest of lowering cost or making better use of time and energy costs, redirecting or conserving energy directed at the competencies of a particular business, or to make more efficient use of land, labor, capital, (information) technology and resources. _____ became part of the business lexicon during the 1980s.

a. Averch-Johnson effect
b. Additional Funds Needed
c. Electronic business
d. Outsourcing

58. _____ in economic theory is the use of modern economic tools to study problems that are traditionally in the province of political science.

In particular, it studies the behavior of politicians and government officials as mostly self-interested agents and their interactions in the social system either as such or under alternative constitutional rules. These can be represented a number of ways, including standard constrained utility maximization, game theory, or decision theory.

a. Rational ignorance
b. Paradox of voting
c. Public interest theory
d. Public choice

59. A _____ or labor union is an organization of workers who have banded together to achieve common goals in key areas and working conditions. The _____, through its leadership, bargains with the employer on behalf of union members (rank and file members) and negotiates labor contracts (Collective bargaining) with employers. This may include the negotiation of wages, work rules, complaint procedures, rules governing hiring, firing and promotion of workers, benefits, workplace safety and policies.

a. Case-Shiller Home Price Indices
b. Trade union
c. Guaranteed investment contracts
d. Consumer goods

60. _____ refers to confiscation of private property with the stated purpose of establishing social equality.

Unlike eminent domain, _____ takes place beyond the common law legal systems and refers to socially-motivated confiscations of any property rather than to taking away the real estate. Just compensation to owners is given.

a. AD-IA Model
b. ACEA agreement
c. ACCRA Cost of Living Index
d. Expropriation

Chapter 5. The Public Sector and Public Choice

61. A _____ is:

- Rewrite _____, in generative grammar and computer science
- Standardization, a formal and widely-accepted statement, fact, definition, or qualification
- Operation, a determinate _____ for performing a mathematical operation and obtaining a certain result (Mathematics, Logic)
    - Unary operation
    - Binary operation
- _____ of inference, a function from sets of formulae to formulae (Mathematics, Logic)
- _____ of thumb, principle with broad application that is not intended to be strictly accurate or reliable for every situation. Also often simply referred to as a _____
- Moral, an atomic element of a moral code for guiding choices in human behavior
- Heuristic, a quantized '_____' which shows a tendency or probability for successful function
- A regulation, as in sports
- A Production _____, as in computer science
- Procedural law, a _____ set governing the application of laws to cases
    - A law, which may informally be called a '_____'
    - A court ruling, a decision by a court
- In the U.S. Government, a regulation mandated by Congress, but written or expanded upon by the Executive Branch.
- Norm (sociology), an informal but widely accepted _____, concept, truth, definition, or qualification (social norms, legal norms, coding norms)
- Norm (philosophy), a kind of sentence or a reason to act, feel or believe
- 'Rulership' is the concept of governance by a government:
    - Military _____, governance by a military body
    - Monastic _____, a collection of precepts that guides the life of monks or nuns in a religious order where the superior holds the place of Christ
- Slide _____

- '_____,' a song by Ayumi Hamasaki
- '_____,' a song by rapper Nas
- '_____s,' an album by the band The Whitest Boy Alive
- _____s: Pyaar Ka Superhit Formula, a 2003 Bollywood film
- ruler, an instrument for measuring lengths
- _____, a component of an astrolabe, circumferator or similar instrument
- The _____s, a bestselling self-help book
- _____ Project (Run Up-to-date Linux Everywhere), a project that aims to use up-to-date Linux software on old PCs
- _____ engine, a software system that helps managing business _____s
- Ja _____, a hip hop artist
    - R.U.L.E., a 2005 greatest hits album by rapper Ja _____
- '_____s,' a KMFDM song

a. Technocracy
b. Demand
c. Procter ' Gamble
d. Rule

62. In economics, a _____ is a good that is non-rivaled and non-excludable. This means, respectively, that consumption of the good by one individual does not reduce availability of the good for consumption by others; and that no one can be effectively excluded from using the good. In the real world, there may be no such thing as an absolutely non-rivaled and non-excludable good; but economists think that some goods approximate the concept closely enough for the analysis to be economically useful.

   a. Neoclassical synthesis

   b. Demand-pull theory

   c. Public good

   d. Happiness economics

Chapter 6. Taxes, Transfers, and Public Spending

1. _____s is the social science that studies the production, distribution, and consumption of goods and services. The term _____s comes from the Ancient Greek oá¼°κονομῖα from oá¼¶κος (oikos, 'house') + νΊŒµος (nomos, 'custom' or 'law'), hence 'rules of the house(hold)'. Current _____ models developed out of the broader field of political economy in the late 19th century, owing to a desire to use an empirical approach more akin to the physical sciences.

   a. Inflation
   b. Energy economics
   c. Economic
   d. Opportunity cost

2. The _____ is the audit, evaluation, and investigative arm of the United States Congress. It is located in the Legislative branch of the United States government.

   The _____ was established as the General Accounting Office by the Budget and Accounting Act of 1921 (Pub.L.

   a. 100-year flood
   b. 1921 recession
   c. Government Accountability Office
   d. 130-30 fund

3. In economic theory, _____ is the competitive situation in any market where the conditions necessary for perfect competition are not satisfied. It is a market structure that does not meet the conditions of perfect competition.

   Forms of _____ include:

   - Monopoly, in which there is only one seller of a good.
   - Oligopoly, in which there is a small number of sellers.
   - Monopolistic competition, in which there are many sellers producing highly differentiated goods.
   - Monopsony, in which there is only one buyer of a good.
   - Oligopsony, in which there is a small number of buyers.

   There may also be _____ in markets due to buyers or sellers lacking information about prices and the goods being traded.

   There may also be _____ due to a time lag in a market.

   a. ACCRA Cost of Living Index
   b. AD-IA Model
   c. ACEA agreement
   d. Imperfect Competition

4. To _____ is to impose a financial charge or other levy upon a taxpayer by a state or the functional equivalent of a state.

   _____es are also imposed by many subnational entities. _____es consist of direct _____ or indirect _____, and may be paid in money or as its labour equivalent (often but not always unpaid.)

   a. 1921 recession
   b. 130-30 fund
   c. 100-year flood
   d. Tax

5. To tax is to impose a financial charge or other levy upon a taxpayer by a state or the functional equivalent of a state.

_____ are also imposed by many subnational entities. _____ consist of direct tax or indirect tax, and may be paid in money or as its labour equivalent (often but not always unpaid.)

a. 1921 recession
b. Taxes
c. 100-year flood
d. 130-30 fund

6. In economics and especially in the theory of competition, _____ are obstacles in the path of a firm that make it difficult to enter a given market.

_____ are the source of a firm's pricing power - the ability of a firm to raise prices without losing all its customers.

The term refers to hindrances that an individual may face while trying to gain entrance into a profession or trade.

a. Social dumping
b. Limit price
c. Barriers to entry
d. Group boycott

7. A _____ represents the combinations of goods and services that a consumer can purchase given current prices and his income. Consumer theory uses the concepts of a _____ and a preference map to analyze consumer choices. Both concepts have a ready graphical representation in the two-good case.

a. Joint demand
b. Revealed preference
c. Quality bias
d. Budget constraint

8. A _____ is a legal document that is often passed by the legislature, and approved by the chief executive-or president. For example, only certain types of revenue may be imposed and collected. Property tax is frequently the basis for municipal and county revenues, while sales tax and/or income tax are the basis for state revenues, and income tax and corporate tax are the basis for national revenues.

a. Right-financing
b. Lump-sum tax
c. Structural deficit
d. Government budget

9. _____ are the income that is gained by governments because of taxation of the people.

Just as there are different types of tax, the form in which _____ is collected also differs; furthermore, the agency that collects the tax may not be part of central government, but may be an alternative third-party licenced to collect tax which they themselves will use. For example:

- In the UK, the DVLA collects road tax, which is then passed on the treasury.

_____s on purchases can come from two forms: 'tax' itself is a percentage of the price added to the purchase (such as sales tax in US states, or VAT in the UK), while 'duty' is a fixed amount added to the purchase price (such as is commonly found on cigarettes.) In order to calculate the total tax raised from these sales, we must work out the effective tax rate multiplied by the quantity supplied.

Chapter 6. Taxes, Transfers, and Public Spending

a. Tax and spend
b. Tax revenue
c. Taxation as slavery
d. Taxable wage

10. A _____ is a charge for the use of a product or service.

A _____ may apply per use of the good or service or charge the user for use of the good or service. The first is a charge for each time while the second is a charge for bulk or time-limited use.

a. User charge
b. Ad valorem tax
c. Indirect tax
d. Optimal tax theory

11. In economics, the _____ of a good or of a service is the utility of the specific use to which an agent would put a given increase in that good or service, or of the specific use that would be abandoned in response to a given decrease. In other words, _____ is the utility of the marginal use -- which, on the assumption of economic rationality, would be the least urgent use of the good or service, from the best feasible combination of actions in which its use is included. Under the mainstream assumptions, the _____ of a good or service is the posited quantified change in utility obtained by increasing or by decreasing use of that good or service.

a. 130-30 fund
b. 1921 recession
c. Marginal utility
d. 100-year flood

12. _____ was a predominant American integrated oil producing, transporting, refining, and marketing company. Established in 1870 as an Ohio Corporation, it was the largest oil refiner in the world and operated as a major company trust and was one of the world's first and largest multinational corporations until it was broken up by the United States Supreme Court in 1911. John D. Rockefeller was a founder, chairman and major shareholder, and the company made him a billionaire and eventually the richest man in history.

a. 1921 recession
b. 100-year flood
c. 130-30 fund
d. Standard Oil

13. In economics, _____ refers to the ability of a party to produce a good or service using fewer real resources than another entity producing the same good or service..A party has an _____ when using the same input as another party, it can produce a greater output. Since _____ is determined by a simple comparison of labor productivities, it is possible for a a party to have no _____ in anything. It can be contrasted with the concept of comparative advantage which refers to the ability to produce a particular good at a lower opportunity cost.

a. International economics
b. ACCRA Cost of Living Index
c. Index number
d. Absolute advantage

14. A _____ is a consumption tax charged at the point of purchase for certain goods and services. The tax is usually set as a percentage by the government charging the tax. There is usually a list of exemptions.

a. 1921 recession
b. 100-year flood
c. 130-30 fund
d. Sales tax

15. In economics, _____ is a measure of the relative satisfaction from consumption of various goods and services. Given this measure, one may speak meaningfully of increasing or decreasing _____, and thereby explain economic behavior in terms of attempts to increase one's _____. For illustrative purposes, changes in _____ are sometimes expressed in units called utils.

a. Expected utility hypothesis
b. Ordinal utility
c. Utility function
d. Utility

16. An _____ is a tax levied on the financial income of people, corporations, or other legal entities. Various _____ systems exist, with varying degrees of tax incidence. Income taxation can be progressive, proportional, or regressive.
   a. AD-IA Model
   b. ACEA agreement
   c. ACCRA Cost of Living Index
   d. Income tax

17. The U.S. _____ is a federal agency whose goal is ending employment discrimination. The _____ investigates discrimination complaints based on an individual's race, color, national origin, religion, sex, age, disability and retaliation for reporting and/or opposing a discriminatory practice. The Commission is also tasked with filing suits on behalf of alleged victim(s) of discrimination against employers and as an adjudicatory for claims of discrimination brought against federal agencies.
   a. ACCRA Cost of Living Index
   b. ACEA agreement
   c. AD-IA Model
   d. Equal Employment Opportunity Commission

18. In finance, the _____s between two currencies specifies how much one currency is worth in terms of the other. It is the value of a foreign natione;s currency in terms of the home natione;s currency. For example an _____ of 102 Japanese yen to the United States dollar means that JPY 102 is worth the same as USD 1.
   a. Interbank market
   b. ACEA agreement
   c. Exchange rate
   d. ACCRA Cost of Living Index

19. _____ is an economic concept with commonplace familiarity. It is the price that a good or service is offered at, or will fetch, in the marketplace. It is of interest mainly in the study of microeconomics.
   a. Noisy market hypothesis
   b. Paper trading
   c. Market anomaly
   d. Market price

20. _____ in economics and business is the result of an exchange and from that trade we assign a numerical monetary value to a good, service or asset. If Alice trades Bob 4 apples for an orange, the _____ of an orange is 4 apples. Inversely, the _____ of an apple is 1/4 oranges.
   a. Price book
   b. Price
   c. Price war
   d. Premium pricing

21. _____ or government expenditure is classified by economists into three main types. Government purchases of goods and services for current use are classed as government consumption. Government purchases of goods and services intended to create future benefits, such as infrastructure investment or research spending, are classed as government investment.
   a. 130-30 fund
   b. 1921 recession
   c. 100-year flood
   d. Government spending

22. _____ is a common concept in economics, and gives rise to derived concepts such as consumer debt. Generally _____ is defined by opposition to production. But the precise definition can vary because different schools of economists define production quite differently.

Chapter 6. Taxes, Transfers, and Public Spending 47

a. Federal Reserve Bank Notes
b. Cash or share options
c. Foreclosure data providers
d. Consumption

23. _____, in law and economics, is a form of risk management primarily used to hedge against the risk of a contingent loss. _____ is defined as the equitable transfer of the risk of a loss, from one entity to another, in exchange for a premium, and can be thought of as a guaranteed small loss to prevent a large, possibly devastating loss. An insurer is a company selling the _____; an insured or policyholder is the person or entity buying the _____.
   a. AD-IA Model
   b. ACEA agreement
   c. Insurance
   d. ACCRA Cost of Living Index

24. A trade union or _____ is an organization of workers who have banded together to achieve common goals in key areas and working conditions. The trade union, through its leadership, bargains with the employer on behalf of union members (rank and file members) and negotiates labor contracts (Collective bargaining) with employers. This may include the negotiation of wages, work rules, complaint procedures, rules governing hiring, firing and promotion of workers, benefits, workplace safety and policies.
   a. Basis of futures
   b. Business valuation standards
   c. Demand-side technologies
   d. Labor union

25. _____ is an equity (stock) exchange located at 11 Wall Street in lower Manhattan, New York, USA. It is the largest stock exchange in the world by dollar value of its listed companies' securities. As of October 2008, the combined capitalization of all domestic _____ listed companies was US$10.1 trillion.
   a. 1921 recession
   b. 130-30 fund
   c. 100-year flood
   d. New York Stock Exchange

26. A _____ is a group of people who share or are motivated by at least one common issue or interest, or work together on a specific project(s) to achieve a common objective. _____s are also characterised by attempts to share and exercise political and social power and to make decisions on a consensus-driven and egalitarian basis. _____s differ from cooperatives in that they are not necessarily focused upon an economic benefit or saving (but can be that as well.)
   a. 130-30 fund
   b. 100-year flood
   c. Collective
   d. 1921 recession

27. _____ or financing is to provide capital (funds), which means money for a project, a person, a business or any other private or public institutions.

Those funds can be allocated for either short term or long term purposes. The health fund is a new way of _____ private healthcare centers.

   a. Customer retention
   b. Funding
   c. No-bid contract
   d. Business transformation

28. A _____ or labor union is an organization of workers who have banded together to achieve common goals in key areas and working conditions. The _____, through its leadership, bargains with the employer on behalf of union members (rank and file members) and negotiates labor contracts (Collective bargaining) with employers. This may include the negotiation of wages, work rules, complaint procedures, rules governing hiring, firing and promotion of workers, benefits, workplace safety and policies.

Chapter 6. Taxes, Transfers, and Public Spending

a. Case-Shiller Home Price Indices
c. Consumer goods
b. Guaranteed investment contracts
d. Trade union

29. _____ are the inflation-indexed bonds issued by the U.S. Treasury. The principal is adjusted to the Consumer Price Index, the commonly used measure of inflation. The coupon rate is constant, but generates a different amount of interest when multiplied by the inflation-adjusted principal, thus protecting the holder against inflation.
   a. 130-30 fund
   c. 100-year flood
   b. 1921 recession
   d. Treasury Inflation-Protected Securities

30. In finance, _____ rate of profit or sometimes just return, is the ratio of money gained or lost on an investment relative to the amount of money invested. The amount of money gained or lost may be referred to as interest, profit/loss, gain/loss, or net income/loss. The money invested may be referred to as the asset, capital, principal, or the cost basis of the investment.
   a. Cost accrual ratio
   c. Rate of return
   b. Sortino ratio
   d. Current ratio

31. The _____ is an international organization that oversees the global financial system by following the macroeconomic policies of its member countries, in particular those with an impact on exchange rates and the balance of payments. It is an organization formed to stabilize international exchange rates and facilitate development. It also offers financial and technical assistance to its members, making it an international lender of last resort.
   a. ACEA agreement
   c. Office of Thrift Supervision
   b. International Monetary Fund
   d. ACCRA Cost of Living Index

32. Under the system of feudalism, a _____, fief, feud, feoff often consisted of inheritable lands or revenue-producing property granted by a liege lord, generally to a vassal, in return for a form of allegiance, originally to give him the means to fulfill his military duties when called upon. However anything of value could be held in fief, such as an office, a right of exploitation (e.g., hunting, fishing) or any other type of revenue, rather than the land it comes from.

Originally, the feudal institution of vassalage did not imply the giving or receiving of landholdings (which were granted only as a reward for loyalty), but by the eighth century the giving of a landholding was becoming standard.

   a. 100-year flood
   c. Fiefdom
   b. 1921 recession
   d. 130-30 fund

Chapter 7. Consumer Choice

1. The _____ proposed by John L. Lewis in 1932, was a federation of unions that organized workers in industrial unions in the United States and Canada from 1935 to 1955. The Taft-Hartley Act of 1947 required union leaders to swear that they were not Communists. Many CIO leaders refused to obey that requirement, later found unconstitutional.
   a. Multinational corporation
   b. Chinese correction
   c. Congress of Industrial Organizations
   d. Foreign direct investment

2. _____ is a field of economics that studies the strategic behavior of firms, the structure of markets and their interactions. The study of _____ adds to the perfectly competitive model real-world frictions such as limited information, transaction cost, cost of adjusting prices, government actions, and barriers to entry by new firms into a market. It then considers how firms are organized and how they compete.
   a. Inflation
   b. Industrial Organization
   c. Economic ideology
   d. Economic

3. In economics, the _____ of a good or of a service is the utility of the specific use to which an agent would put a given increase in that good or service, or of the specific use that would be abandoned in response to a given decrease. In other words, _____ is the utility of the marginal use -- which, on the assumption of economic rationality, would be the least urgent use of the good or service, from the best feasible combination of actions in which its use is included. Under the mainstream assumptions, the _____ of a good or service is the posited quantified change in utility obtained by increasing or by decreasing use of that good or service.
   a. 100-year flood
   b. 1921 recession
   c. 130-30 fund
   d. Marginal utility

4. In economics, _____ is a measure of the relative satisfaction from consumption of various goods and services. Given this measure, one may speak meaningfully of increasing or decreasing _____, and thereby explain economic behavior in terms of attempts to increase one's _____. For illustrative purposes, changes in _____ are sometimes expressed in units called utils.
   a. Ordinal utility
   b. Utility function
   c. Expected utility hypothesis
   d. Utility

5. In finance, the _____s between two currencies specifies how much one currency is worth in terms of the other. It is the value of a foreign natione;s currency in terms of the home natione;s currency. For example an _____ of 102 Japanese yen to the United States dollar means that JPY 102 is worth the same as USD 1.
   a. ACCRA Cost of Living Index
   b. ACEA agreement
   c. Interbank market
   d. Exchange rate

6. In economics, and cost accounting, _____ describes the total economic cost of production and is made up of variable costs, which vary according to the quantity of a good produced and include inputs such as labor and raw materials, plus fixed costs, which are independent of the quantity of a good produced and include inputs (capital) that cannot be varied in the short term, such as buildings and machinery. _____ in economics includes the total opportunity cost of each factor of production in addition to fixed and variable costs.

The rate at which _____ changes as the amount produced changes is called marginal cost.

   a. 1921 recession
   b. Total cost
   c. 100-year flood
   d. 130-30 fund

7. _____ is the total money received from the sale of any given quantity of output.

The _____ is calculated by taking the price of the sale times the quantity sold, i.e.

_____ = price X quantity.

    a. Market development funds
    c. Ceteris paribus
    b. Small numbers game
    d. Total revenue

8. _____ is an economics term to describe a firms variable costs (labor, electricity, etc.) divided by the quantity (Q) of total units of output.

$$AVC = \frac{TVC}{Q}$$

Where:

- TVC = Total Variable Cost
- _____ = Average variable cost
- Q = Quantity of Units Produced

_____ plus average fixed cost equals average total cost:

    _____ + AFC = ATC.

    a. Average variable cost
    c. Explicit cost
    b. Average fixed cost
    d. Inventory valuation

9. _____ is a broad label that refers to any individuals or households that use goods and services generated within the economy. The concept of a _____ is used in different contexts, so that the usage and significance of the term may vary.

Typically when business people and economists talk of _____s they are talking about person as _____, an aggregated commodity item with little individuality other than that expressed in the buy/not-buy decision.

    a. 100-year flood
    c. 1921 recession
    b. Consumer
    d. 130-30 fund

10. In economics, _____ are the resources employed to produce goods and services. They facilitate production but do not become part of the product (as with raw materials) or significantly transformed by the production process (as with fuel used to power machinery.) To 19th century economists, the _____ were land (natural resources, gifts from nature), labor (the ability to work), and capital goods (human-made tools and equipment.)

Chapter 7. Consumer Choice

a. Product Pipeline
b. Long-run
c. Hicks-neutral technical change
d. Factors of production

11. _____ is the term denoting either an entrance or changes which are inserted into a system and which activate/modify a process. It is an abstract concept, used in the modeling, system(s) design and system(s) exploitation. It is usually connected with other terms, e.g., _____ field, _____ variable, _____ parameter, _____ value, _____ signal, _____ device and _____ file.
   a. AD-IA Model
   b. ACCRA Cost of Living Index
   c. ACEA agreement
   d. Input

12. In microeconomics, _____ is quite simply the conversion of inputs into outputs. It is an economic process that uses resources to create a good or service that is suitable for exchange. This can include manufacturing, storing, shipping, and packaging.
   a. MET
   b. Red Guards
   c. Solved
   d. Production

13. _____s are expenses that change in proportion to the activity of a business. In other words, _____ is the sum of marginal costs. It can also be considered normal costs.
   a. Quality costs
   b. Cost-Volume-Profit Analysis
   c. Cost allocation
   d. Variable cost

14. _____ is an equity (stock) exchange located at 11 Wall Street in lower Manhattan, New York, USA. It is the largest stock exchange in the world by dollar value of its listed companies' securities. As of October 2008, the combined capitalization of all domestic _____ listed companies was US$10.1 trillion.
   a. 100-year flood
   b. 1921 recession
   c. New York Stock Exchange
   d. 130-30 fund

15. _____ in economics and business is the result of an exchange and from that trade we assign a numerical monetary value to a good, service or asset. If Alice trades Bob 4 apples for an orange, the _____ of an orange is 4 apples. Inversely, the _____ of an apple is 1/4 oranges.
   a. Price war
   b. Premium pricing
   c. Price book
   d. Price

16. _____ refers to a business or organization attempting to acquire goods or services to accomplish the goals of the enterprise. Though there are several organizations that attempt to set standards in the _____ process, processes can vary greatly between organizations. Typically the word '_____' is not used interchangeably with the word 'procurement', since procurement typically includes Expediting, Supplier Quality, and Traffic and Logistics (T'L) in addition to _____.
   a. 130-30 fund
   b. Free port
   c. 100-year flood
   d. Purchasing

17. _____ is the number of goods/services that can be purchased with a unit of currency. For example, if you had taken one dollar to a store in the 1950s, you would have been able to buy a greater number of items than you would today, indicating that you would have had a greater _____ in the 1950s. Currency can be either a commodity money, like gold or silver, or fiat currency like US dollars.

Chapter 7. Consumer Choice

a. Genuine progress indicator
c. Human Poverty Index

b. Purchasing power
d. Compliance cost

18. _____ was a survey conducted by the U.S. Department of Justice to gauge the prevalence of alcohol and illegal drug use among prior arrestees. It was a reformulation of the prior Drug Use Forecasting (DUF) program, focused on five drugs in particular: cocaine, marijuana, methamphetamine, opiates, and PCP.

Participants were randomly selected from arrest records in major metropolitan areas; because no personally identifying information is taken from each record chosen, the resulting data can be correlated to arrest rates, but not to the total population of persons charged.

a. AD-IA Model
c. ACEA agreement

b. ACCRA Cost of Living Index
d. Arrestee Drug Abuse Monitoring

19. _____ was a Scottish moral philosopher and a pioneer of political economy. One of the key figures of the Scottish Enlightenment, Smith is the author of The Theory of Moral Sentiments and An Inquiry into the Nature and Causes of the Wealth of Nations. The latter, usually abbreviated as The Wealth of Nations, is considered his magnum opus and the first modern work of economics.

a. Adam Smith
c. Alan Greenspan

b. Adolph Fischer
d. Adolf Hitler

20. Economics:

- _____, the desire to own something and the ability to pay for it
- _____ curve, a graphic representation of a _____ schedule
- _____ deposit, the money in checking accounts
- _____ pull theory, the theory that inflation occurs when _____ for goods and services exceeds existing supplies
- _____ schedule, a table that lists the quantity of a good a person will buy it each different price
- _____ side economics, the school of economics at believes government spending and tax cuts open economy by raising _____

a. Variability
c. Demand

b. Production
d. McKesson ' Robbins scandal

21. In economics, the _____ is an economic law that states that consumers buy more of a good when its price decreases and less when its price increases.

There are certain goods which do not follow this law. These include Veblen and Giffen goods

a. Law of demand
c. Market failure

b. Financial crisis
d. Georgism

Chapter 7. Consumer Choice

22. The _____ is the apparent contradiction that although water is on the whole more useful, in terms of survival, than diamonds, diamonds command a higher price in the market. The economist Adam Smith is often considered to be the classic presenter of this paradox. Nicolaus Copernicus, John Locke, John Law and others had previously tried to explain the disparity.
   a. St. Petersburg paradox
   b. 130-30 fund
   c. Paradox of value
   d. 100-year flood

23. In microeconomic theory, an _____ is a graph showing different bundles of goods, each measured as to quantity, between which a consumer is indifferent. That is, at each point on the curve, the consumer has no preference for one bundle over another. In other words, they are all equally preferred.
   a. Indifference map
   b. Expenditure minimization problem
   c. Engel curve
   d. Indifference curve

24. In microeconomic theory a preference map or _____ is the collection of indifference curves possessed by an individual. Similar in nature to a topographical map, the contour lines of such a map demonstrating progressively more desirable options as they move upward or to the right. Because of the nature of indifference curves they cannot intersect and are effectively infinite in number, their sum defining all possible combinations of values.
   a. Engel curve
   b. Indifference map
   c. Elasticity of substitution
   d. Expenditure minimization problem

25. In economics, the _____ is the rate at which a consumer is ready to give up one good in exchange for another good while maintaining the same level of satisfaction.

Under the standard assumption of neoclassical economics that goods and services are continuously divisible, the marginal rates of substitution will be the same regardless of the direction of exchange, and will correspond to the slope of an indifference curve (more precisely, to the slope multiplied by -1) passing through the consumption bundle in question, at that point: mathematically, it is the implicit derivative. MRS of Y for X is the amount of Y for which a consumer is willing to exchange for X locally.

   a. Quality bias
   b. Supply and demand
   c. Marginal rate of substitution
   d. Demand vacuum

26. _____ is subcontracting a process, such as product design or manufacturing, to a third-party company. The decision to outsource is often made in the interest of lowering cost or making better use of time and energy costs, redirecting or conserving energy directed at the competencies of a particular business, or to make more efficient use of land, labor, capital, (information) technology and resources. _____ became part of the business lexicon during the 1980s.
   a. Electronic business
   b. Averch-Johnson effect
   c. Additional Funds Needed
   d. Outsourcing

27. A _____ represents the combinations of goods and services that a consumer can purchase given current prices and his income. Consumer theory uses the concepts of a _____ and a preference map to analyze consumer choices. Both concepts have a ready graphical representation in the two-good case.
   a. Joint demand
   b. Quality bias
   c. Budget constraint
   d. Revealed preference

28. _____ is a common concept in economics, and gives rise to derived concepts such as consumer debt. Generally _____ is defined by opposition to production. But the precise definition can vary because different schools of economists define production quite differently.
   a. Foreclosure data providers
   b. Federal Reserve Bank Notes
   c. Cash or share options
   d. Consumption

Chapter 8. Demand and Supply Elasticity

1. _____ is a common concept in economics, and gives rise to derived concepts such as consumer debt. Generally _____ is defined by opposition to production. But the precise definition can vary because different schools of economists define production quite differently.
   - a. Foreclosure data providers
   - b. Federal Reserve Bank Notes
   - c. Consumption
   - d. Cash or share options

2. Economics:
   - _____, the desire to own something and the ability to pay for it
   - _____ curve, a graphic representation of a _____ schedule
   - _____ deposit, the money in checking accounts
   - _____ pull theory, the theory that inflation occurs when _____ for goods and services exceeds existing supplies
   - _____ schedule, a table that lists the quantity of a good a person will buy it each different price
   - _____ side economics, the school of economics at believes government spending and tax cuts open economy by raising _____

   - a. Demand
   - b. McKesson ' Robbins scandal
   - c. Production
   - d. Variability

3. In economics, the _____ is an economic law that states that consumers buy more of a good when its price decreases and less when its price increases.

   There are certain goods which do not follow this law. These include Veblen and Giffen goods
   - a. Market failure
   - b. Financial crisis
   - c. Law of demand
   - d. Georgism

4. In economics, _____ is the ratio of the percent change in one variable to the percent change in another variable. It is a tool for measuring the responsiveness of a function to changes in parameters in a relative way. Commonly analyzed are _____ of substitution, price and wealth.
   - a. ACEA agreement
   - b. ACCRA Cost of Living Index
   - c. Elasticity of demand
   - d. Elasticity

5. Price _____ is defined as the measure of responsiveness in the quantity demanded for a commodity as a result of change in price of the same commodity. It is a measure of how consumers react to a change in price. In other words, it is percentage change in quantity demanded by the percentage change in price of the same commodity.
   - a. ACCRA Cost of Living Index
   - b. ACEA agreement
   - c. Elasticity
   - d. Elasticity of demand

6. _____ in economics and business is the result of an exchange and from that trade we assign a numerical monetary value to a good, service or asset. If Alice trades Bob 4 apples for an orange, the _____ of an orange is 4 apples. Inversely, the _____ of an apple is 1/4 oranges.
   - a. Premium pricing
   - b. Price war
   - c. Price book
   - d. Price

Chapter 8. Demand and Supply Elasticity

7. _____ is defined as the measure of responsiveness in the quantity demanded for a commodity as a result of change in price of the same commodity. It is a measure of how consumers react to a change in price. In other words, it is percentage change in quantity demanded as per the percentage change in price of the same commodity.
   a. 1921 recession
   b. 130-30 fund
   c. 100-year flood
   d. Price elasticity of demand

8. In neoclassical economics and microeconomics, _____ describes the perfect being a market in which there are many small firms, all producing homogeneous goods. In the short term, such markets are productively inefficient as output will not occur where mc is equal to ac, but allocatively efficient, as output under _____ will always occur where mc is equal to mr, and therefore where mc equals ar. However, in the long term, such markets are both allocatively and productively efficient.
   a. Co-operative economics
   b. Law of supply
   c. General equilibrium
   d. Perfect competition

9. In economics, market concentration is a function of the number of firms and their respective shares of the total production (alternatively, total capacity or total reserves) in a market. Alternative terms are _____ and Seller concentration.

Market concentration is related to the concept of industrial concentration, which concerns the distribution of production within an industry, as opposed to a market.

   a. ACCRA Cost of Living Index
   b. ACEA agreement
   c. AD-IA Model
   d. Industry concentration

10. In economics, _____ describes demand that is not very sensitive to a change in price.
    a. Effective unemployment rate
    b. Inflation hedge
    c. Export-led growth
    d. Inelastic

11. To _____ is to impose a financial charge or other levy upon a taxpayer by a state or the functional equivalent of a state.

    _____es are also imposed by many subnational entities. _____es consist of direct _____ or indirect _____, and may be paid in money or as its labour equivalent (often but not always unpaid.)

    a. 130-30 fund
    b. 1921 recession
    c. 100-year flood
    d. Tax

12. To tax is to impose a financial charge or other levy upon a taxpayer by a state or the functional equivalent of a state.

    _____ are also imposed by many subnational entities. _____ consist of direct tax or indirect tax, and may be paid in money or as its labour equivalent (often but not always unpaid.)

    a. 1921 recession
    b. Taxes
    c. 130-30 fund
    d. 100-year flood

Chapter 8. Demand and Supply Elasticity

13. A _____ or labor union is an organization of workers who have banded together to achieve common goals in key areas and working conditions. The _____, through its leadership, bargains with the employer on behalf of union members (rank and file members) and negotiates labor contracts (Collective bargaining) with employers. This may include the negotiation of wages, work rules, complaint procedures, rules governing hiring, firing and promotion of workers, benefits, workplace safety and policies.

   a. Consumer goods
   b. Trade union
   c. Case-Shiller Home Price Indices
   d. Guaranteed investment contracts

14. In economics, and cost accounting, _____ describes the total economic cost of production and is made up of variable costs, which vary according to the quantity of a good produced and include inputs such as labor and raw materials, plus fixed costs, which are independent of the quantity of a good produced and include inputs (capital) that cannot be varied in the short term, such as buildings and machinery. _____ in economics includes the total opportunity cost of each factor of production in addition to fixed and variable costs.

   The rate at which _____ changes as the amount produced changes is called marginal cost.

   a. Total cost
   b. 100-year flood
   c. 1921 recession
   d. 130-30 fund

15. _____ is the total money received from the sale of any given quantity of output.

   The _____ is calculated by taking the price of the sale times the quantity sold, i.e.

   _____ = price X quantity.

   a. Market development funds
   b. Small numbers game
   c. Ceteris paribus
   d. Total revenue

16. _____ is an equity (stock) exchange located at 11 Wall Street in lower Manhattan, New York, USA. It is the largest stock exchange in the world by dollar value of its listed companies' securities. As of October 2008, the combined capitalization of all domestic _____ listed companies was US$10.1 trillion.

   a. 1921 recession
   b. New York Stock Exchange
   c. 100-year flood
   d. 130-30 fund

17. _____ was a survey conducted by the U.S. Department of Justice to gauge the prevalence of alcohol and illegal drug use among prior arrestees. It was a reformulation of the prior Drug Use Forecasting (DUF) program, focused on five drugs in particular: cocaine, marijuana, methamphetamine, opiates, and PCP.

   Participants were randomly selected from arrest records in major metropolitan areas; because no personally identifying information is taken from each record chosen, the resulting data can be correlated to arrest rates, but not to the total population of persons charged.

   a. AD-IA Model
   b. ACCRA Cost of Living Index
   c. ACEA agreement
   d. Arrestee Drug Abuse Monitoring

Chapter 8. Demand and Supply Elasticity

18. In economic models, the _____ time frame assumes no fixed factors of production. Firms can enter or leave the marketplace, and the cost (and availability) of land, labor, raw materials, and capital goods can be assumed to vary. In contrast, in the short-run time frame, certain factors are assumed to be fixed, because there is not sufficient time for them to change.
   a. Long-run
   b. Price/performance ratio
   c. Productivity world
   d. Diseconomies of scale

19. In economics, the concept of the _____ refers to the decision-making time frame of a firm in which at least one factor of production is fixed. Costs which are fixed in the _____ have no impact on a firms decisions. For example a firm can raise output by increasing the amount of labour through overtime.
   a. Hicks-neutral technical change
   b. Productivity model
   c. Short-run
   d. Product Pipeline

20. The _____ is an international organization that oversees the global financial system by following the macroeconomic policies of its member countries, in particular those with an impact on exchange rates and the balance of payments. It is an organization formed to stabilize international exchange rates and facilitate development. It also offers financial and technical assistance to its members, making it an international lender of last resort.
   a. ACCRA Cost of Living Index
   b. ACEA agreement
   c. Office of Thrift Supervision
   d. International Monetary Fund

21. In economics, the _____ of demand measures the responsiveness of the demand of a good to the change in the income of the people demanding the good. It is calculated as the ratio of the percent change in demand to the percent change in income. For example, if, in response to a 10% increase in income, the demand of a good increased by 20%, the _____ of demand would be 20%/10% = 2.
   a. ACEA agreement
   b. AD-IA Model
   c. ACCRA Cost of Living Index
   d. Income elasticity

22. In economics, the _____ measures the responsiveness of the demand of a good to the change in the income of the people demanding the good. It is calculated as the ratio of the percent change in demand to the percent change in income. For example, if, in response to a 10% increase in income, the demand of a good increased by 20%, the _____ would be 20%/10% = 2.
   a. Expenditure minimization problem
   b. Elasticity of substitution
   c. Indifference map
   d. Income elasticity of demand

23. In finance, the _____s between two currencies specifies how much one currency is worth in terms of the other. It is the value of a foreign natione;s currency in terms of the home natione;s currency. For example an _____ of 102 Japanese yen to the United States dollar means that JPY 102 is worth the same as USD 1.
   a. ACCRA Cost of Living Index
   b. ACEA agreement
   c. Interbank market
   d. Exchange rate

24. In economics, the _____ is defined as a numerical measure of the responsiveness of the quantity supplied of product (A) to a change in price of product (A) alone. It is the measure of the way quantity supplied reacts to a change in price.

For example, if, in response to a 10% rise in the price of a good, the quantity supplied increases by 20%, the _____ would be 20%/10% = 2.

a. Passive income
b. Hedonimetry
c. Demand shaping
d. Price elasticity of supply

Chapter 9. Rents, Profits, and the Financial Environment of Business

1. A _____ refers to any type debt instrument, such as a loan, bond, mortgage that does not have a fixed rate of interest over the life of the instrument. Such debt typically uses an index or other base rate for establishing the interest rate for each relevant period. One of the most common rates to use as the basis for applying interest rates is the London Inter-bank Offered Rate, or LIBOR
   - a. Disposal tax effect
   - b. Moneylender
   - c. Money market
   - d. Floating interest rate

2. The United States federal _____ is a refundable tax credit. For tax year 2008, a claimant with one qualifying child can receive a maximum credit of $2,917. For two or more qualifying children, the maximum credit is $4,824.
   - a. AD-IA Model
   - b. ACEA agreement
   - c. ACCRA Cost of Living Index
   - d. Earned Income Tax Credit

3. An _____ is a tax levied on the financial income of people, corporations, or other legal entities. Various _____ systems exist, with varying degrees of tax incidence. Income taxation can be progressive, proportional, or regressive.
   - a. ACEA agreement
   - b. ACCRA Cost of Living Index
   - c. AD-IA Model
   - d. Income Tax

4. In microeconomics, _____ is the extra revenue that an additional unit of product will bring. It is the additional income from selling one more unit of a good; sometimes equal to price. It can also be described as the change in total revenue/change in number of units sold.
   - a. Market demand schedule
   - b. Reservation price
   - c. Long term
   - d. Marginal revenue

5. To _____ is to impose a financial charge or other levy upon a taxpayer by a state or the functional equivalent of a state.

   _____es are also imposed by many subnational entities. _____es consist of direct _____ or indirect _____, and may be paid in money or as its labour equivalent (often but not always unpaid.)

   - a. 1921 recession
   - b. 130-30 fund
   - c. 100-year flood
   - d. Tax

6. The term _____ describes two different concepts:

   - The first is a recognition of partial payment already made towards taxes due.
   - The second is a state benefit paid to workers through the tax system, which has the effect of increasing (rather than reducing) net income.

   Within the Australian, Canadian, United Kingdom, and United States tax systems, a _____ is a recognition of partial payment already made towards taxes due. A similar concept exists (fr:Avoir fiscal) in the French tax system. This situation arises, for example, when standard rate tax has been deducted at source, but the tax-payer is subject to further taxation at a higher rate. It also applies in dividend imputation systems.

   - a. 1921 recession
   - b. 100-year flood
   - c. 130-30 fund
   - d. Tax Credit

Chapter 9. Rents, Profits, and the Financial Environment of Business

7. _____s is the social science that studies the production, distribution, and consumption of goods and services. The term _____s comes from the Ancient Greek oá¼°κονομῖα from οá¼¶κος (oikos, 'house') + νÏŒμος (nomos, 'custom' or 'law'), hence 'rules of the house(hold)'. Current _____ models developed out of the broader field of political economy in the late 19th century, owing to a desire to use an empirical approach more akin to the physical sciences.
   a. Energy economics
   b. Inflation
   c. Opportunity cost
   d. Economic

8. In economics supernormal profit _____ or pure profit or excess profits, is a profit exceeding the normal profit. Normal profit equals the opportunity cost of labour and capital, while supernormal profit is the amount exceeds the normal return from these input factors in production.

   _____ is usually generated by an oligopoly or a monopoly; however, these firms often try to hide this from the market to reduce risk of competition or antitrust investigation.

   a. Abnormal profit
   b. Economic profit
   c. ACCRA Cost of Living Index
   d. Accounting profit

9. Economic _____ is defined as an excess distribution to any factor in a production process above that which is required to induce the factor into the process or any excess above that which is necessary to keep the factor in its current use..

   Classical Factor _____ is primarily concerned with the fee paid for the use of fixed (e.g. natural) resources. The classical definition is expressed as any excess payment above that required to induce or provide for production.

   a. 100-year flood
   b. 1921 recession
   c. 130-30 fund
   d. Rent

10. In microeconomics, _____ is quite simply the conversion of inputs into outputs. It is an economic process that uses resources to create a good or service that is suitable for exchange. This can include manufacturing, storing, shipping, and packaging.
    a. Production
    b. MET
    c. Solved
    d. Red Guards

11. In economics, _____ is how a natione;s total economy is distributed among its population. ._____ has always been a central concern of economic theory and economic policy. Classical economists such as Adam Smith, Thomas Malthus and David Ricardo were mainly concerned with factor _____, that is, the distribution of income between the main factors of production, land, labour and capital.
    a. Eco commerce
    b. Equipment trust certificate
    c. Income distribution
    d. Authorised capital

12. A _____, or simply proprietorship is a type of business entity which legally has no separate existence from its owner. Hence, the limitations of liability enjoyed by a corporation and limited liability partnerships do not apply to sole proprietors. All debts of the business are debts of the owner.

Chapter 9. Rents, Profits, and the Financial Environment of Business

a. Sole proprietorship
b. Golden parachute
c. Golden hello
d. Corporate tax

13. _____ is a broad label that refers to any individuals or households that use goods and services generated within the economy. The concept of a _____ is used in different contexts, so that the usage and significance of the term may vary.

Typically when business people and economists talk of _____s they are talking about person as _____, an aggregated commodity item with little individuality other than that expressed in the buy/not-buy decision.

a. Consumer
b. 130-30 fund
c. 1921 recession
d. 100-year flood

14. The _____ consists of a number of economic theories which describe the nature of the firm, company including its existence, its behaviour, and its relationship with the market.

In simplified terms, the _____ aims to answer these questions:

1. Existence - why do firms emerge, why are not all transactions in the economy mediated over the market?
2. Boundaries - why the boundary between firms and the market is located exactly there? Which transactions are performed internally and which are negotiated on the market?
3. Organization - why are firms structured in such specific way? What is the interplay of formal and informal relationships?

Despite looking simple, these questions are not answered by the established economic theory, which usually views firms as given, and treats them as black boxes without any internal structure.

The First World War period saw a change of emphasis in economic theory away from industry-level analysis which mainly included analysing markets to analysis at the level of the firm, as it became increasingly clear that perfect competition was no longer an adequate model of how firms behaved. Economic theory till then had focussed on trying to understand markets alone and there had been little study on understanding why firms or organisations exist.

a. Technology gap
b. Khazzoom-Brookes postulate
c. Policy Ineffectiveness Proposition
d. Theory of the firm

15. _____s are payments made by a corporation to its shareholders. It is the portion of corporate profits paid out to stockholders. When a corporation earns a profit or surplus, that money can be put to two uses: it can either be re-invested in the business (called retained earnings), or it can be paid to the shareholders as a _____.

a. Dividend puzzle
b. Dividend
c. Dividend yield
d. Dividend cover

Chapter 9. Rents, Profits, and the Financial Environment of Business

16. _____ is a concept whereby a person's financial liability is limited to a fixed sum, most commonly the value of a person's investment in a company or partnership with _____. A shareholder in a limited company is not personally liable for any of the debts of the company, other than for the value of his investment in that company. The same is true for the members of a _____ partnership and the limited partners in a limited partnership.
   a. Personal Responsibility and Work Opportunity Reconciliation Act of 1996
   b. Deficiency judgment
   c. Nexus of contracts
   d. Limited liability

17. A mutual _____ or stockholder is an individual or company (including a corporation) that legally owns one or more shares of stock in a joint stock company. A company's _____s collectively own that company. Thus, the typical goal of such companies is to enhance _____ value.
   a. Prime Standard
   b. Shareholder
   c. Profit warning
   d. Relative valuation

18. In economics, _____ is equal to total cost divided by the number of goods produced (the output quantity, Q.) It is also equal to the sum of average variable costs (total variable costs divided by Q) plus average fixed costs (total fixed costs divided by Q.) _____s may be dependent on the time period considered (increasing production may be expensive or impossible in the short term, for example.)
   a. Average variable cost
   b. Average fixed cost
   c. Explicit cost
   d. Average cost

19. In finance, a _____ is a debt security, in which the authorized issuer owes the holders a debt and, depending on the terms of the _____, is obliged to pay interest (the coupon) and/or to repay the principal at a later date, termed maturity. A _____ is a formal contract to repay borrowed money with interest at fixed intervals.

Thus a _____ is like a loan: the issuer is the borrower (debtor), the holder is the lender (creditor), and the coupon is the interest.
   a. Prize Bond
   b. Callable
   c. Zero-coupon
   d. Bond

20. The _____ is an international organization that oversees the global financial system by following the macroeconomic policies of its member countries, in particular those with an impact on exchange rates and the balance of payments. It is an organization formed to stabilize international exchange rates and facilitate development. It also offers financial and technical assistance to its members, making it an international lender of last resort.
   a. ACCRA Cost of Living Index
   b. Office of Thrift Supervision
   c. ACEA agreement
   d. International Monetary Fund

21. In economics and finance, _____ is the change in total cost that arises when the quantity produced changes by one unit. It is the cost of producing one more unit of a good. Mathematically, the _____ function is expressed as the first derivative of the total cost (TC) function with respect to quantity (Q.)
   a. Khozraschyot
   b. Quality costs
   c. Variable cost
   d. Marginal cost

Chapter 9. Rents, Profits, and the Financial Environment of Business

22. _____ or economic opportunity loss is the value of the next best alternative foregone as the result of making a decision. _____ analysis is an important part of a company's decision-making processes but is not treated as an actual cost in any financial statement. The next best thing that a person can engage in is referred to as the _____ of doing the best thing and ignoring the next best thing to be done.
   a. Economic ideology
   b. Industrial organization
   c. Economic
   d. Opportunity cost

23. A security is a fungible, negotiable instrument representing financial value. _____ are broadly categorized into debt _____; equity _____, e.g., common stocks; and derivative (finance) contracts such as forwards, futures, options and swaps. The company or other entity issuing the security is called the issuer.
   a. Settlement risk
   b. Red herring prospectus
   c. Pass-Through Certificates
   d. Securities

24. The U.S. _____ is an independent agency of the United States government which holds primary responsibility for enforcing the federal securities laws and regulating the securities industry, the nation's stock and options exchanges, and other electronic securities markets. The SEC was created by section 4 of the Securities Exchange Act of 1934 (now codified as 15 U.S.C. Â§ 78d and commonly referred to as the 1934 Act.)
   a. 130-30 fund
   b. 100-year flood
   c. 1921 recession
   d. Securities and Exchange Commission

25. In economics, _____ refers to the ability of a party to produce a good or service using fewer real resources than another entity producing the same good or service..A party has an _____ when using the same input as another party, it can produce a greater output. Since _____ is determined by a simple comparison of labor productivities, it is possible for a a party to have no _____ in anything. It can be contrasted with the concept of comparative advantage which refers to the ability to produce a particular good at a lower opportunity cost.
   a. ACCRA Cost of Living Index
   b. Index number
   c. International economics
   d. Absolute advantage

26. _____ is the difference between price and the costs of bringing to market whatever it is that is accounted as an enterprise (whether by harvest, extraction, manufacture, or purchase) in terms of the component costs of delivered goods and/or services and any operating or other expenses.

A key difficulty in measuring profit is in defining costs. Pure economic monetary profits can be zero or negative even in competitive equilibrium when accounted monetized costs exceed monetized price.

   a. ACCRA Cost of Living Index
   b. Economic profit
   c. Operating profit
   d. Accounting profit

27. An _____ is an easy accounted cost, such as wage, rent and materials. It can be transacted in the form of money payment and is lost directly, as opposed to monetary implicit costs.
   a. Average variable cost
   b. Average fixed cost
   c. Inventory valuation
   d. Explicit cost

Chapter 9. Rents, Profits, and the Financial Environment of Business

28. In economics, an _____ occurs when one foregoes an alternative action but does not make an actual payment. (For instance, the explicit cost of a night at the movies includes the moviegoer's ticket and soda, but the _____ includes the pay he would have earned if he had chosen to work instead.) _____s are related to forgone benefits of any single transaction.
    a. Implicit cost
    b. External sector
    c. Overnight trade
    d. Ostrich strategy

29. To tax is to impose a financial charge or other levy upon a taxpayer by a state or the functional equivalent of a state.

    _____ are also imposed by many subnational entities. _____ consist of direct tax or indirect tax, and may be paid in money or as its labour equivalent (often but not always unpaid.)

    a. 100-year flood
    b. 1921 recession
    c. 130-30 fund
    d. Taxes

30. In economics, _____ is the difference between a company's total revenue and its opportunity costs. It is the increase in wealth that an investor has from making an investment, taking into consideration all costs associated with that investment including the opportunity cost of capital.

    Profit is the factor income of the entrepreneur.

    a. Operating profit
    b. Accounting profit
    c. ACCRA Cost of Living Index
    d. Economic profit

31. _____ is a fee paid on borrowed assets. It is the price paid for the use of borrowed money, or, money earned by deposited funds. Assets that are sometimes lent with _____ include money, shares, consumer goods through hire purchase, major assets such as aircraft, and even entire factories in finance lease arrangements.
    a. Asset protection
    b. Internal debt
    c. Insolvency
    d. Interest

32. An _____ is the price a borrower pays for the use of money they do not own, for instance a small company might borrow from a bank to kick start their business, and the return a lender receives for deferring the use of funds, by lending it to the borrower. _____s are normally expressed as a percentage rate over the period of one year.

    _____s targets are also a vital tool of monetary policy and are used to control variables like investment, inflation, and unemployment.

    a. Arrow-Debreu model
    b. ACCRA Cost of Living Index
    c. Interest rate
    d. Enterprise value

33. In economics, the _____ of a good or of a service is the utility of the specific use to which an agent would put a given increase in that good or service, or of the specific use that would be abandoned in response to a given decrease. In other words, _____ is the utility of the marginal use -- which, on the assumption of economic rationality, would be the least urgent use of the good or service, from the best feasible combination of actions in which its use is included. Under the mainstream assumptions, the _____ of a good or service is the posited quantified change in utility obtained by increasing or by decreasing use of that good or service.

66 *Chapter 9. Rents, Profits, and the Financial Environment of Business*

    a. Marginal utility
    b. 130-30 fund
    c. 1921 recession
    d. 100-year flood

34. _____ is the value on a given date of a future payment or series of future payments, discounted to reflect the time value of money and other factors such as investment risk. _____ calculations are widely used in business and economics to provide a means to compare cash flows at different times on a meaningful 'like to like' basis.

Money value fluctuates over time: $100 today are not worth $100 in five years.

    a. Present value of costs
    b. Future value
    c. Tax shield
    d. Present value

35. In economics, _____ is a measure of the relative satisfaction from consumption of various goods and services. Given this measure, one may speak meaningfully of increasing or decreasing _____, and thereby explain economic behavior in terms of attempts to increase one's _____. For illustrative purposes, changes in _____ are sometimes expressed in units called utils.

    a. Expected utility hypothesis
    b. Utility function
    c. Ordinal utility
    d. Utility

36. _____ is the a method of technical and economic research of the systems for purpose to optimize a parity between system's consumer functions or properties and expenses to achieve those functions or properties.

This methodology for continuous perfection of production, industrial technologies, organizational structures was developed by Juryj Sobolev in 1948 at the 'Perm telephone factory'

- 1948 Juryj Sobolev - the first success in application of a method analysis at the 'Perm telephone factory'.
- 1949 - the first application for the invention as result of use of the new method.

Today in economically developed countries practically each enterprise or the company use methodology of the kind of functional-cost analysis as a practice of the quality management, most full satisfying to principles of standards of series ISO 9000.

- Interest of consumer not in products itself, but the advantage which it will receive from its usage.
- The consumer aspires to reduce his expenses
- Functions needed by consumer can be executed in the various ways, and, hence, with various efficiency and expenses. Among possible alternatives of realization of functions exist such in which the parity of quality and the price is the optimal for the consumer.

The goal of _____ is achievement of the highest consumer satisfaction of production at simultaneous decrease in all kinds of industrial expenses Classical _____ has three English synonyms - Value Engineering, Value Management, Value Analysis.

    a. Monopoly wage
    b. Willingness to pay
    c. Staple financing
    d. Function cost analysis

Chapter 9. Rents, Profits, and the Financial Environment of Business

37. Discounting is a financial mechanism in which a debtor obtains the right to delay payments to a creditor, for a defined period of time, in exchange for a charge or fee. Essentially, the party that owes money in the present purchases the right to delay the payment until some future date. The _____, or charge, is simply the difference between the original amount owed in the present and the amount that has to be paid in the future to settle the debt.
- a. Reliability theory
- b. Certified Risk Manager
- c. Discount
- d. Reinsurance

38. The _____ is an interest rate a central bank charges depository institutions that borrow reserves from it.

The term _____ has two meanings:

- the same as interest rate; the term 'discount' does not refer to the meaning of the word, but to the purpose of using the quantity, such as computations of present value, e.g. net present value or discounted cash flow

- the annual effective _____, which is the annual interest divided by the capital including that interest; this rate is lower than the interest rate; it corresponds to using the value after a year as the nominal value, and seeing the initial value as the nominal value minus a discount; it is used for Treasury Bills and similar financial instruments

The annual effective _____ is the annual interest divided by the capital including that interest, which is the interest rate divided by 100% plus the interest rate. It is the annual discount factor to be applied to the future cash flow, to find the discount, subtracted from a future value to find the value one year earlier.

For example, suppose there is a government bond that sells for $95 and pays $100 in a year's time.
- a. Johansen test
- b. Perpetuity
- c. Stochastic volatility
- d. Discount rate

39. _____ is a financial mechanism in which a debtor obtains the right to delay payments to a creditor, for a defined period of time, in exchange for a charge or fee. Essentially, the party that owes money in the present purchases the right to delay the payment until some future date. The discount, or charge, is simply the difference between the original amount owed in the present and the amount that has to be paid in the future to settle the debt.
- a. Maximum life span
- b. Certified Risk Manager
- c. Generalized linear model
- d. Discounting

40. The _____ was a trading company, which was established in 1602, when the States-General of the Netherlands granted it a 21-year monopoly to carry out colonial activities in Asia. It was the first multinational corporation in the world and the first company to issue stock. It was also arguably the world's first megacorporation, possessing quasi-governmental powers, including the ability to wage war, negotiate treaties, coin money, and establish colonies.
- a. 100-year flood
- b. 1921 recession
- c. Dutch East India Company
- d. 130-30 fund

Chapter 9. Rents, Profits, and the Financial Environment of Business

41. The _____ was an early English joint-stock company that was formed initially for pursuing trade with the East Indies, but that ended up trading with the Indian subcontinent and China. The oldest among several similarly formed European East India Companies, the Company was granted an English Royal Charter, under the name Governor and Company of Merchants of London Trading into the East Indies, by Elizabeth I on 31 December 1600. After a rival English company challenged its monopoly in the late 17th century, the two companies were merged in 1708 to form the United Company of Merchants of England Trading to the East Indies, commonly styled the Honourable _____, and abbreviated, HEast India Company; the Company was colloquially referred to as John Company, and in India as Company Bahadur .
   a. AD-IA Model
   b. ACEA agreement
   c. ACCRA Cost of Living Index
   d. East India Company

42. _____ is an equity (stock) exchange located at 11 Wall Street in lower Manhattan, New York, USA. It is the largest stock exchange in the world by dollar value of its listed companies' securities. As of October 2008, the combined capitalization of all domestic _____ listed companies was US$10.1 trillion.
   a. 100-year flood
   b. 130-30 fund
   c. 1921 recession
   d. New York Stock Exchange

43. _____ describes a set of laws relating to domestic agriculture and imports of foreign agricultural products. Governments usually implement agricultural policies with the goal of achieving a specific outcome in the domestic agricultural product markets. Outcomes can involve, for example, a guaranteed supply level, price stability, product quality, product selection, land use or employment.
   a. ACCRA Cost of Living Index
   b. ACEA agreement
   c. Intercropping
   d. Agricultural Policy

44. A _____ is the transfer of wealth from one party (such as a person or company) to another. A _____ is usually made in exchange for the provision of goods, services or both, or to fulfill a legal obligation.

The simplest and oldest form of _____ is barter, the exchange of one good or service for another.

   a. Social gravity
   b. Soft count
   c. Going concern
   d. Payment

45. The _____ is an American stock exchange. It is the largest electronic screen-based equity securities trading market in the United States. With approximately 3,800 companies, it has more trading volume per hour than any other stock exchange in the world.
   a. 1921 recession
   b. 130-30 fund
   c. 100-year flood
   d. Nasdaq

46. _____ was a predominant American integrated oil producing, transporting, refining, and marketing company. Established in 1870 as an Ohio Corporation, it was the largest oil refiner in the world and operated as a major company trust and was one of the world's first and largest multinational corporations until it was broken up by the United States Supreme Court in 1911. John D. Rockefeller was a founder, chairman and major shareholder, and the company made him a billionaire and eventually the richest man in history.
   a. 100-year flood
   b. 130-30 fund
   c. 1921 recession
   d. Standard Oil

Chapter 9. Rents, Profits, and the Financial Environment of Business

47. _____ is one of the four Ps of the marketing mix. The other three aspects are product, promotion, and place. It is also a key variable in microeconomic price allocation theory.
   a. Guaranteed Maximum Price
   b. Premium pricing
   c. Point of total assumption
   d. Pricing

48. _____ is a concept with somewhat disparate meanings in several fields. It also has a common meaning which has a loose connection with some of those more definite meanings.

Casually, it is typically used to denote a lack of order, or purpose, or cause.

   a. 100-year flood
   b. 1921 recession
   c. 130-30 fund
   d. Randomness

49. A _____, sometimes denoted _____, is a mathematical formalization of a trajectory that consists of taking successive random steps. The results of _____ analysis have been applied to computer science, physics, ecology, economics, and a number of other fields as a fundamental model for random processes in time. For example, the path traced by a molecule as it travels in a liquid or a gas, the search path of a foraging animal, the price of a fluctuating stock and the financial status of a gambler can all be modeled as _____s.
   a. 100-year flood
   b. Random walk
   c. 130-30 fund
   d. 1921 recession

50. A _____ is a corporation or mutual organization which provides trading facilities for stock brokers and traders, to trade stocks and other securities. It may be a physical trading room where the traders gather, or a formalised communications network. Creation of a _____ is a strategy of economic development.
   a. SEAQ
   b. 100-year flood
   c. Primary shares
   d. Stock exchange

51. A _____ is a public market for the trading of company stock and derivatives at an agreed price; these are securities listed on a stock exchange as well as those only traded privately.

The size of the world _____ was estimated at about $36.6 trillion US at the beginning of October 2008 . The total world derivatives market has been estimated at about $791 trillion face or nominal value, 11 times the size of the entire world economy.

   a. Adolf Hitler
   b. Adolph Fischer
   c. Adam Smith
   d. Stock market

52. In neoclassical economics and microeconomics, _____ describes the perfect being a market in which there are many small firms, all producing homogeneous goods. In the short term, such markets are productively inefficient as output will not occur where mc is equal to ac, but allocatively efficient, as output under _____ will always occur where mc is equal to mr, and therefore where mc equals ar. However, in the long term, such markets are both allocatively and productively efficient.
   a. General equilibrium
   b. Law of supply
   c. Co-operative economics
   d. Perfect competition

Chapter 9. Rents, Profits, and the Financial Environment of Business

53. _____ are the inflation-indexed bonds issued by the U.S. Treasury. The principal is adjusted to the Consumer Price Index, the commonly used measure of inflation. The coupon rate is constant, but generates a different amount of interest when multiplied by the inflation-adjusted principal, thus protecting the holder against inflation.
   a. 1921 recession
   b. 130-30 fund
   c. 100-year flood
   d. Treasury Inflation-Protected Securities

54. In economics, market concentration is a function of the number of firms and their respective shares of the total production (alternatively, total capacity or total reserves) in a market. Alternative terms are _____ and Seller concentration.

Market concentration is related to the concept of industrial concentration, which concerns the distribution of production within an industry, as opposed to a market.

   a. AD-IA Model
   b. ACCRA Cost of Living Index
   c. Industry concentration
   d. ACEA agreement

Chapter 10. The Firm: Cost and Output Determination

1. _____ is an economics term to describe a firms variable costs (labor, electricity, etc.) divided by the quantity (Q) of total units of output.

$$AVC = \frac{TVC}{Q}$$

Where:

- TVC = Total Variable Cost
- _____ = Average variable cost
- Q = Quantity of Units Produced

_____ plus average fixed cost equals average total cost:

_____ + AFC = ATC.

a. Explicit cost
b. Average variable cost
c. Inventory valuation
d. Average fixed cost

2. In economics, _____ are the resources employed to produce goods and services. They facilitate production but do not become part of the product (as with raw materials) or significantly transformed by the production process (as with fuel used to power machinery.) To 19th century economists, the _____ were land (natural resources, gifts from nature), labor (the ability to work), and capital goods (human-made tools and equipment.)

a. Hicks-neutral technical change
b. Product Pipeline
c. Long-run
d. Factors of production

3. In economics, _____ is how a natione;s total economy is distributed among its population. . _____ has always been a central concern of economic theory and economic policy. Classical economists such as Adam Smith, Thomas Malthus and David Ricardo were mainly concerned with factor _____, that is, the distribution of income between the main factors of production, land, labour and capital.

a. Authorised capital
b. Income distribution
c. Eco commerce
d. Equipment trust certificate

4. _____ is the term denoting either an entrance or changes which are inserted into a system and which activate/modify a process. It is an abstract concept, used in the modeling, system(s) design and system(s) exploitation. It is usually connected with other terms, e.g., _____ field, _____ variable, _____ parameter, _____ value, _____ signal, _____ device and _____ file.

a. AD-IA Model
b. ACEA agreement
c. ACCRA Cost of Living Index
d. Input

5. In microeconomics, _____ is quite simply the conversion of inputs into outputs. It is an economic process that uses resources to create a good or service that is suitable for exchange. This can include manufacturing, storing, shipping, and packaging.

Chapter 10. The Firm: Cost and Output Determination

    a. MET
    b. Solved
    c. Red Guards
    d. Production

6. _____s are expenses that change in proportion to the activity of a business. In other words, _____ is the sum of marginal costs. It can also be considered normal costs.
    a. Quality costs
    b. Cost-Volume-Profit Analysis
    c. Cost allocation
    d. Variable cost

7. _____ are the inflation-indexed bonds issued by the U.S. Treasury. The principal is adjusted to the Consumer Price Index, the commonly used measure of inflation. The coupon rate is constant, but generates a different amount of interest when multiplied by the inflation-adjusted principal, thus protecting the holder against inflation.
    a. 100-year flood
    b. 130-30 fund
    c. 1921 recession
    d. Treasury Inflation-Protected Securities

8. In economics, _____ refers to how the marginal contribution of a factor of production usually decreases as more of the factor is used. According to this relationship, in a production system with fixed and variable inputs, beyond some point, each additional unit of the variable input yields smaller and smaller increases in output. Conversely, producing one more unit of output costs more and more in variable inputs.
    a. Community property
    b. Patent troll
    c. Derivatives law
    d. Diminishing returns

9. In finance, the _____s between two currencies specifies how much one currency is worth in terms of the other. It is the value of a foreign natione;s currency in terms of the home natione;s currency. For example an _____ of 102 Japanese yen to the United States dollar means that JPY 102 is worth the same as USD 1.
    a. ACCRA Cost of Living Index
    b. ACEA agreement
    c. Exchange rate
    d. Interbank market

10. _____ is a broad label that refers to any individuals or households that use goods and services generated within the economy. The concept of a _____ is used in different contexts, so that the usage and significance of the term may vary.

Typically when business people and economists talk of _____s they are talking about person as _____, an aggregated commodity item with little individuality other than that expressed in the buy/not-buy decision.

    a. 1921 recession
    b. 130-30 fund
    c. 100-year flood
    d. Consumer

11. In economics, _____ are business expenses that are not dependent on the activities of the business They tend to be time-related, such as salaries or rents being paid per month. This is in contrast to variable costs, which are volume-related (and are paid per quantity.)

In management accounting, _____ are defined as expenses that do not change in proportion to the activity of a business, within the relevant period or scale of production.

Chapter 10. The Firm: Cost and Output Determination

a. Cost of poor quality
b. Fixed costs
c. Cost-Volume-Profit Analysis
d. Quality costs

12. In economics, the concept of the _____ refers to the decision-making time frame of a firm in which at least one factor of production is fixed. Costs which are fixed in the _____ have no impact on a firms decisions. For example a firm can raise output by increasing the amount of labour through overtime.
   a. Productivity model
   b. Product Pipeline
   c. Hicks-neutral technical change
   d. Short-run

13. In economics, and cost accounting, _____ describes the total economic cost of production and is made up of variable costs, which vary according to the quantity of a good produced and include inputs such as labor and raw materials, plus fixed costs, which are independent of the quantity of a good produced and include inputs (capital) that cannot be varied in the short term, such as buildings and machinery. _____ in economics includes the total opportunity cost of each factor of production in addition to fixed and variable costs.

The rate at which _____ changes as the amount produced changes is called marginal cost.

   a. 100-year flood
   b. 130-30 fund
   c. 1921 recession
   d. Total cost

14. In economics, the _____ of a good or of a service is the utility of the specific use to which an agent would put a given increase in that good or service, or of the specific use that would be abandoned in response to a given decrease. In other words, _____ is the utility of the marginal use -- which, on the assumption of economic rationality, would be the least urgent use of the good or service, from the best feasible combination of actions in which its use is included. Under the mainstream assumptions, the _____ of a good or service is the posited quantified change in utility obtained by increasing or by decreasing use of that good or service.
   a. 1921 recession
   b. 100-year flood
   c. 130-30 fund
   d. Marginal utility

15. In economics, _____ is equal to total cost divided by the number of goods produced (the output quantity, Q.) It is also equal to the sum of average variable costs (total variable costs divided by Q) plus average fixed costs (total fixed costs divided by Q.) _____s may be dependent on the time period considered (increasing production may be expensive or impossible in the short term, for example.)
   a. Average variable cost
   b. Average fixed cost
   c. Explicit cost
   d. Average cost

16. _____ is an economics term used to describe the total fixed costs (TFC) divided by the quantity (Q) of units produced.

$$AFC = \frac{TFC}{Q}$$

_____ is a per-unit measure of fixed costs. As the total number of goods produced increases, the _____ decreases because the same amount of fixed costs are being spread over a larger number of units.

a. Inventory valuation
b. Average variable cost
c. Explicit cost
d. Average fixed cost

17. In economics, _____ is a measure of the relative satisfaction from consumption of various goods and services. Given this measure, one may speak meaningfully of increasing or decreasing _____, and thereby explain economic behavior in terms of attempts to increase one's _____. For illustrative purposes, changes in _____ are sometimes expressed in units called utils.
   a. Utility function
   b. Ordinal utility
   c. Expected utility hypothesis
   d. Utility

18. The _____ is an independent agency of the United States government, established in 1914 by the _____ Act. Its principal mission is the promotion of 'consumer protection' and the elimination and prevention of what regulators perceive to be harmfully 'anti-competitive' business practices, such as coercive monopoly.

The _____ Act was one of President Wilson's major acts against trusts.

   a. 1921 recession
   b. Federal Trade Commission
   c. 100-year flood
   d. 130-30 fund

19. The _____ of 1914 (15 U.S.C §§ 41-58, as amended) established the Federal Trade Commission (FTC), a bipartisan body of five members appointed by the President of the United States for seven year terms. This Commission was authorized to issue Cease and Desist orders to large corporations to curb unfair trade practices. This Act also gave more flexibility to the US congress for judicial matters.
   a. Minimum wage law
   b. Federal Trade Commission Act
   c. Buydown
   d. Competition law theory

20. A _____ is the transfer of wealth from one party (such as a person or company) to another. A _____ is usually made in exchange for the provision of goods, services or both, or to fulfill a legal obligation.

The simplest and oldest form of _____ is barter, the exchange of one good or service for another.

   a. Soft count
   b. Social gravity
   c. Going concern
   d. Payment

21. In economics, a _____ is a redistribution of income in the market system. These payments are considered to be nonexhaustive because they do not directly absorb resources or create output. Examples of certain _____s include welfare (financial aid), social security, and government subsidies for certain businesses (firms.)
   a. 1921 recession
   b. 100-year flood
   c. 130-30 fund
   d. Transfer payment

22. In economics and finance, _____ is the change in total cost that arises when the quantity produced changes by one unit. It is the cost of producing one more unit of a good. Mathematically, the _____ function is expressed as the first derivative of the total cost (TC) function with respect to quantity (Q.)
   a. Variable cost
   b. Quality costs
   c. Khozraschyot
   d. Marginal cost

Chapter 10. The Firm: Cost and Output Determination

23. In economics, a _____ is a graph of the costs of production as a function of total quantity produced. In a free market economy, productively efficient firms use these curves to find the optimal point of production, where they make the most profits. There are a few different types of _____s, each relevant to a different area of economics.
   a. Kuznets curve
   b. Phillips curve
   c. Demand curve
   d. Cost curve

24. In economic models, the _____ time frame assumes no fixed factors of production. Firms can enter or leave the marketplace, and the cost (and availability) of land, labor, raw materials, and capital goods can be assumed to vary. In contrast, in the short-run time frame, certain factors are assumed to be fixed, because there is not sufficient time for them to change.
   a. Productivity world
   b. Diseconomies of scale
   c. Price/performance ratio
   d. Long-run

25. The _____ proposed by John L. Lewis in 1932, was a federation of unions that organized workers in industrial unions in the United States and Canada from 1935 to 1955. The Taft-Hartley Act of 1947 required union leaders to swear that they were not Communists. Many CIO leaders refused to obey that requirement, later found unconstitutional.
   a. Foreign direct investment
   b. Multinational corporation
   c. Chinese correction
   d. Congress of Industrial Organizations

26. _____s is the social science that studies the production, distribution, and consumption of goods and services. The term _____s comes from the Ancient Greek oá¼°κονομῖα from oá¼¶κος (oikos, 'house') + vĺŒμος (nomos, 'custom' or 'law'), hence 'rules of the house(hold)'. Current _____ models developed out of the broader field of political economy in the late 19th century, owing to a desire to use an empirical approach more akin to the physical sciences.
   a. Inflation
   b. Opportunity cost
   c. Energy economics
   d. Economic

27. In economic theory, _____ is the competitive situation in any market where the conditions necessary for perfect competition are not satisfied. It is a market structure that does not meet the conditions of perfect competition.

Forms of _____ include:

- Monopoly, in which there is only one seller of a good.
- Oligopoly, in which there is a small number of sellers.
- Monopolistic competition, in which there are many sellers producing highly differentiated goods.
- Monopsony, in which there is only one buyer of a good.
- Oligopsony, in which there is a small number of buyers.

There may also be _____ in markets due to buyers or sellers lacking information about prices and the goods being traded.

There may also be _____ due to a time lag in a market.

   a. ACEA agreement
   b. AD-IA Model
   c. ACCRA Cost of Living Index
   d. Imperfect Competition

28. _____ is a field of economics that studies the strategic behavior of firms, the structure of markets and their interactions. The study of _____ adds to the perfectly competitive model real-world frictions such as limited information, transaction cost, cost of adjusting prices, government actions, and barriers to entry by new firms into a market. It then considers how firms are organized and how they compete.
   a. Economic ideology
   b. Economic
   c. Inflation
   d. Industrial Organization

29. In production, returns to scale refers to changes in output subsequent to a proportional change in all inputs (where all inputs increase by a constant factor.) If output increases by that same proportional change then there are _____ If output increases by less than that proportional change, there are decreasing returns to scale (DRS.)
   a. Long term
   b. Lexicographic preferences
   c. Consumer sovereignty
   d. Constant returns to scale

30. _____ are the forces that cause larger firms to produce goods and services at increased per-unit costs. They are less well known than what economists have long understood as 'economies of scale', the forces which enable larger firms to produce goods and services at reduced per-unit costs.

Some of the forces which cause a diseconomy of scale are listed below:

Ideally, all employees of a firm would have one-on-one communication with each other so they know exactly what the other workers are doing.

   a. Marginal physical product
   b. Productive capacity
   c. Factors of production
   d. Diseconomies of scale

31. _____, in microeconomics, are the cost advantages that a business obtains due to expansion. They are factors that cause a producere;s average cost per unit to fall as scale is increased. _____ is a long run concept and refers to reductions in unit cost as the size of a facility, or scale, increases.
   a. Isoquant
   b. Economies of scale
   c. Economic production quantity
   d. Underinvestment employment relationship

32. In economics, _____ and economies of scale are related terms that describe what happens as the scale of production increases. They are different terms and should not be used interchangeably.

_____ refers to a technical property of production that examines changes in output subsequent to a proportional change in all inputs (where all inputs increase by a constant factor.)

   a. Necessity good
   b. Returns to scale
   c. Customer equity
   d. Constant returns to scale

33. In economics, _____ refers to the ability of a person or a country to produce a particular good at a lower marginal cost and opportunity cost than another person or country. It is the ability to produce a product most efficiently given all the other products that could be produced. It can be contrasted with absolute advantage which refers to the ability of a person or a country to produce a particular good at a lower absolute cost than another.

a. Triffin dilemma
b. Gravity model of trade
c. Hot money
d. Comparative advantage

Chapter 11. Perfect Competition

1. _____s is the social science that studies the production, distribution, and consumption of goods and services. The term _____s comes from the Ancient Greek oá¼°κονομῖα from oá¼¶κος (oikos, 'house') + vÏŒμος (nomos, 'custom' or 'law'), hence 'rules of the house(hold)'. Current _____ models developed out of the broader field of political economy in the late 19th century, owing to a desire to use an empirical approach more akin to the physical sciences.

 a. Energy economics   b. Inflation
 c. Opportunity cost   d. Economic

2. In economic theory, _____ is the competitive situation in any market where the conditions necessary for perfect competition are not satisfied. It is a market structure that does not meet the conditions of perfect competition.

Forms of _____ include:

- Monopoly, in which there is only one seller of a good.
- Oligopoly, in which there is a small number of sellers.
- Monopolistic competition, in which there are many sellers producing highly differentiated goods.
- Monopsony, in which there is only one buyer of a good.
- Oligopsony, in which there is a small number of buyers.

There may also be _____ in markets due to buyers or sellers lacking information about prices and the goods being traded.

There may also be _____ due to a time lag in a market.

 a. Imperfect Competition   b. ACCRA Cost of Living Index
 c. ACEA agreement   d. AD-IA Model

3. In economics, and cost accounting, _____ describes the total economic cost of production and is made up of variable costs, which vary according to the quantity of a good produced and include inputs such as labor and raw materials, plus fixed costs, which are independent of the quantity of a good produced and include inputs (capital) that cannot be varied in the short term, such as buildings and machinery. _____ in economics includes the total opportunity cost of each factor of production in addition to fixed and variable costs.

The rate at which _____ changes as the amount produced changes is called marginal cost.

 a. 1921 recession   b. 100-year flood
 c. 130-30 fund   d. Total cost

4. _____ is the total money received from the sale of any given quantity of output.

The _____ is calculated by taking the price of the sale times the quantity sold, i.e.

_____ = price X quantity.

Chapter 11. Perfect Competition

a. Small numbers game
b. Market development funds
c. Ceteris paribus
d. Total revenue

5. _____ is a broad label that refers to any individuals or households that use goods and services generated within the economy. The concept of a _____ is used in different contexts, so that the usage and significance of the term may vary.

Typically when business people and economists talk of _____s they are talking about person as _____, an aggregated commodity item with little individuality other than that expressed in the buy/not-buy decision.

a. Consumer
b. 100-year flood
c. 1921 recession
d. 130-30 fund

6. _____ are the inflation-indexed bonds issued by the U.S. Treasury. The principal is adjusted to the Consumer Price Index, the commonly used measure of inflation. The coupon rate is constant, but generates a different amount of interest when multiplied by the inflation-adjusted principal, thus protecting the holder against inflation.

a. 130-30 fund
b. 100-year flood
c. 1921 recession
d. Treasury Inflation-Protected Securities

7. In finance, the _____s between two currencies specifies how much one currency is worth in terms of the other. It is the value of a foreign natione;s currency in terms of the home natione;s currency. For example an _____ of 102 Japanese yen to the United States dollar means that JPY 102 is worth the same as USD 1.

a. ACCRA Cost of Living Index
b. ACEA agreement
c. Interbank market
d. Exchange rate

8. In economics, the concept of the _____ refers to the decision-making time frame of a firm in which at least one factor of production is fixed. Costs which are fixed in the _____ have no impact on a firms decisions. For example a firm can raise output by increasing the amount of labour through overtime.

a. Productivity model
b. Hicks-neutral technical change
c. Product Pipeline
d. Short-run

9. A _____ refers to any type debt instrument, such as a loan, bond, mortgage that does not have a fixed rate of interest over the life of the instrument. Such debt typically uses an index or other base rate for establishing the interest rate for each relevant period. One of the most common rates to use as the basis for applying interest rates is the London Inter-bank Offered Rate, or LIBOR

a. Moneylender
b. Money market
c. Disposal tax effect
d. Floating interest rate

10. The United States federal _____ is a refundable tax credit. For tax year 2008, a claimant with one qualifying child can receive a maximum credit of $2,917. For two or more qualifying children, the maximum credit is $4,824.

a. Earned Income Tax Credit
b. ACCRA Cost of Living Index
c. ACEA agreement
d. AD-IA Model

Chapter 11. Perfect Competition

11. An _____ is a tax levied on the financial income of people, corporations, or other legal entities. Various _____ systems exist, with varying degrees of tax incidence. Income taxation can be progressive, proportional, or regressive.
    a. ACEA agreement
    b. AD-IA Model
    c. ACCRA Cost of Living Index
    d. Income Tax

12. To _____ is to impose a financial charge or other levy upon a taxpayer by a state or the functional equivalent of a state.

    _____es are also imposed by many subnational entities. _____es consist of direct _____ or indirect _____, and may be paid in money or as its labour equivalent (often but not always unpaid.)

    a. 100-year flood
    b. Tax
    c. 1921 recession
    d. 130-30 fund

13. The term _____ describes two different concepts:

    - The first is a recognition of partial payment already made towards taxes due.
    - The second is a state benefit paid to workers through the tax system, which has the effect of increasing (rather than reducing) net income.

    Within the Australian, Canadian, United Kingdom, and United States tax systems, a _____ is a recognition of partial payment already made towards taxes due. A similar concept exists (fr:Avoir fiscal) in the French tax system. This situation arises, for example, when standard rate tax has been deducted at source, but the tax-payer is subject to further taxation at a higher rate. It also applies in dividend imputation systems.

    a. 100-year flood
    b. 130-30 fund
    c. 1921 recession
    d. Tax Credit

14. _____ in economics and business is the result of an exchange and from that trade we assign a numerical monetary value to a good, service or asset. If Alice trades Bob 4 apples for an orange, the _____ of an orange is 4 apples. Inversely, the _____ of an apple is 1/4 oranges.
    a. Price war
    b. Premium pricing
    c. Price book
    d. Price

15. In economics and business, specifically cost accounting, the _____ point (BEP) is the point at which cost or expenses and revenue are equal: there is no net loss or gain, and one has 'broken even'. A profit or a loss has not been made, although opportunity costs have been paid, and capital has received the risk-adjusted, expected return.

    For example, if the business sells less than 200 tables each month, it will make a loss, if it sells more, it will be a profit.

    a. Buffer stock scheme
    b. Break-even
    c. Nonmarket
    d. Small numbers game

Chapter 11. Perfect Competition

16. In economics, _____ is the difference between a company's total revenue and its opportunity costs. It is the increase in wealth that an investor has from making an investment, taking into consideration all costs associated with that investment including the opportunity cost of capital.

Profit is the factor income of the entrepreneur.

   a. Operating profit
   b. Accounting profit
   c. ACCRA Cost of Living Index
   d. Economic profit

17. In economics, an _____ is any good or commodity, transported from one country to another country in a legitimate fashion, typically for use in trade. _____ goods or services are provided to foreign consumers by domestic producers. _____ is an important part of international trade.
   a. AD-IA Model
   b. ACCRA Cost of Living Index
   c. Export
   d. ACEA agreement

18. In neoclassical economics and microeconomics, _____ describes the perfect being a market in which there are many small firms, all producing homogeneous goods. In the short term, such markets are productively inefficient as output will not occur where mc is equal to ac, but allocatively efficient, as output under _____ will always occur where mc is equal to mr, and therefore where mc equals ar. However, in the long term, such markets are both allocatively and productively efficient.
   a. Co-operative economics
   b. General equilibrium
   c. Law of supply
   d. Perfect competition

19. In economics, market concentration is a function of the number of firms and their respective shares of the total production (alternatively, total capacity or total reserves) in a market. Alternative terms are _____ and Seller concentration.

Market concentration is related to the concept of industrial concentration, which concerns the distribution of production within an industry, as opposed to a market.

   a. Industry concentration
   b. ACCRA Cost of Living Index
   c. AD-IA Model
   d. ACEA agreement

20. _____ describes a set of laws relating to domestic agriculture and imports of foreign agricultural products. Governments usually implement agricultural policies with the goal of achieving a specific outcome in the domestic agricultural product markets. Outcomes can involve, for example, a guaranteed supply level, price stability, product quality, product selection, land use or employment.
   a. ACCRA Cost of Living Index
   b. Agricultural Policy
   c. Intercropping
   d. ACEA agreement

21. The U.S. _____ is a federal agency whose goal is ending employment discrimination. The _____ investigates discrimination complaints based on an individual's race, color, national origin, religion, sex, age, disability and retaliation for reporting and/or opposing a discriminatory practice. The Commission is also tasked with filing suits on behalf of alleged victim(s) of discrimination against employers and as an adjudicatory for claims of discrimination brought against federal agencies.

Chapter 11. Perfect Competition

a. ACEA agreement
b. AD-IA Model
c. ACCRA Cost of Living Index
d. Equal Employment Opportunity Commission

22. In economic models, the _____ time frame assumes no fixed factors of production. Firms can enter or leave the marketplace, and the cost (and availability) of land, labor, raw materials, and capital goods can be assumed to vary. In contrast, in the short-run time frame, certain factors are assumed to be fixed, because there is not sufficient time for them to change.
   a. Long-run
   b. Price/performance ratio
   c. Diseconomies of scale
   d. Productivity world

23. To tax is to impose a financial charge or other levy upon a taxpayer by a state or the functional equivalent of a state. _____ are also imposed by many subnational entities. _____ consist of direct tax or indirect tax, and may be paid in money or as its labour equivalent (often but not always unpaid.)
   a. 130-30 fund
   b. 100-year flood
   c. 1921 recession
   d. Taxes

24. The _____ proposed by John L. Lewis in 1932, was a federation of unions that organized workers in industrial unions in the United States and Canada from 1935 to 1955. The Taft-Hartley Act of 1947 required union leaders to swear that they were not Communists. Many CIO leaders refused to obey that requirement, later found unconstitutional.
   a. Congress of Industrial Organizations
   b. Multinational corporation
   c. Foreign direct investment
   d. Chinese correction

25. _____ is a field of economics that studies the strategic behavior of firms, the structure of markets and their interactions. The study of _____ adds to the perfectly competitive model real-world frictions such as limited information, transaction cost, cost of adjusting prices, government actions, and barriers to entry by new firms into a market. It then considers how firms are organized and how they compete.
   a. Economic ideology
   b. Economic
   c. Inflation
   d. Industrial Organization

26. _____ describes a deliberate attempt to interfere with the free and fair operation of the market and create artificial, false or misleading appearances with respect to the price of a security, commodity or currency. _____ is prohibited under Section 9(a)(2) of the Securities Exchange Act of 1934, and in Australia under Section s 1041A of the Corporations Act 2001. The Act defines _____ as transactions which create an artificial price or maintain an artificial price for a tradable security.
   a. Managerial economics
   b. Net domestic product
   c. Legal monopoly
   d. Market manipulation

27. In economics, _____ is equal to total cost divided by the number of goods produced (the output quantity, Q.) It is also equal to the sum of average variable costs (total variable costs divided by Q) plus average fixed costs (total fixed costs divided by Q.) _____s may be dependent on the time period considered (increasing production may be expensive or impossible in the short term, for example.)
   a. Average cost
   b. Average variable cost
   c. Average fixed cost
   d. Explicit cost

Chapter 11. Perfect Competition

28. In economics, a _____ is a graph of the costs of production as a function of total quantity produced. In a free market economy, productively efficient firms use these curves to find the optimal point of production, where they make the most profits. There are a few different types of _____s, each relevant to a different area of economics.
    a. Cost curve
    b. Demand curve
    c. Phillips curve
    d. Kuznets curve

29. The U.S. _____ (EEOC) is a federal agency whose goal is ending employment discrimination. The _____ investigates discrimination complaints based on an individual's race, color, national origin, religion, sex, age, disability and retaliation for reporting and/or opposing a discriminatory practice. The Commission is also tasked with filing suits on behalf of alleged victim(s) of discrimination against employers and as an adjudicatory for claims of discrimination brought against federal agencies.
    a. ACCRA Cost of Living Index
    b. AD-IA Model
    c. ACEA agreement
    d. EEOC

30. _____ is used to refer to a number of related concepts. It is the using resources in such a way as to maximize the production of goods and services. A system can be called economically efficient if:

    - No one can be made better off without making someone else worse off.
    - More output cannot be obtained without increasing the amount of inputs.
    - Production proceeds at the lowest possible per-unit cost.

    These definitions of efficiency are not equivalent, but they are all encompassed by the idea that nothing more can be achieved given the resources available.

    An economic system is more efficient if it can provide more goods and services for society without using more resources.

    a. ACCRA Cost of Living Index
    b. Efficient contract theory
    c. Economic efficiency
    d. ACEA agreement

31. In economics and finance, _____ is the change in total cost that arises when the quantity produced changes by one unit. It is the cost of producing one more unit of a good. Mathematically, the _____ function is expressed as the first derivative of the total cost (TC) function with respect to quantity (Q.)
    a. Quality costs
    b. Khozraschyot
    c. Variable cost
    d. Marginal cost

32. _____ is one of the four Ps of the marketing mix. The other three aspects are product, promotion, and place. It is also a key variable in microeconomic price allocation theory.
    a. Guaranteed Maximum Price
    b. Premium pricing
    c. Point of total assumption
    d. Pricing

33. In economics, a _____ exists when the production or use of goods and services by the market is not efficient. That is, there exists another outcome where all involved can be made better off. _____s can be viewed as scenarios where individuals' pursuit of pure self-interest leads to results that are not efficient - that can be improved upon from the societal point-of-view.

a. Fixed exchange rate
b. General equilibrium
c. Financial economics
d. Market failure

Chapter 12. Monopoly

1. Competition law, known in the United States as _____ law, has three main elements:

   - prohibiting agreements or practices that restrict free trading and competition between business entities. This includes in particular the repression of cartels.
   - banning abusive behaviour by a firm dominating a market, or anti-competitive practices that tend to lead to such a dominant position. Practices controlled in this way may include predatory pricing, tying, price gouging, refusal to deal, and many others.
   - supervising the mergers and acquisitions of large corporations, including some joint ventures. Transactions that are considered to threaten the competitive process can be prohibited altogether, or approved subject to 'remedies' such as an obligation to divest part of the merged business or to offer licences or access to facilities to enable other businesses to continue competing.

   The substance and practice of competition law varies from jurisdiction to jurisdiction. Protecting the interests of consumers (consumer welfare) and ensuring that entrepreneurs have an opportunity to compete in the market economy are often treated as important objectives. Competition law is closely connected with law on deregulation of access to markets, state aids and subsidies, the privatisation of state owned assets and the establishment of independent sector regulators. In recent decades, competition law has been viewed as a way to provide better public services.

   a. Intellectual property law
   b. Anti-Inflation Act
   c. United Kingdom competition law
   d. Antitrust

2.

   The _____ was the first United States Federal statute to limit cartels and monopolies. It falls under antitrust law.

   The Act provides: 'Every contract, combination in the form of trust or otherwise, or conspiracy, in restraint of trade or commerce among the several States, or with foreign nations, is declared to be illegal'. The Act also provides: 'Every person who shall monopolize, or attempt to monopolize, or combine or conspire with any other person or persons, to monopolize any part of the trade or commerce among the several States, or with foreign nations, shall be deemed guilty of a felony [. . .]' The Act put responsibility upon government attorneys and district courts to pursue and investigate trusts, companies and organizations suspected of violating the Act. The Clayton Act extended the right to sue under the antitrust laws to 'any person who shall be injured in his business or property by reason of anything forbidden in the antitrust laws.' Under the Clayton Act, private parties may sue in U.S. district court and should they prevail, they may be awarded treble damages and the cost of suit, including reasonable attorney's fees.

   a. Sherman Antitrust Act
   b. 100-year flood
   c. 1921 recession
   d. 130-30 fund

3. _____ is a voluntary transfer of resources from one country to another, given at least partly with the objective of benefiting the recipient country. It may have other functions as well: it may be given as a signal of diplomatic approval, or to strengthen a military ally, to reward a government for behaviour desired by the donor, to extend the donor's cultural influence, to provide infrastructure needed by the donor for resource extraction from the recipient country, or to gain other kinds of commercial access. Humanitarianism and altruism are, nevertheless, significant motivations for the giving of _____.

Chapter 12. Monopoly

a. ACEA agreement
c. AD-IA Model
b. ACCRA Cost of Living Index
d. Aid

4. In economics and especially in the theory of competition, _____ are obstacles in the path of a firm that make it difficult to enter a given market.

_____ are the source of a firm's pricing power - the ability of a firm to raise prices without losing all its customers.

The term refers to hindrances that an individual may face while trying to gain entrance into a profession or trade.

a. Group boycott
c. Social dumping
b. Limit price
d. Barriers to entry

5. In finance, the _____s between two currencies specifies how much one currency is worth in terms of the other. It is the value of a foreign natione;s currency in terms of the home natione;s currency. For example an _____ of 102 Japanese yen to the United States dollar means that JPY 102 is worth the same as USD 1.

a. ACEA agreement
c. Interbank market
b. ACCRA Cost of Living Index
d. Exchange rate

6. A _____ strategy is the planned method of delivering goods or services to a target market and distributing them there. When importing or exporting services, it refers to establishing and managing contracts in a foreign country.

Many companies successfully operate in a niche market without ever expanding into new markets.

a. Customer centricity
c. Forfaiting
b. Deep discount broker
d. Market entry

7. _____s (economically referred to as land or raw materials) occur naturally within environments that exist relatively undisturbed by mankind, in a natural form. A _____'s is often characterized by amounts of biodiversity existent in various ecosystems.

Mining, petroleum extraction, fishing, hunting, and forestry are generally considered natural-resource industries.

a. 130-30 fund
c. 100-year flood
b. 1921 recession
d. Natural resource

8. _____ is a broad label that refers to any individuals or households that use goods and services generated within the economy. The concept of a _____ is used in different contexts, so that the usage and significance of the term may vary.

Typically when business people and economists talk of _____s they are talking about person as _____, an aggregated commodity item with little individuality other than that expressed in the buy/not-buy decision.

a. 130-30 fund
b. 100-year flood
c. 1921 recession
d. Consumer

9. _____s is the social science that studies the production, distribution, and consumption of goods and services. The term _____s comes from the Ancient Greek oá¼°κονομῖα from oá¼¶κος (oikos, 'house') + vÏŒμος (nomos, 'custom' or 'law'), hence 'rules of the house(hold)'. Current _____ models developed out of the broader field of political economy in the late 19th century, owing to a desire to use an empirical approach more akin to the physical sciences.
  a. Economic
  b. Opportunity cost
  c. Energy economics
  d. Inflation

10. In economic theory, _____ is the competitive situation in any market where the conditions necessary for perfect competition are not satisfied. It is a market structure that does not meet the conditions of perfect competition.

Forms of _____ include:

- Monopoly, in which there is only one seller of a good.
- Oligopoly, in which there is a small number of sellers.
- Monopolistic competition, in which there are many sellers producing highly differentiated goods.
- Monopsony, in which there is only one buyer of a good.
- Oligopsony, in which there is a small number of buyers.

There may also be _____ in markets due to buyers or sellers lacking information about prices and the goods being traded.

There may also be _____ due to a time lag in a market.

  a. AD-IA Model
  b. Imperfect Competition
  c. ACEA agreement
  d. ACCRA Cost of Living Index

11. In economics, _____ is equal to total cost divided by the number of goods produced (the output quantity, Q.) It is also equal to the sum of average variable costs (total variable costs divided by Q) plus average fixed costs (total fixed costs divided by Q.) _____s may be dependent on the time period considered (increasing production may be expensive or impossible in the short term, for example.)
  a. Average variable cost
  b. Average fixed cost
  c. Explicit cost
  d. Average cost

12. In economics, a _____ is a graph of the costs of production as a function of total quantity produced. In a free market economy, productively efficient firms use these curves to find the optimal point of production, where they make the most profits. There are a few different types of _____s, each relevant to a different area of economics.
  a. Phillips curve
  b. Kuznets curve
  c. Demand curve
  d. Cost curve

13. _____, in microeconomics, are the cost advantages that a business obtains due to expansion. They are factors that cause a producere;s average cost per unit to fall as scale is increased. _____ is a long run concept and refers to reductions in unit cost as the size of a facility, or scale, increases.

Chapter 12. Monopoly

a. Economic production quantity
b. Economies of scale
c. Isoquant
d. Underinvestment employment relationship

14. In economic models, the _____ time frame assumes no fixed factors of production. Firms can enter or leave the marketplace, and the cost (and availability) of land, labor, raw materials, and capital goods can be assumed to vary. In contrast, in the short-run time frame, certain factors are assumed to be fixed, because there is not sufficient time for them to change.
   a. Productivity world
   b. Diseconomies of scale
   c. Price/performance ratio
   d. Long-run

15. In economics and finance, _____ is the change in total cost that arises when the quantity produced changes by one unit. It is the cost of producing one more unit of a good. Mathematically, the _____ function is expressed as the first derivative of the total cost (TC) function with respect to quantity (Q.)
   a. Variable cost
   b. Quality costs
   c. Khozraschyot
   d. Marginal cost

16. In economics, _____ is how a natione;s total economy is distributed among its population. ._____ has always been a central concern of economic theory and economic policy. Classical economists such as Adam Smith, Thomas Malthus and David Ricardo were mainly concerned with factor _____, that is, the distribution of income between the main factors of production, land, labour and capital.
   a. Authorised capital
   b. Equipment trust certificate
   c. Eco commerce
   d. Income distribution

17. To _____ is to impose a financial charge or other levy upon a taxpayer by a state or the functional equivalent of a state.

_____es are also imposed by many subnational entities. _____es consist of direct _____ or indirect _____, and may be paid in money or as its labour equivalent (often but not always unpaid.)

   a. 1921 recession
   b. Tax
   c. 130-30 fund
   d. 100-year flood

18. To tax is to impose a financial charge or other levy upon a taxpayer by a state or the functional equivalent of a state.

_____ are also imposed by many subnational entities. _____ consist of direct tax or indirect tax, and may be paid in money or as its labour equivalent (often but not always unpaid.)

   a. 130-30 fund
   b. 1921 recession
   c. 100-year flood
   d. Taxes

19. A _____ is a counterfeit agreement among industries. It is an informal organization of producers that agree to coordinate prices and production. _____s usually occur in an oligopolistic industry, where there is a small number of sellers and usually involve homogeneous products.
   a. Cartel
   b. 100-year flood
   c. Shill
   d. Shanzhai

Chapter 12. Monopoly

20. _____ is the transition of a national economy from monopoly control by groups of large businesses to a free market economy. This change rarely arises naturally, and is generally the result of regulation by a governing body.

A modern example of _____ is the economic restructuring of Germany after the fall of the Third Reich in 1945.

  a. Monopolization
  c. Complementary monopoly
  b. Market power
  d. Decartelization

21. A _____ is a duty imposed on goods when they are moved across a political boundary. They are usually associated with protectionism, the economic policy of restraining trade between nations. For political reasons, _____s are usually imposed on imported goods, although they may also be imposed on exported goods.

  a. 130-30 fund
  c. 100-year flood
  b. Tariff
  d. 1921 recession

22. Economics:

- _____, the desire to own something and the ability to pay for it
- _____ curve, a graphic representation of a _____ schedule
- _____ deposit, the money in checking accounts
- _____ pull theory, the theory that inflation occurs when _____ for goods and services exceeds existing supplies
- _____ schedule, a table that lists the quantity of a good a person will buy it each different price
- _____ side economics, the school of economics at believes government spending and tax cuts open economy by raising _____

  a. Demand
  c. McKesson ' Robbins scandal
  b. Production
  d. Variability

23. In economics, the _____ can be defined as the graph depicting the relationship between the price of a certain commodity, and the amount of it that consumers are willing and able to purchase at that given price. It is a graphic representation of a demand schedule. The _____ for all consumers together follows from the _____ of every individual consumer: the individual demands at each price are added together.

  a. Kuznets curve
  c. Cost curve
  b. Wage curve
  d. Demand curve

24. In microeconomics, _____ is the extra revenue that an additional unit of product will bring. It is the additional income from selling one more unit of a good; sometimes equal to price. It can also be described as the change in total revenue/change in number of units sold.

  a. Long term
  c. Market demand schedule
  b. Reservation price
  d. Marginal revenue

25. In economics, _____ is the ratio of the percent change in one variable to the percent change in another variable. It is a tool for measuring the responsiveness of a function to changes in parameters in a relative way. Commonly analyzed are _____ of substitution, price and wealth.

a. ACCRA Cost of Living Index
b. ACEA agreement
c. Elasticity of demand
d. Elasticity

26. Price _____ is defined as the measure of responsiveness in the quantity demanded for a commodity as a result of change in price of the same commodity. It is a measure of how consumers react to a change in price. In other words, it is percentage change in quantity demanded by the percentage change in price of the same commodity.
a. Elasticity
b. ACCRA Cost of Living Index
c. ACEA agreement
d. Elasticity of demand

27. _____ in economics and business is the result of an exchange and from that trade we assign a numerical monetary value to a good, service or asset. If Alice trades Bob 4 apples for an orange, the _____ of an orange is 4 apples. Inversely, the _____ of an apple is 1/4 oranges.
a. Price war
b. Price book
c. Premium pricing
d. Price

28. _____ is defined as the measure of responsiveness in the quantity demanded for a commodity as a result of change in price of the same commodity. It is a measure of how consumers react to a change in price. In other words, it is percentage change in quantity demanded as per the percentage change in price of the same commodity.
a. Price elasticity of demand
b. 100-year flood
c. 1921 recession
d. 130-30 fund

29. _____ are the inflation-indexed bonds issued by the U.S. Treasury. The principal is adjusted to the Consumer Price Index, the commonly used measure of inflation. The coupon rate is constant, but generates a different amount of interest when multiplied by the inflation-adjusted principal, thus protecting the holder against inflation.
a. 100-year flood
b. 1921 recession
c. 130-30 fund
d. Treasury Inflation-Protected Securities

30. In economics, a _____ exists when a specific individual or enterprise has sufficient control over a particular product or service to determine significantly the terms on which other individuals shall have access to it. Monopolies are thus characterized by a lack of economic competition for the good or service that they provide and a lack of viable substitute goods. The verb 'monopolize' refers to the process by which a firm gains persistently greater market share than what is expected under perfect competition.
a. 1921 recession
b. Monopoly
c. 100-year flood
d. 130-30 fund

31. In economics, a firm is said to reap _____s when a lack of viable market competition allows it to set its prices above the equilibrium price for a good or service without losing profits to competitors. _____ is a type of economic profit, that is, it is a profit greater than the normal profit that is typical in a perfectly competitive industry. The resulting price is known as the monopoly price.
a. Cleanup clause
b. Borrowing base
c. Monopoly profit
d. First-price sealed-bid auction

32. In economics, _____ is the process by which a firm determines the price and output level that returns the greatest profit. There are several approaches to this problem. The total revenue--total cost method relies on the fact that profit equals revenue minus cost, and the marginal revenue--marginal cost method is based on the fact that total profit in a perfectly competitive market reaches its maximum point where marginal revenue equals marginal cost.

Chapter 12. Monopoly

a. Profit maximization
b. Profit margin
c. 100-year flood
d. Normal profit

33. In economics, and cost accounting, _____ describes the total economic cost of production and is made up of variable costs, which vary according to the quantity of a good produced and include inputs such as labor and raw materials, plus fixed costs, which are independent of the quantity of a good produced and include inputs (capital) that cannot be varied in the short term, such as buildings and machinery. _____ in economics includes the total opportunity cost of each factor of production in addition to fixed and variable costs.

The rate at which _____ changes as the amount produced changes is called marginal cost.

a. Total cost
b. 1921 recession
c. 100-year flood
d. 130-30 fund

34. _____ is the total money received from the sale of any given quantity of output.

The _____ is calculated by taking the price of the sale times the quantity sold, i.e.

_____ = price X quantity.

a. Ceteris paribus
b. Small numbers game
c. Market development funds
d. Total revenue

35. A trade union or _____ is an organization of workers who have banded together to achieve common goals in key areas and working conditions. The trade union, through its leadership, bargains with the employer on behalf of union members (rank and file members) and negotiates labor contracts (Collective bargaining) with employers. This may include the negotiation of wages, work rules, complaint procedures, rules governing hiring, firing and promotion of workers, benefits, workplace safety and policies.

a. Basis of futures
b. Labor union
c. Business valuation standards
d. Demand-side technologies

36. A _____ is a group of people who share or are motivated by at least one common issue or interest, or work together on a specific project(s) to achieve a common objective. _____s are also characterised by attempts to share and exercise political and social power and to make decisions on a consensus-driven and egalitarian basis. _____s differ from cooperatives in that they are not necessarily focused upon an economic benefit or saving (but can be that as well.)

a. 1921 recession
b. 130-30 fund
c. 100-year flood
d. Collective

37. _____ exists when sales of identical goods or services are transacted at different prices from the same provider. In a theoretical market with perfect information, no transaction costs or prohibition on secondary exchange (or re-selling) to prevent arbitrage, _____ can only be a feature of monopoly and oligopoly markets, where market power can be exercised. Otherwise, the moment the seller tries to sell the same good at different prices, the buyer at the lower price can arbitrage by selling to the consumer buying at the higher price but with a tiny discount.

a. Price discrimination
c. Lerner Index
b. Transfer pricing
d. Loss leader

38. A _____ or labor union is an organization of workers who have banded together to achieve common goals in key areas and working conditions. The _____, through its leadership, bargains with the employer on behalf of union members (rank and file members) and negotiates labor contracts (Collective bargaining) with employers. This may include the negotiation of wages, work rules, complaint procedures, rules governing hiring, firing and promotion of workers, benefits, workplace safety and policies.

a. Case-Shiller Home Price Indices
c. Trade union
b. Consumer goods
d. Guaranteed investment contracts

39. In economics _____ is defined as the sum of private and external costs. Economic theorists ascribe individual decision-making to a calculation costs and benefits. Rational choice theory assumes that individuals only consider their own private costs when making decisions, not the costs that may be borne by others.

a. Khozraschyot
c. Psychic cost
b. Cost-Volume-Profit Analysis
d. Social cost

40. A _____ is a set of exclusive rights granted by a state to an inventor or his assignee for a limited period of time in exchange for a disclosure of an invention.

The procedure for granting _____s, the requirements placed on the _____ee and the extent of the exclusive rights vary widely between countries according to national laws and international agreements. Typically, however, a _____ application must include one or more claims defining the invention which must be new, inventive, and useful or industrially applicable.

a. Bona fide occupational qualification
c. Patent
b. Bank regulation
d. Long service leave

Chapter 13. Monopolistic Competition

1. To _____ is to impose a financial charge or other levy upon a taxpayer by a state or the functional equivalent of a state.

   _____es are also imposed by many subnational entities. _____es consist of direct _____ or indirect _____, and may be paid in money or as its labour equivalent (often but not always unpaid.)

   a. Tax
   b. 100-year flood
   c. 1921 recession
   d. 130-30 fund

2. To tax is to impose a financial charge or other levy upon a taxpayer by a state or the functional equivalent of a state.

   _____ are also imposed by many subnational entities. _____ consist of direct tax or indirect tax, and may be paid in money or as its labour equivalent (often but not always unpaid.)

   a. Taxes
   b. 100-year flood
   c. 130-30 fund
   d. 1921 recession

3. Competition law, known in the United States as _____ law, has three main elements:

   - prohibiting agreements or practices that restrict free trading and competition between business entities. This includes in particular the repression of cartels.
   - banning abusive behaviour by a firm dominating a market, or anti-competitive practices that tend to lead to such a dominant position. Practices controlled in this way may include predatory pricing, tying, price gouging, refusal to deal, and many others.
   - supervising the mergers and acquisitions of large corporations, including some joint ventures. Transactions that are considered to threaten the competitive process can be prohibited altogether, or approved subject to 'remedies' such as an obligation to divest part of the merged business or to offer licences or access to facilities to enable other businesses to continue competing.

   The substance and practice of competition law varies from jurisdiction to jurisdiction. Protecting the interests of consumers (consumer welfare) and ensuring that entrepreneurs have an opportunity to compete in the market economy are often treated as important objectives. Competition law is closely connected with law on deregulation of access to markets, state aids and subsidies, the privatisation of state owned assets and the establishment of independent sector regulators. In recent decades, competition law has been viewed as a way to provide better public services.

   a. United Kingdom competition law
   b. Intellectual property law
   c. Antitrust
   d. Anti-Inflation Act

4. _____s is the social science that studies the production, distribution, and consumption of goods and services. The term _____s comes from the Ancient Greek οἰκονομία from οἶκος (oikos, 'house') + νόμος (nomos, 'custom' or 'law'), hence 'rules of the house(hold)'. Current _____ models developed out of the broader field of political economy in the late 19th century, owing to a desire to use an empirical approach more akin to the physical sciences.

   a. Opportunity cost
   b. Energy economics
   c. Inflation
   d. Economic

Chapter 13. Monopolistic Competition

5. In economic theory, _____ is the competitive situation in any market where the conditions necessary for perfect competition are not satisfied. It is a market structure that does not meet the conditions of perfect competition.

Forms of _____ include:

- Monopoly, in which there is only one seller of a good.
- Oligopoly, in which there is a small number of sellers.
- Monopolistic competition, in which there are many sellers producing highly differentiated goods.
- Monopsony, in which there is only one buyer of a good.
- Oligopsony, in which there is a small number of buyers.

There may also be _____ in markets due to buyers or sellers lacking information about prices and the goods being traded.

There may also be _____ due to a time lag in a market.

    a. ACCRA Cost of Living Index   b. Imperfect Competition
    c. AD-IA Model   d. ACEA agreement

6. A trade union or _____ is an organization of workers who have banded together to achieve common goals in key areas and working conditions. The trade union, through its leadership, bargains with the employer on behalf of union members (rank and file members) and negotiates labor contracts (Collective bargaining) with employers. This may include the negotiation of wages, work rules, complaint procedures, rules governing hiring, firing and promotion of workers, benefits, workplace safety and policies.

    a. Labor union   b. Business valuation standards
    c. Basis of futures   d. Demand-side technologies

7.

The _____ was the first United States Federal statute to limit cartels and monopolies. It falls under antitrust law.

The Act provides: 'Every contract, combination in the form of trust or otherwise, or conspiracy, in restraint of trade or commerce among the several States, or with foreign nations, is declared to be illegal'. The Act also provides: 'Every person who shall monopolize, or attempt to monopolize, or combine or conspire with any other person or persons, to monopolize any part of the trade or commerce among the several States, or with foreign nations, shall be deemed guilty of a felony [. . .]' The Act put responsibility upon government attorneys and district courts to pursue and investigate trusts, companies and organizations suspected of violating the Act. The Clayton Act extended the right to sue under the antitrust laws to 'any person who shall be injured in his business or property by reason of anything forbidden in the antitrust laws.' Under the Clayton Act, private parties may sue in U.S. district court and should they prevail, they may be awarded treble damages and the cost of suit, including reasonable attorney's fees.

Chapter 13. Monopolistic Competition

a. 1921 recession
b. 100-year flood
c. 130-30 fund
d. Sherman Antitrust Act

8. A _____ is a group of people who share or are motivated by at least one common issue or interest, or work together on a specific project(s) to achieve a common objective. _____s are also characterised by attempts to share and exercise political and social power and to make decisions on a consensus-driven and egalitarian basis. _____s differ from cooperatives in that they are not necessarily focused upon an economic benefit or saving (but can be that as well.)

a. 100-year flood
b. 130-30 fund
c. Collective
d. 1921 recession

9. _____ is an agreement, usually secretive, which occurs between two or more persons to deceive, mislead or to obtain an objective forbidden by law typically involving fraud or gaining an unfair advantage. It is an agreement among firms to divide the market, set prices kickbacks, or misrepresenting the independence of the relationship between the colluding parties.' All acts effected by _____ are considered void.

a. Bid rigging
b. Collusion
c. Net Book Agreement
d. Dividing territories

10. In finance, the _____s between two currencies specifies how much one currency is worth in terms of the other. It is the value of a foreign natione;s currency in terms of the home natione;s currency. For example an _____ of 102 Japanese yen to the United States dollar means that JPY 102 is worth the same as USD 1.

a. ACCRA Cost of Living Index
b. Interbank market
c. Exchange rate
d. ACEA agreement

11. _____, in strategic management and marketing is, according to Carlton O'Neal, the percentage or proportion of the total available market or market segment that is being serviced by a company. It can be expressed as a company's sales revenue (from that market) divided by the total sales revenue available in that market. It can also be expressed as a company's unit sales volume (in a market) divided by the total volume of units sold in that market.

a. Market share
b. Product differentiation
c. Customer to customer
d. Pricing science

12. _____ is a common market structure where many competing producers sell products that are differentiated from one another (ie. the products are substitutes, but are not exactly alike.) Many markets are monopolistically competitive, common examples include the markets for restaurants, cereal, clothing, shoes and service industries in large cities.

a. Financial crisis
b. Mathematical economics
c. Perfect competition
d. Monopolistic competition

13. A _____ or labor union is an organization of workers who have banded together to achieve common goals in key areas and working conditions. The _____, through its leadership, bargains with the employer on behalf of union members (rank and file members) and negotiates labor contracts (Collective bargaining) with employers. This may include the negotiation of wages, work rules, complaint procedures, rules governing hiring, firing and promotion of workers, benefits, workplace safety and policies.

a. Guaranteed investment contracts
b. Case-Shiller Home Price Indices
c. Consumer goods
d. Trade union

Chapter 13. Monopolistic Competition

14. _____ are the inflation-indexed bonds issued by the U.S. Treasury. The principal is adjusted to the Consumer Price Index, the commonly used measure of inflation. The coupon rate is constant, but generates a different amount of interest when multiplied by the inflation-adjusted principal, thus protecting the holder against inflation.
   a. 130-30 fund
   b. 1921 recession
   c. Treasury Inflation-Protected Securities
   d. 100-year flood

15. _____ was a survey conducted by the U.S. Department of Justice to gauge the prevalence of alcohol and illegal drug use among prior arrestees. It was a reformulation of the prior Drug Use Forecasting (DUF) program, focused on five drugs in particular: cocaine, marijuana, methamphetamine, opiates, and PCP.

Participants were randomly selected from arrest records in major metropolitan areas; because no personally identifying information is taken from each record chosen, the resulting data can be correlated to arrest rates, but not to the total population of persons charged.

   a. AD-IA Model
   b. ACCRA Cost of Living Index
   c. ACEA agreement
   d. Arrestee Drug Abuse Monitoring

16. _____ is an equity (stock) exchange located at 11 Wall Street in lower Manhattan, New York, USA. It is the largest stock exchange in the world by dollar value of its listed companies' securities. As of October 2008, the combined capitalization of all domestic _____ listed companies was US$10.1 trillion.
   a. 100-year flood
   b. 1921 recession
   c. 130-30 fund
   d. New York Stock Exchange

17. In economics, _____ refers to the ability of a person or a country to produce a particular good at a lower marginal cost and opportunity cost than another person or country. It is the ability to produce a product most efficiently given all the other products that could be produced. It can be contrasted with absolute advantage which refers to the ability of a person or a country to produce a particular good at a lower absolute cost than another.
   a. Triffin dilemma
   b. Comparative advantage
   c. Hot money
   d. Gravity model of trade

18. A _____ strategy is the planned method of delivering goods or services to a target market and distributing them there. When importing or exporting services, it refers to establishing and managing contracts in a foreign country.

Many companies successfully operate in a niche market without ever expanding into new markets.

   a. Customer centricity
   b. Market entry
   c. Forfaiting
   d. Deep discount broker

19. The U.S. _____ is a federal agency whose goal is ending employment discrimination. The _____ investigates discrimination complaints based on an individual's race, color, national origin, religion, sex, age, disability and retaliation for reporting and/or opposing a discriminatory practice. The Commission is also tasked with filing suits on behalf of alleged victim(s) of discrimination against employers and as an adjudicatory for claims of discrimination brought against federal agencies.
   a. ACCRA Cost of Living Index
   b. AD-IA Model
   c. Equal Employment Opportunity Commission
   d. ACEA agreement

Chapter 13. Monopolistic Competition

20. _____ in economics and business is the result of an exchange and from that trade we assign a numerical monetary value to a good, service or asset. If Alice trades Bob 4 apples for an orange, the _____ of an orange is 4 apples. Inversely, the _____ of an apple is 1/4 oranges.
    a. Premium pricing
    b. Price war
    c. Price book
    d. Price

21. In economics, the concept of the _____ refers to the decision-making time frame of a firm in which at least one factor of production is fixed. Costs which are fixed in the _____ have no impact on a firms decisions. For example a firm can raise output by increasing the amount of labour through overtime.
    a. Productivity model
    b. Product Pipeline
    c. Hicks-neutral technical change
    d. Short-run

22. In economic models, the _____ time frame assumes no fixed factors of production. Firms can enter or leave the marketplace, and the cost (and availability) of land, labor, raw materials, and capital goods can be assumed to vary. In contrast, in the short-run time frame, certain factors are assumed to be fixed, because there is not sufficient time for them to change.
    a. Price/performance ratio
    b. Productivity world
    c. Diseconomies of scale
    d. Long-run

23. In neoclassical economics and microeconomics, _____ describes the perfect being a market in which there are many small firms, all producing homogeneous goods. In the short term, such markets are productively inefficient as output will not occur where mc is equal to ac, but allocatively efficient, as output under _____ will always occur where mc is equal to mr, and therefore where mc equals ar. However, in the long term, such markets are both allocatively and productively efficient.
    a. Co-operative economics
    b. Law of supply
    c. General equilibrium
    d. Perfect competition

24. A _____ is a term used in economics for a good whose utility impact is difficult or impossible for the consumer to ascertain. In contrast to experience goods, the utility gain or loss of _____s is difficult to measure after consumption as well. The seller of the good knows the utility impact of the good, creating a situation of asymmetric information.
    a. Search good
    b. Credence good
    c. Composite good
    d. Pie method

25. In economics, an _____ is a product or service where product characteristics such as quality or price are difficult to observe in advance, but these characteristics can be ascertained upon consumption. The concept is originally due to Philip Nelson, who contrasted an _____ with a search good.

    _____s pose difficulties for consumers in accurately making consumption choices.

    a. Independent goods
    b. Export-oriented
    c. Experience good
    d. Information good

26. A _____ is an object whose consumption increases the utility of the consumer, for which the quantity demanded exceeds the quantity supplied at zero price. _____s are usually modeled as having diminishing marginal utility. The first individual purchase has high utility; the second has less.

a. Composite good
b. Pie method
c. Merit good
d. Good

27. In economics, a _____ is a product or service with features and characteristics easily evaluated before purchase. In a distinction originally due to Philip Nelson, a _____ is contrasted with an experience good.

_____s are more subject to substitution and price competition, as consumers can easily verify the price of the product and alternatives at other outlets and make sure that the products are comparable.

a. Substitute good
b. Superior goods
c. Search good
d. Luxury good

28. _____ is a broad label that refers to any individuals or households that use goods and services generated within the economy. The concept of a _____ is used in different contexts, so that the usage and significance of the term may vary.

Typically when business people and economists talk of _____s they are talking about person as _____, an aggregated commodity item with little individuality other than that expressed in the buy/not-buy decision.

a. 100-year flood
b. 130-30 fund
c. Consumer
d. 1921 recession

29. _____ or economic opportunity loss is the value of the next best alternative foregone as the result of making a decision. _____ analysis is an important part of a company's decision-making processes but is not treated as an actual cost in any financial statement. The next best thing that a person can engage in is referred to as the _____ of doing the best thing and ignoring the next best thing to be done.

a. Economic ideology
b. Industrial organization
c. Economic
d. Opportunity cost

Chapter 14. Oligopoly and Strategic Behavior

1. The _____ is an independent agency of the United States government, established in 1914 by the _____ Act. Its principal mission is the promotion of 'consumer protection' and the elimination and prevention of what regulators perceive to be harmfully 'anti-competitive' business practices, such as coercive monopoly.

The _____ Act was one of President Wilson's major acts against trusts.

a. 100-year flood
b. Federal Trade Commission
c. 1921 recession
d. 130-30 fund

2. The _____ of 1914 (15 U.S.C §§ 41-58, as amended) established the Federal Trade Commission (FTC), a bipartisan body of five members appointed by the President of the United States for seven year terms. This Commission was authorized to issue Cease and Desist orders to large corporations to curb unfair trade practices. This Act also gave more flexibility to the US congress for judicial matters.

a. Minimum wage law
b. Buydown
c. Competition law theory
d. Federal Trade Commission Act

3. A _____ is the transfer of wealth from one party (such as a person or company) to another. A _____ is usually made in exchange for the provision of goods, services or both, or to fulfill a legal obligation.

The simplest and oldest form of _____ is barter, the exchange of one good or service for another.

a. Social gravity
b. Going concern
c. Soft count
d. Payment

4. In economics, a _____ is a redistribution of income in the market system. These payments are considered to be nonexhaustive because they do not directly absorb resources or create output. Examples of certain _____s include welfare (financial aid), social security, and government subsidies for certain businesses (firms.)

a. Transfer payment
b. 1921 recession
c. 130-30 fund
d. 100-year flood

5. _____ is an equity (stock) exchange located at 11 Wall Street in lower Manhattan, New York, USA. It is the largest stock exchange in the world by dollar value of its listed companies' securities. As of October 2008, the combined capitalization of all domestic _____ listed companies was US$10.1 trillion.

a. 130-30 fund
b. 100-year flood
c. 1921 recession
d. New York Stock Exchange

6. _____s is the social science that studies the production, distribution, and consumption of goods and services. The term _____s comes from the Ancient Greek οἰκονομία from οἶκος (oikos, 'house') + νόμος (nomos, 'custom' or 'law'), hence 'rules of the house(hold)'. Current _____ models developed out of the broader field of political economy in the late 19th century, owing to a desire to use an empirical approach more akin to the physical sciences.

a. Inflation
b. Economic
c. Opportunity cost
d. Energy economics

7. In economic theory, _____ is the competitive situation in any market where the conditions necessary for perfect competition are not satisfied. It is a market structure that does not meet the conditions of perfect competition.

Chapter 14. Oligopoly and Strategic Behavior

Forms of _____ include:

- Monopoly, in which there is only one seller of a good.
- Oligopoly, in which there is a small number of sellers.
- Monopolistic competition, in which there are many sellers producing highly differentiated goods.
- Monopsony, in which there is only one buyer of a good.
- Oligopsony, in which there is a small number of buyers.

There may also be _____ in markets due to buyers or sellers lacking information about prices and the goods being traded.

There may also be _____ due to a time lag in a market.

a. ACEA agreement
c. ACCRA Cost of Living Index
b. AD-IA Model
d. Imperfect Competition

8. In economics and especially in the theory of competition, _____ are obstacles in the path of a firm that make it difficult to enter a given market.

_____ are the source of a firm's pricing power - the ability of a firm to raise prices without losing all its customers.

The term refers to hindrances that an individual may face while trying to gain entrance into a profession or trade.

a. Barriers to entry
c. Social dumping
b. Group boycott
d. Limit price

9. A true _____ is a specific type of oligopoly where only two producers exist in one market. In reality, this definition is generally used where only two firms have dominant control over a market. In the field of industrial organization, it is the most commonly studied form of oligopoly due to its simplicity.

a. 130-30 fund
c. Megacorpstate
b. 100-year flood
d. Duopoly

10. _____, in microeconomics, are the cost advantages that a business obtains due to expansion. They are factors that cause a producere;s average cost per unit to fall as scale is increased. _____ is a long run concept and refers to reductions in unit cost as the size of a facility, or scale, increases.

a. Economies of scale
c. Isoquant
b. Economic production quantity
d. Underinvestment employment relationship

11. In finance, the _____s between two currencies specifies how much one currency is worth in terms of the other. It is the value of a foreign natione;s currency in terms of the home natione;s currency. For example an _____ of 102 Japanese yen to the United States dollar means that JPY 102 is worth the same as USD 1.

a. Interbank market
b. Exchange rate
c. ACCRA Cost of Living Index
d. ACEA agreement

12. A _____ strategy is the planned method of delivering goods or services to a target market and distributing them there. When importing or exporting services, it refers to establishing and managing contracts in a foreign country.

Many companies successfully operate in a niche market without ever expanding into new markets.

a. Deep discount broker
b. Customer centricity
c. Market entry
d. Forfaiting

13. _____ describes a set of laws relating to domestic agriculture and imports of foreign agricultural products. Governments usually implement agricultural policies with the goal of achieving a specific outcome in the domestic agricultural product markets. Outcomes can involve, for example, a guaranteed supply level, price stability, product quality, product selection, land use or employment.

a. Intercropping
b. ACCRA Cost of Living Index
c. ACEA agreement
d. Agricultural Policy

14. In neoclassical economics and microeconomics, _____ describes the perfect being a market in which there are many small firms, all producing homogeneous goods. In the short term, such markets are productively inefficient as output will not occur where mc is equal to ac, but allocatively efficient, as output under _____ will always occur where mc is equal to mr, and therefore where mc equals ar. However, in the long term, such markets are both allocatively and productively efficient.

a. Law of supply
b. Co-operative economics
c. General equilibrium
d. Perfect competition

15. In economics, the _____ of an industry is used as an indicator of the relative size of firms in relation to the industry as a whole. It is calculated as the sum of the percent market share of the top n industries. This may also assist in determining the market structure of the industry.

a. Quasi-rent
b. Pacman conjecture
c. Monopolization
d. Concentration ratio

16. In economics, a _____ is the combination of two or more firms competing in the same market with the same good or service. See Horizontal integration.

a. Market dominance
b. Federal Reserve districts
c. Horizontal merger
d. Financial system

17. In economics, market concentration is a function of the number of firms and their respective shares of the total production (alternatively, total capacity or total reserves) in a market. Alternative terms are _____ and Seller concentration.

Market concentration is related to the concept of industrial concentration, which concerns the distribution of production within an industry, as opposed to a market.

Chapter 14. Oligopoly and Strategic Behavior

a. ACCRA Cost of Living Index
b. Industry concentration
c. AD-IA Model
d. ACEA agreement

18. The phrase _____ and acquisitions refers to the aspect of corporate strategy, corporate finance and management dealing with the buying, selling and combining of different companies that can aid, finance, or help a growing company in a given industry grow rapidly without having to create another business entity.

An acquisition, also known as a takeover or a buyout, is the buying of one company (the 'target') by another. An acquisition may be friendly or hostile.

a. Political economy
b. Peace dividend
c. Differential accumulation
d. Mergers

19. A _____ is an expression that compares quantities relative to each other. The most common examples involve two quantities, but any number of quantities can be compared. _____s are represented mathematically by separating each quantity with a colon, for example the _____ 2:3, which is read as the _____ 'two to three'.

a. Y-intercept
b. 100-year flood
c. 130-30 fund
d. Ratio

20. In economics, _____ are the resources employed to produce goods and services. They facilitate production but do not become part of the product (as with raw materials) or significantly transformed by the production process (as with fuel used to power machinery.) To 19th century economists, the _____ were land (natural resources, gifts from nature), labor (the ability to work), and capital goods (human-made tools and equipment.)

a. Hicks-neutral technical change
b. Factors of production
c. Product Pipeline
d. Long-run

21. In economics, _____ is the ability of a firm to alter the market price of a good or service. A firm with _____ can raise prices without losing all customers to competitors.

When a firm has _____ it faces a downward-sloping demand curve.

a. Market power
b. Pacman conjecture
c. Revenue-cap regulation
d. Price makers

22. In microeconomics, _____ is quite simply the conversion of inputs into outputs. It is an economic process that uses resources to create a good or service that is suitable for exchange. This can include manufacturing, storing, shipping, and packaging.

a. Red Guards
b. Solved
c. MET
d. Production

23. _____ is a broad label that refers to any individuals or households that use goods and services generated within the economy. The concept of a _____ is used in different contexts, so that the usage and significance of the term may vary.

Chapter 14. Oligopoly and Strategic Behavior 103

Typically when business people and economists talk of _____s they are talking about person as _____, an aggregated commodity item with little individuality other than that expressed in the buy/not-buy decision.

a. 100-year flood
c. 130-30 fund
b. 1921 recession
d. Consumer

24. _____ is a branch of applied mathematics that is used in the social sciences (most notably economics), biology, engineering, political science, international relations, computer science, and philosophy. _____ attempts to mathematically capture behavior in strategic situations, in which an individual's success in making choices depends on the choices of others. While initially developed to analyze competitions in which one individual does better at another's expense (zero sum games), it has been expanded to treat a wide class of interactions, which are classified according to several criteria.

a. Proper equilibrium
c. Discriminatory price auction
b. Dollar auction
d. Game theory

25. A trade union or _____ is an organization of workers who have banded together to achieve common goals in key areas and working conditions. The trade union, through its leadership, bargains with the employer on behalf of union members (rank and file members) and negotiates labor contracts (Collective bargaining) with employers. This may include the negotiation of wages, work rules, complaint procedures, rules governing hiring, firing and promotion of workers, benefits, workplace safety and policies.

a. Labor union
c. Business valuation standards
b. Basis of futures
d. Demand-side technologies

26. A _____ is a group of people who share or are motivated by at least one common issue or interest, or work together on a specific project(s) to achieve a common objective. _____s are also characterised by attempts to share and exercise political and social power and to make decisions on a consensus-driven and egalitarian basis. _____s differ from cooperatives in that they are not necessarily focused upon an economic benefit or saving (but can be that as well.)

a. 100-year flood
c. 1921 recession
b. 130-30 fund
d. Collective

27. A _____ or labor union is an organization of workers who have banded together to achieve common goals in key areas and working conditions. The _____, through its leadership, bargains with the employer on behalf of union members (rank and file members) and negotiates labor contracts (Collective bargaining) with employers. This may include the negotiation of wages, work rules, complaint procedures, rules governing hiring, firing and promotion of workers, benefits, workplace safety and policies.

a. Trade union
c. Consumer goods
b. Case-Shiller Home Price Indices
d. Guaranteed investment contracts

28. The concept was first developed in game theory and consequently zero-sum situations are often called _____s though this does not imply that the concept applies only to what are commonly referred to as games.

For 2-player finite _____s, the different game theoretic Solution concepts of Nash equilibrium, minimax, and maximin all give the same solution. In the solution, players play a mixed strategy.

a. Cash or share options
b. General purpose technologies
c. Zero-sum game
d. Gordon growth model

29. The _____ consists of a number of economic theories which describe the nature of the firm, company including its existence, its behaviour, and its relationship with the market.

In simplified terms, the _____ aims to answer these questions:

1. Existence - why do firms emerge, why are not all transactions in the economy mediated over the market?
2. Boundaries - why the boundary between firms and the market is located exactly there? Which transactions are performed internally and which are negotiated on the market?
3. Organization - why are firms structured in such specific way? What is the interplay of formal and informal relationships?

Despite looking simple, these questions are not answered by the established economic theory, which usually views firms as given, and treats them as black boxes without any internal structure.

The First World War period saw a change of emphasis in economic theory away from industry-level analysis which mainly included analysing markets to analysis at the level of the firm, as it became increasingly clear that perfect competition was no longer an adequate model of how firms behaved. Economic theory till then had focussed on trying to understand markets alone and there had been little study on understanding why firms or organisations exist.

a. Khazzoom-Brookes postulate
b. Policy Ineffectiveness Proposition
c. Technology gap
d. Theory of the firm

30. _____ are the inflation-indexed bonds issued by the U.S. Treasury. The principal is adjusted to the Consumer Price Index, the commonly used measure of inflation. The coupon rate is constant, but generates a different amount of interest when multiplied by the inflation-adjusted principal, thus protecting the holder against inflation.

a. 130-30 fund
b. Treasury Inflation-Protected Securities
c. 100-year flood
d. 1921 recession

31. Economics:

- _____ ,the desire to own something and the ability to pay for it
- _____ curve,a graphic representation of a _____ schedule
- _____ deposit, the money in checking accounts
- _____ pull theory,the theory that inflation occurs when _____ for goods and services exceeds existing supplies
- _____ schedule,a table that lists the quantity of a good a person will buy it each different price
- _____ side economics,the school of economics at believes government spending and tax cuts open economy by raising _____

a. McKesson ' Robbins scandal
c. Production
b. Variability
d. Demand

32. In economics, the _____ can be defined as the graph depicting the relationship between the price of a certain commodity, and the amount of it that consumers are willing and able to purchase at that given price. It is a graphic representation of a demand schedule. The _____ for all consumers together follows from the _____ of every individual consumer: the individual demands at each price are added together.
   a. Cost curve
   b. Demand curve
   c. Wage curve
   d. Kuznets curve

33. The _____ curve theory is an economic theory regarding oligopoly and monopolistic competition. When it was created, the idea fundamentally challenged classical economic tenets such as efficient markets and rapidly-changing prices, ideas that underly basic supply and demand models. _____ was an initial attempt to explain sticky prices.
   a. Precautionary demand
   b. Kinked demand curve
   c. Marginal demand
   d. Kinked demand

34. The _____ theory is an economic theory regarding oligopoly and monopolistic competition. When it was created, the idea fundamentally challenged classical economic tenets such as efficient markets and rapidly-changing prices, ideas that underly basic supply and demand models. Kinked demand was an initial attempt to explain sticky prices.
   a. Hicksian demand function
   b. Kinked demand
   c. Precautionary demand
   d. Kinked demand curve

35. _____ in economics and business is the result of an exchange and from that trade we assign a numerical monetary value to a good, service or asset. If Alice trades Bob 4 apples for an orange, the _____ of an orange is 4 apples. Inversely, the _____ of an apple is 1/4 oranges.
   a. Price war
   b. Price book
   c. Premium pricing
   d. Price

36. In economics, _____ is how a natione;s total economy is distributed among its population. . _____ has always been a central concern of economic theory and economic policy. Classical economists such as Adam Smith, Thomas Malthus and David Ricardo were mainly concerned with factor _____, that is, the distribution of income between the main factors of production, land, labour and capital.
   a. Authorised capital
   b. Income distribution
   c. Equipment trust certificate
   d. Eco commerce

37. In economics and business, a _____ is the effect that one user of a good or service has on the value of that product to other people.

The classic example is the telephone. The more people own telephones, the more valuable the telephone is to each owner.

   a. Penn effect
   b. Pigou effect
   c. Cluster effect
   d. Network effect

Chapter 14. Oligopoly and Strategic Behavior

38. A _____ refers to any type debt instrument, such as a loan, bond, mortgage that does not have a fixed rate of interest over the life of the instrument. Such debt typically uses an index or other base rate for establishing the interest rate for each relevant period. One of the most common rates to use as the basis for applying interest rates is the London Inter-bank Offered Rate, or LIBOR

   a. Money market
   b. Floating interest rate
   c. Moneylender
   d. Disposal tax effect

39. The United States federal _____ is a refundable tax credit. For tax year 2008, a claimant with one qualifying child can receive a maximum credit of $2,917. For two or more qualifying children, the maximum credit is $4,824.

   a. ACCRA Cost of Living Index
   b. ACEA agreement
   c. Earned Income Tax Credit
   d. AD-IA Model

40. An _____ is a tax levied on the financial income of people, corporations, or other legal entities. Various _____ systems exist, with varying degrees of tax incidence. Income taxation can be progressive, proportional, or regressive.

   a. Income Tax
   b. ACEA agreement
   c. AD-IA Model
   d. ACCRA Cost of Living Index

41. To _____ is to impose a financial charge or other levy upon a taxpayer by a state or the functional equivalent of a state.

   _____es are also imposed by many subnational entities. _____es consist of direct _____ or indirect _____, and may be paid in money or as its labour equivalent (often but not always unpaid.)

   a. Tax
   b. 130-30 fund
   c. 1921 recession
   d. 100-year flood

42. The term _____ describes two different concepts:

   - The first is a recognition of partial payment already made towards taxes due.
   - The second is a state benefit paid to workers through the tax system, which has the effect of increasing (rather than reducing) net income.

Within the Australian, Canadian, United Kingdom, and United States tax systems, a _____ is a recognition of partial payment already made towards taxes due. A similar concept exists (fr:Avoir fiscal) in the French tax system. This situation arises, for example, when standard rate tax has been deducted at source , but the tax-payer is subject to further taxation at a higher rate. It also applies in dividend imputation systems.

   a. 1921 recession
   b. 100-year flood
   c. Tax Credit
   d. 130-30 fund

43. To tax is to impose a financial charge or other levy upon a taxpayer by a state or the functional equivalent of a state.

   _____ are also imposed by many subnational entities. _____ consist of direct tax or indirect tax, and may be paid in money or as its labour equivalent (often but not always unpaid.)

a. 1921 recession
b. 130-30 fund
c. 100-year flood
d. Taxes

44. Competition law, known in the United States as _____ law, has three main elements:

- prohibiting agreements or practices that restrict free trading and competition between business entities. This includes in particular the repression of cartels.
- banning abusive behaviour by a firm dominating a market, or anti-competitive practices that tend to lead to such a dominant position. Practices controlled in this way may include predatory pricing, tying, price gouging, refusal to deal, and many others.
- supervising the mergers and acquisitions of large corporations, including some joint ventures. Transactions that are considered to threaten the competitive process can be prohibited altogether, or approved subject to 'remedies' such as an obligation to divest part of the merged business or to offer licences or access to facilities to enable other businesses to continue competing.

The substance and practice of competition law varies from jurisdiction to jurisdiction. Protecting the interests of consumers (consumer welfare) and ensuring that entrepreneurs have an opportunity to compete in the market economy are often treated as important objectives. Competition law is closely connected with law on deregulation of access to markets, state aids and subsidies, the privatisation of state owned assets and the establishment of independent sector regulators. In recent decades, competition law has been viewed as a way to provide better public services.

a. Anti-Inflation Act
b. Intellectual property law
c. United Kingdom competition law
d. Antitrust

45.

The _____ was the first United States Federal statute to limit cartels and monopolies. It falls under antitrust law.

The Act provides: 'Every contract, combination in the form of trust or otherwise, or conspiracy, in restraint of trade or commerce among the several States, or with foreign nations, is declared to be illegal'. The Act also provides: 'Every person who shall monopolize, or attempt to monopolize, or combine or conspire with any other person or persons, to monopolize any part of the trade or commerce among the several States, or with foreign nations, shall be deemed guilty of a felony [. . .]' The Act put responsibility upon government attorneys and district courts to pursue and investigate trusts, companies and organizations suspected of violating the Act. The Clayton Act extended the right to sue under the antitrust laws to 'any person who shall be injured in his business or property by reason of anything forbidden in the antitrust laws.' Under the Clayton Act, private parties may sue in U.S. district court and should they prevail, they may be awarded treble damages and the cost of suit, including reasonable attorney's fees.

a. 130-30 fund
b. 1921 recession
c. 100-year flood
d. Sherman Antitrust Act

Chapter 15. Regulation and Antitrust Policy in a Globalized Economy

1. To _____ is to impose a financial charge or other levy upon a taxpayer by a state or the functional equivalent of a state.

    _____es are also imposed by many subnational entities. _____es consist of direct _____ or indirect _____, and may be paid in money or as its labour equivalent (often but not always unpaid.)

    a. 100-year flood
    b. 1921 recession
    c. Tax
    d. 130-30 fund

2. To tax is to impose a financial charge or other levy upon a taxpayer by a state or the functional equivalent of a state.

    _____ are also imposed by many subnational entities. _____ consist of direct tax or indirect tax, and may be paid in money or as its labour equivalent (often but not always unpaid.)

    a. 1921 recession
    b. Taxes
    c. 100-year flood
    d. 130-30 fund

3. In economics and especially in the theory of competition, _____ are obstacles in the path of a firm that make it difficult to enter a given market.

    _____ are the source of a firm's pricing power - the ability of a firm to raise prices without losing all its customers.

    The term refers to hindrances that an individual may face while trying to gain entrance into a profession or trade.

    a. Social dumping
    b. Group boycott
    c. Limit price
    d. Barriers to entry

4. In economics, _____ is how a natione;s total economy is distributed among its population. ._____ has always been a central concern of economic theory and economic policy. Classical economists such as Adam Smith, Thomas Malthus and David Ricardo were mainly concerned with factor _____, that is, the distribution of income between the main factors of production, land, labour and capital.

    a. Authorised capital
    b. Equipment trust certificate
    c. Income distribution
    d. Eco commerce

5. The term '_____' refers to the concept of collecting information and attempting to spot a pattern in the information. In some fields of study, the term '_____' has more formally-defined meanings.

    In project management _____ is a mathematical technique that uses historical results to predict future outcome.

    a. Quantile regression
    b. Probit model
    c. Coefficient of determination
    d. Trend analysis

6. _____ was a survey conducted by the U.S. Department of Justice to gauge the prevalence of alcohol and illegal drug use among prior arrestees. It was a reformulation of the prior Drug Use Forecasting (DUF) program, focused on five drugs in particular: cocaine, marijuana, methamphetamine, opiates, and PCP.

Participants were randomly selected from arrest records in major metropolitan areas; because no personally identifying information is taken from each record chosen, the resulting data can be correlated to arrest rates, but not to the total population of persons charged.

a. ACEA agreement
b. Arrestee Drug Abuse Monitoring
c. ACCRA Cost of Living Index
d. AD-IA Model

7. In finance, a _____ is a debt security, in which the authorized issuer owes the holders a debt and, depending on the terms of the _____, is obliged to pay interest (the coupon) and/or to repay the principal at a later date, termed maturity. A _____ is a formal contract to repay borrowed money with interest at fixed intervals.

Thus a _____ is like a loan: the issuer is the borrower (debtor), the holder is the lender (creditor), and the coupon is the interest.

a. Prize Bond
b. Callable
c. Zero-coupon
d. Bond

8. The _____ consists of a number of economic theories which describe the nature of the firm, company including its existence, its behaviour, and its relationship with the market.

In simplified terms, the _____ aims to answer these questions:

1. Existence - why do firms emerge, why are not all transactions in the economy mediated over the market?
2. Boundaries - why the boundary between firms and the market is located exactly there? Which transactions are performed internally and which are negotiated on the market?
3. Organization - why are firms structured in such specific way? What is the interplay of formal and informal relationships?

Despite looking simple, these questions are not answered by the established economic theory, which usually views firms as given, and treats them as black boxes without any internal structure.

The First World War period saw a change of emphasis in economic theory away from industry-level analysis which mainly included analysing markets to analysis at the level of the firm, as it became increasingly clear that perfect competition was no longer an adequate model of how firms behaved. Economic theory till then had focussed on trying to understand markets alone and there had been little study on understanding why firms or organisations exist.

a. Technology gap
b. Khazzoom-Brookes postulate
c. Policy Ineffectiveness Proposition
d. Theory of the firm

9. A _____ refers to any type debt instrument, such as a loan, bond, mortgage that does not have a fixed rate of interest over the life of the instrument. Such debt typically uses an index or other base rate for establishing the interest rate for each relevant period. One of the most common rates to use as the basis for applying interest rates is the London Inter-bank Offered Rate, or LIBOR

a. Money market
b. Moneylender
c. Floating interest rate
d. Disposal tax effect

10. The United States federal _____ is a refundable tax credit. For tax year 2008, a claimant with one qualifying child can receive a maximum credit of $2,917. For two or more qualifying children, the maximum credit is $4,824.
  a. ACEA agreement
  b. ACCRA Cost of Living Index
  c. Earned Income Tax Credit
  d. AD-IA Model

11. The _____ is a United States government corporation created by the Glass-Steagall Act of 1933. It provides deposit insurance, which guarantees the safety of deposits in member banks, currently up to $250,000 per depositor per bank. Funds in non-interest bearing transaction accounts are fully insured, with no limit, under the temporary Transaction Account Guarantee Program.
  a. Great Leap Forward
  b. Federal Deposit Insurance Corporation
  c. Foreign direct investment
  d. Luxembourg Income Study

12.

The _____ is an independent agency of the United States government, created, directed, and empowered by Congressional statute , and with the majority of its commissioners appointed by the current President. The _____ works towards six strategic goals in the areas of broadband, competition, the spectrum, the media, public safety and homeland security, and modernizing the _____.

  a. 130-30 fund
  b. 1921 recession
  c. 100-year flood
  d. Federal Communications Commission

13. An _____ is a tax levied on the financial income of people, corporations, or other legal entities. Various _____ systems exist, with varying degrees of tax incidence. Income taxation can be progressive, proportional, or regressive.
  a. ACEA agreement
  b. AD-IA Model
  c. ACCRA Cost of Living Index
  d. Income Tax

14. _____, in law and economics, is a form of risk management primarily used to hedge against the risk of a contingent loss. _____ is defined as the equitable transfer of the risk of a loss, from one entity to another, in exchange for a premium, and can be thought of as a guaranteed small loss to prevent a large, possibly devastating loss. An insurer is a company selling the _____; an insured or policyholder is the person or entity buying the _____.
  a. ACCRA Cost of Living Index
  b. Insurance
  c. AD-IA Model
  d. ACEA agreement

15. The U.S. _____ is an independent agency of the United States government which holds primary responsibility for enforcing the federal securities laws and regulating the securities industry, the nation's stock and options exchanges, and other electronic securities markets. The SEC was created by section 4 of the Securities Exchange Act of 1934 (now codified as 15 U.S.C. § 78d and commonly referred to as the 1934 Act.)
  a. 130-30 fund
  b. Securities and Exchange Commission
  c. 100-year flood
  d. 1921 recession

Chapter 15. Regulation and Antitrust Policy in a Globalized Economy

16. A security is a fungible, negotiable instrument representing financial value. _____ are broadly categorized into debt _____; equity _____, e.g., common stocks; and derivative (finance) contracts such as forwards, futures, options and swaps. The company or other entity issuing the security is called the issuer.
    a. Securities
    b. Pass-Through Certificates
    c. Red herring prospectus
    d. Settlement risk

17. _____ was a Scottish moral philosopher and a pioneer of political economy. One of the key figures of the Scottish Enlightenment, Smith is the author of The Theory of Moral Sentiments and An Inquiry into the Nature and Causes of the Wealth of Nations. The latter, usually abbreviated as The Wealth of Nations, is considered his magnum opus and the first modern work of economics.
    a. Adolf Hitler
    b. Adolph Fischer
    c. Alan Greenspan
    d. Adam Smith

18. The term _____ describes two different concepts:

    - The first is a recognition of partial payment already made towards taxes due.
    - The second is a state benefit paid to workers through the tax system, which has the effect of increasing (rather than reducing) net income.

    Within the Australian, Canadian, United Kingdom, and United States tax systems, a _____ is a recognition of partial payment already made towards taxes due. A similar concept exists (fr:Avoir fiscal) in the French tax system. This situation arises, for example, when standard rate tax has been deducted at source, but the tax-payer is subject to further taxation at a higher rate. It also applies in dividend imputation systems.

    a. 100-year flood
    b. 1921 recession
    c. Tax Credit
    d. 130-30 fund

19. _____s is the social science that studies the production, distribution, and consumption of goods and services. The term _____s comes from the Ancient Greek οἰκονομία from οἶκος (oikos, 'house') + νόμος (nomos, 'custom' or 'law'), hence 'rules of the house(hold)'. Current _____ models developed out of the broader field of political economy in the late 19th century, owing to a desire to use an empirical approach more akin to the physical sciences.
    a. Energy economics
    b. Opportunity cost
    c. Inflation
    d. Economic

20. A _____ association is a financial institution that specializes in accepting savings deposits and making mortgage and other loans. The S'L or thrift term is mainly used in the United States; similar institutions in the United Kingdom, Ireland and some Commonwealth countries include building societies and trustee savings banks.

    They are often mutually held, meaning that the depositors and borrowers are members with voting rights, and have the ability to direct the financial and managerial goals of the organization, similar to the policyholders of a mutual insurance company.

    a. Collective investment scheme
    b. Participating policy
    c. Fonds commun de placement
    d. Savings and loan

21. A _____ or labor union is an organization of workers who have banded together to achieve common goals in key areas and working conditions. The _____, through its leadership, bargains with the employer on behalf of union members (rank and file members) and negotiates labor contracts (Collective bargaining) with employers. This may include the negotiation of wages, work rules, complaint procedures, rules governing hiring, firing and promotion of workers, benefits, workplace safety and policies.

    a. Trade union
    b. Consumer goods
    c. Guaranteed investment contracts
    d. Case-Shiller Home Price Indices

22. _____ is a broad label that refers to any individuals or households that use goods and services generated within the economy. The concept of a _____ is used in different contexts, so that the usage and significance of the term may vary.

Typically when business people and economists talk of _____s they are talking about person as _____, an aggregated commodity item with little individuality other than that expressed in the buy/not-buy decision.

    a. 1921 recession
    b. Consumer
    c. 100-year flood
    d. 130-30 fund

23. The U.S. _____ (EEOC) is a federal agency whose goal is ending employment discrimination. The _____ investigates discrimination complaints based on an individual's race, color, national origin, religion, sex, age, disability and retaliation for reporting and/or opposing a discriminatory practice. The Commission is also tasked with filing suits on behalf of alleged victim(s) of discrimination against employers and as an adjudicatory for claims of discrimination brought against federal agencies.

    a. ACCRA Cost of Living Index
    b. ACEA agreement
    c. AD-IA Model
    d. EEOC

24. _____ is a practice of protecting the environment, on individual, organisational or governmental level, for the benefit of the natural environment and (or) humans.

Due to the pressures of population and technology the biophysical environment is being degraded, sometimes permanently. This has been recognised and governments began placing restraints on activities that caused environmental degradation.

    a. ACEA agreement
    b. ACCRA Cost of Living Index
    c. AD-IA Model
    d. Environmental Protection

25. The U.S. _____ is a federal agency whose goal is ending employment discrimination. The _____ investigates discrimination complaints based on an individual's race, color, national origin, religion, sex, age, disability and retaliation for reporting and/or opposing a discriminatory practice. The Commission is also tasked with filing suits on behalf of alleged victim(s) of discrimination against employers and as an adjudicatory for claims of discrimination brought against federal agencies.

    a. ACCRA Cost of Living Index
    b. ACEA agreement
    c. AD-IA Model
    d. Equal Employment Opportunity Commission

Chapter 15. Regulation and Antitrust Policy in a Globalized Economy

26. The _____ is an independent agency of the United States government, established in 1914 by the _____ Act. Its principal mission is the promotion of 'consumer protection' and the elimination and prevention of what regulators perceive to be harmfully 'anti-competitive' business practices, such as coercive monopoly.

The _____ Act was one of President Wilson's major acts against trusts.

  a. 130-30 fund
  c. 1921 recession
  b. 100-year flood
  d. Federal Trade Commission

27. In finance, the _____s between two currencies specifies how much one currency is worth in terms of the other. It is the value of a foreign natione;s currency in terms of the home natione;s currency. For example an _____ of 102 Japanese yen to the United States dollar means that JPY 102 is worth the same as USD 1.
  a. ACEA agreement
  c. Exchange rate
  b. ACCRA Cost of Living Index
  d. Interbank market

28. _____ laws are designed to ensure fair competition and the free flow of truthful information in the marketplace. The laws are designed to prevent businesses that engage in fraud or specified unfair practices from gaining an advantage over competitors and may provide additional protection for the weak and unable to take care of themselves. _____ laws are a form of government regulation which protects the interests of consumers.
  a. Dow Jones Industrial Average
  c. Global warming
  b. History of minimum wage
  d. Consumer protection

29. _____ are the inflation-indexed bonds issued by the U.S. Treasury. The principal is adjusted to the Consumer Price Index, the commonly used measure of inflation. The coupon rate is constant, but generates a different amount of interest when multiplied by the inflation-adjusted principal, thus protecting the holder against inflation.
  a. 1921 recession
  c. 100-year flood
  b. 130-30 fund
  d. Treasury Inflation-Protected Securities

30. A _____ is a term used in economics for a good whose utility impact is difficult or impossible for the consumer to ascertain. In contrast to experience goods, the utility gain or loss of _____s is difficult to measure after consumption as well. The seller of the good knows the utility impact of the good, creating a situation of asymmetric information.
  a. Pie method
  c. Composite good
  b. Search good
  d. Credence good

31. A _____ is an object whose consumption increases the utility of the consumer, for which the quantity demanded exceeds the quantity supplied at zero price. _____s are usually modeled as having diminishing marginal utility. The first individual purchase has high utility; the second has less.
  a. Merit good
  c. Composite good
  b. Pie method
  d. Good

32. In economics, a _____ exists when the production or use of goods and services by the market is not efficient. That is, there exists another outcome where all involved can be made better off. _____s can be viewed as scenarios where individuals' pursuit of pure self-interest leads to results that are not efficient - that can be improved upon from the societal point-of-view.

a. Financial economics
b. Fixed exchange rate
c. General equilibrium
d. Market failure

33. The _____ of 1914 (15 U.S.C §§ 41-58, as amended) established the Federal Trade Commission (FTC), a bipartisan body of five members appointed by the President of the United States for seven year terms. This Commission was authorized to issue Cease and Desist orders to large corporations to curb unfair trade practices. This Act also gave more flexibility to the US congress for judicial matters.

   a. Competition law theory
   b. Federal Trade Commission Act
   c. Buydown
   d. Minimum wage law

34. A mutual _____ or stockholder is an individual or company (including a corporation) that legally owns one or more shares of stock in a joint stock company. A company's _____s collectively own that company. Thus, the typical goal of such companies is to enhance _____ value.

   a. Profit warning
   b. Relative valuation
   c. Prime Standard
   d. Shareholder

35. _____ is a common concept in economics, and gives rise to derived concepts such as consumer debt. Generally _____ is defined by opposition to production. But the precise definition can vary because different schools of economists define production quite differently.

   a. Consumption
   b. Foreclosure data providers
   c. Federal Reserve Bank Notes
   d. Cash or share options

36. Competition law, known in the United States as _____ law, has three main elements:

   - prohibiting agreements or practices that restrict free trading and competition between business entities. This includes in particular the repression of cartels.
   - banning abusive behaviour by a firm dominating a market, or anti-competitive practices that tend to lead to such a dominant position. Practices controlled in this way may include predatory pricing, tying, price gouging, refusal to deal, and many others.
   - supervising the mergers and acquisitions of large corporations, including some joint ventures. Transactions that are considered to threaten the competitive process can be prohibited altogether, or approved subject to 'remedies' such as an obligation to divest part of the merged business or to offer licences or access to facilities to enable other businesses to continue competing.

The substance and practice of competition law varies from jurisdiction to jurisdiction. Protecting the interests of consumers (consumer welfare) and ensuring that entrepreneurs have an opportunity to compete in the market economy are often treated as important objectives. Competition law is closely connected with law on deregulation of access to markets, state aids and subsidies, the privatisation of state owned assets and the establishment of independent sector regulators. In recent decades, competition law has been viewed as a way to provide better public services.

   a. United Kingdom competition law
   b. Anti-Inflation Act
   c. Antitrust
   d. Intellectual property law

Chapter 15. Regulation and Antitrust Policy in a Globalized Economy

37. The _____ of 1936 (or Anti-Price Discrimination Act, 15 U.S.C. § 13) is a United States federal law that prohibits what were considered, at the time of passage, to be anticompetitive practices by producers, specifically price discrimination. It grew out of practices in which chain stores were allowed to purchase goods at lower prices than other retailers.
   a. Feoffee
   b. Flextime
   c. Contract theory
   d. Robinson-Patman Act

38.

The _____ was the first United States Federal statute to limit cartels and monopolies. It falls under antitrust law.

The Act provides: 'Every contract, combination in the form of trust or otherwise, or conspiracy, in restraint of trade or commerce among the several States, or with foreign nations, is declared to be illegal'. The Act also provides: 'Every person who shall monopolize, or attempt to monopolize, or combine or conspire with any other person or persons, to monopolize any part of the trade or commerce among the several States, or with foreign nations, shall be deemed guilty of a felony [. . .]' The Act put responsibility upon government attorneys and district courts to pursue and investigate trusts, companies and organizations suspected of violating the Act. The Clayton Act extended the right to sue under the antitrust laws to 'any person who shall be injured in his business or property by reason of anything forbidden in the antitrust laws.' Under the Clayton Act, private parties may sue in U.S. district court and should they prevail, they may be awarded treble damages and the cost of suit, including reasonable attorney's fees.

   a. Sherman Antitrust Act
   b. 1921 recession
   c. 100-year flood
   d. 130-30 fund

39. _____, known in the United States as antitrust law, has three main elements:

   - prohibiting agreements or practices that restrict free trading and competition between business entities. This includes in particular the repression of cartels.
   - banning abusive behaviour by a firm dominating a market, or anti-competitive practices that tend to lead to such a dominant position. Practices controlled in this way may include predatory pricing, tying, price gouging, refusal to deal, and many others.
   - supervising the mergers and acquisitions of large corporations, including some joint ventures. Transactions that are considered to threaten the competitive process can be prohibited altogether, or approved subject to 'remedies' such as an obligation to divest part of the merged business or to offer licences or access to facilities to enable other businesses to continue competing.

The substance and practice of _____ varies from jurisdiction to jurisdiction. Protecting the interests of consumers (consumer welfare) and ensuring that entrepreneurs have an opportunity to compete in the market economy are often treated as important objectives. _____ is closely connected with law on deregulation of access to markets, state aids and subsidies, the privatisation of state owned assets and the establishment of independent sector regulators. In recent decades, _____ has been viewed as a way to provide better public services.

a. Competition law
b. Fee simple
c. Due diligence
d. Hostile work environment

40. _____ was a predominant American integrated oil producing, transporting, refining, and marketing company. Established in 1870 as an Ohio Corporation, it was the largest oil refiner in the world and operated as a major company trust and was one of the world's first and largest multinational corporations until it was broken up by the United States Supreme Court in 1911. John D. Rockefeller was a founder, chairman and major shareholder, and the company made him a billionaire and eventually the richest man in history.

a. 1921 recession
b. 100-year flood
c. 130-30 fund
d. Standard Oil

41. A trade union or _____ is an organization of workers who have banded together to achieve common goals in key areas and working conditions. The trade union, through its leadership, bargains with the employer on behalf of union members (rank and file members) and negotiates labor contracts (Collective bargaining) with employers. This may include the negotiation of wages, work rules, complaint procedures, rules governing hiring, firing and promotion of workers, benefits, workplace safety and policies.

a. Basis of futures
b. Labor union
c. Business valuation standards
d. Demand-side technologies

42. The _____ is an economic and political union of 27 member states, located primarily in Europe. It was established by the Treaty of Maastricht on 1 November 1993, upon the foundations of the pre-existing European Economic Community. With a population of almost 500 million, the _____ generates an estimated 30% share (US$18.4 trillion in 2008) of the nominal gross world product.

a. European Union
b. European Court of Justice
c. ACEA agreement
d. ACCRA Cost of Living Index

43. The term _____ refers to an offense under Section 2 of the American Sherman Antitrust Act, passed in 1890. Section 2 states that any person 'who shall monopolize .

a. Bilateral monopoly
b. Complementary monopoly
c. Quasi-rent
d. Monopolization

44. _____ in economics and business is the result of an exchange and from that trade we assign a numerical monetary value to a good, service or asset. If Alice trades Bob 4 apples for an orange, the _____ of an orange is 4 apples. Inversely, the _____ of an apple is 1/4 oranges.

a. Price war
b. Price book
c. Premium pricing
d. Price

45. In economics, a _____ may be either a subsidy or a price control, both with the intended effect of keeping the market price of a good higher than the competitive equilibrium level.

In the case of a price control, a _____ is the minimum legal price a seller may charge, typically placed above equilibrium. It is the support of certain price levels at or above market values by the government.

a. Labor intensity
b. Marginal profit
c. Payment schedule
d. Price support

Chapter 15. Regulation and Antitrust Policy in a Globalized Economy

46. _____, in strategic management and marketing is, according to Carlton O'Neal, the percentage or proportion of the total available market or market segment that is being serviced by a company. It can be expressed as a company's sales revenue (from that market) divided by the total sales revenue available in that market. It can also be expressed as a company's unit sales volume (in a market) divided by the total volume of units sold in that market.
   a. Product differentiation
   b. Pricing science
   c. Market share
   d. Customer to customer

47. In competition law the _____ defines the market in which one or more goods compete. Therefore, the _____ defines whether two or more products can be considered substitute goods and whether they constitute a particular and separate market for competition analysis.

The _____ combines the product market and the geographic market, defined as follows:

1. A relevant product market comprises all those products and/or services which are regarded as interchangeable or substitutable by the consumer by reason of the products' characteristics, their prices and their intended use;
2. A relevant geographic market comprises the area in which the firms concerned are involved in the supply of products or services and in which the conditions of competition are sufficiently homogeneous.

The notion of _____ is used in order to identify the products and undertakings which are directly competing in a business. Therefore, the _____ is the market where the competition takes place.

   a. Relevant market
   b. Competition law
   c. Community property
   d. Greenfield agreement

48. A _____ is a group of people who share or are motivated by at least one common issue or interest, or work together on a specific project(s) to achieve a common objective. _____s are also characterised by attempts to share and exercise political and social power and to make decisions on a consensus-driven and egalitarian basis. _____s differ from cooperatives in that they are not necessarily focused upon an economic benefit or saving (but can be that as well.)
   a. 1921 recession
   b. 130-30 fund
   c. Collective
   d. 100-year flood

118 *Chapter 16. The Labor Market: Demand, Supply, and Outsourcing*

1. Economics:

    - _____, the desire to own something and the ability to pay for it
    - _____ curve, a graphic representation of a _____ schedule
    - _____ deposit, the money in checking accounts
    - _____ pull theory, the theory that inflation occurs when _____ for goods and services exceeds existing supplies
    - _____ schedule, a table that lists the quantity of a good a person will buy it each different price
    - _____ side economics, the school of economics at believes government spending and tax cuts open economy by raising _____

    a. Production
    c. McKesson ' Robbins scandal
    b. Variability
    d. Demand

2. In finance, the _____s between two currencies specifies how much one currency is worth in terms of the other. It is the value of a foreign natione;s currency in terms of the home natione;s currency. For example an _____ of 102 Japanese yen to the United States dollar means that JPY 102 is worth the same as USD 1.
    a. Exchange rate
    c. ACEA agreement
    b. Interbank market
    d. ACCRA Cost of Living Index

3. In economics, the _____ of a good or of a service is the utility of the specific use to which an agent would put a given increase in that good or service, or of the specific use that would be abandoned in response to a given decrease. In other words, _____ is the utility of the marginal use -- which, on the assumption of economic rationality, would be the least urgent use of the good or service, from the best feasible combination of actions in which its use is included. Under the mainstream assumptions, the _____ of a good or service is the posited quantified change in utility obtained by increasing or by decreasing use of that good or service.
    a. 100-year flood
    c. 1921 recession
    b. 130-30 fund
    d. Marginal utility

4. _____ or national income by type of income is a measure of national income or output based on the cost of factors of production, instead of market prices. This allows the effect of any subsidy or indirect tax to be removed from the final measure.
    a. Lehman scale
    c. Corporate synergy
    b. Gross regional domestic product
    d. Factor cost

5. In economics, the _____ or marginal physical product is the extra output produced by one more unit of an input (for instance, the difference in output when a firm's labour is increased from five to six units.) Assuming that no other inputs to production change, the _____ of a given input (X) can be expressed as:

    _____ = $\Delta Y / \Delta X$ = (the change of Y)/(the change of X.)

    -
        o
            ■ Pending approval by Thomas Sowell***

Chapter 16. The Labor Market: Demand, Supply, and Outsourcing

In neoclassical economics, this is the mathematical derivative of the production function.... Note that the 'product' (Y) is typically defined ignoring external costs and benefits.

a. Labor problem
c. Factor prices
b. Marginal product
d. Productive capacity

6. In microeconomics, _____ is the extra revenue that an additional unit of product will bring. It is the additional income from selling one more unit of a good; sometimes equal to price. It can also be described as the change in total revenue/change in number of units sold.

a. Reservation price
c. Long term
b. Market demand schedule
d. Marginal revenue

7. The marginal revenue productivity theory of wages, also referred to as the _____ of labor, is the change in total revenue earned by a firm that results from employing one more unit of labor. It is a neoclassical model that determines, under some conditions, the optimal number of workers to employ at an exogenously determined market wage rate.

The _____ of a worker is equal to the product of the marginal product of labor (MP) and the marginal revenue (MR), given by MR×MP = _____.

a. Marginal revenue product
c. Marginal revenue productivity theory of wages
b. Coal depletion
d. Real prices and ideal prices

120   *Chapter 16. The Labor Market: Demand, Supply, and Outsourcing*

8. A _____ is:

- Rewrite _____, in generative grammar and computer science
- Standardization, a formal and widely-accepted statement, fact, definition, or qualification
- Operation, a determinate _____ for performing a mathematical operation and obtaining a certain result (Mathematics, Logic)
    - Unary operation
    - Binary operation
- _____ of inference, a function from sets of formulae to formulae (Mathematics, Logic)
- _____ of thumb, principle with broad application that is not intended to be strictly accurate or reliable for every situation. Also often simply referred to as a _____
- Moral, an atomic element of a moral code for guiding choices in human behavior
- Heuristic, a quantized '_____' which shows a tendency or probability for successful function
- A regulation, as in sports
- A Production _____, as in computer science
- Procedural law, a _____ set governing the application of laws to cases
    - A law, which may informally be called a '_____'
    - A court ruling, a decision by a court
- In the U.S. Government, a regulation mandated by Congress, but written or expanded upon by the Executive Branch.
- Norm (sociology), an informal but widely accepted _____, concept, truth, definition, or qualification (social norms, legal norms, coding norms)
- Norm (philosophy), a kind of sentence or a reason to act, feel or believe
- 'Rulership' is the concept of governance by a government:
    - Military _____, governance by a military body
    - Monastic _____, a collection of precepts that guides the life of monks or nuns in a religious order where the superior holds the place of Christ
- Slide _____

- '_____,' a song by Ayumi Hamasaki
- '_____,' a song by rapper Nas
- '_____s,' an album by the band The Whitest Boy Alive
- _____s: Pyaar Ka Superhit Formula, a 2003 Bollywood film
- ruler, an instrument for measuring lengths
- _____, a component of an astrolabe, circumferator or similar instrument
- The _____s, a bestselling self-help book
- _____ Project (Run Up-to-date Linux Everywhere), a project that aims to use up-to-date Linux software on old PCs
- _____ engine, a software system that helps managing business _____s
- Ja _____, a hip hop artist
    - R.U.L.E., a 2005 greatest hits album by rapper Ja _____
- '_____s,' a KMFDM song

a. Demand
b. Procter ' Gamble
c. Technocracy
d. Rule

Chapter 16. The Labor Market: Demand, Supply, and Outsourcing

9. In economics, _____ is a measure of the relative satisfaction from consumption of various goods and services. Given this measure, one may speak meaningfully of increasing or decreasing _____, and thereby explain economic behavior in terms of attempts to increase one's _____. For illustrative purposes, changes in _____ are sometimes expressed in units called utils.
   a. Ordinal utility
   b. Expected utility hypothesis
   c. Utility function
   d. Utility

10. _____ is the a method of technical and economic research of the systems for purpose to optimize a parity between system's consumer functions or properties and expenses to achieve those functions or properties.

This methodology for continuous perfection of production, industrial technologies, organizational structures was developed by Juryj Sobolev in 1948 at the 'Perm telephone factory'

- 1948 Juryj Sobolev - the first success in application of a method analysis at the 'Perm telephone factory' .
- 1949 - the first application for the invention as result of use of the new method.

Today in economically developed countries practically each enterprise or the company use methodology of the kind of functional-cost analysis as a practice of the quality management, most full satisfying to principles of standards of series ISO 9000.

- Interest of consumer not in products itself, but the advantage which it will receive from its usage.
- The consumer aspires to reduce his expenses
- Functions needed by consumer can be executed in the various ways, and, hence, with various efficiency and expenses. Among possible alternatives of realization of functions exist such in which the parity of quality and the price is the optimal for the consumer.

The goal of _____ is achievement of the highest consumer satisfaction of production at simultaneous decrease in all kinds of industrial expenses Classical _____ has three English synonyms - Value Engineering, Value Management, Value Analysis.

   a. Staple financing
   b. Willingness to pay
   c. Monopoly wage
   d. Function cost analysis

11. _____ is a term in economics, where demand for one good or service occurs as a result of demand for another. This may occur as the former is a part of production of the second. For example, demand for coal leads to _____ for mining, as coal must be mined for coal to be consumed.
   a. Rate risk
   b. Leontief production function
   c. Days Sales Outstanding
   d. Derived demand

12. The U.S. _____ is a federal agency whose goal is ending employment discrimination. The _____ investigates discrimination complaints based on an individual's race, color, national origin, religion, sex, age, disability and retaliation for reporting and/or opposing a discriminatory practice. The Commission is also tasked with filing suits on behalf of alleged victim(s) of discrimination against employers and as an adjudicatory for claims of discrimination brought against federal agencies.

Chapter 16. The Labor Market: Demand, Supply, and Outsourcing

   a. AD-IA Model
   b. ACCRA Cost of Living Index
   c. ACEA agreement
   d. Equal Employment Opportunity Commission

13. In economics, _____ is the ratio of the percent change in one variable to the percent change in another variable. It is a tool for measuring the responsiveness of a function to changes in parameters in a relative way. Commonly analyzed are _____ of substitution, price and wealth.
   a. ACCRA Cost of Living Index
   b. Elasticity of demand
   c. Elasticity
   d. ACEA agreement

14. In economics, the _____ is defined as a numerical measure of the responsiveness of the quantity supplied of product (A) to a change in price of product (A) alone. It is the measure of the way quantity supplied reacts to a change in price.

For example, if, in response to a 10% rise in the price of a good, the quantity supplied increases by 20%, the _____ would be 20%/10% = 2.

   a. Price elasticity of supply
   b. Passive income
   c. Demand shaping
   d. Hedonimetry

15. _____ in economics and business is the result of an exchange and from that trade we assign a numerical monetary value to a good, service or asset. If Alice trades Bob 4 apples for an orange, the _____ of an orange is 4 apples. Inversely, the _____ of an apple is 1/4 oranges.
   a. Price book
   b. Price
   c. Premium pricing
   d. Price war

16. _____ refers to a business or organization attempting to acquire goods or services to accomplish the goals of the enterprise. Though there are several organizations that attempt to set standards in the _____ process, processes can vary greatly between organizations. Typically the word '_____' is not used interchangeably with the word 'procurement', since procurement typically includes Expediting, Supplier Quality, and Traffic and Logistics (T'L) in addition to _____.
   a. Free port
   b. 130-30 fund
   c. Purchasing
   d. 100-year flood

17. _____ is the number of goods/services that can be purchased with a unit of currency. For example, if you had taken one dollar to a store in the 1950s, you would have been able to buy a greater number of items than you would today, indicating that you would have had a greater _____ in the 1950s. Currency can be either a commodity money, like gold or silver, or fiat currency like US dollars.
   a. Purchasing power
   b. Genuine progress indicator
   c. Compliance cost
   d. Human Poverty Index

18. _____ is an equity (stock) exchange located at 11 Wall Street in lower Manhattan, New York, USA. It is the largest stock exchange in the world by dollar value of its listed companies' securities. As of October 2008, the combined capitalization of all domestic _____ listed companies was US$10.1 trillion.

Chapter 16. The Labor Market: Demand, Supply, and Outsourcing

a. 100-year flood
b. 130-30 fund
c. New York Stock Exchange
d. 1921 recession

19. In economics, _____ refers to the ability of a person or a country to produce a particular good at a lower marginal cost and opportunity cost than another person or country. It is the ability to produce a product most efficiently given all the other products that could be produced. It can be contrasted with absolute advantage which refers to the ability of a person or a country to produce a particular good at a lower absolute cost than another.
   a. Hot money
   b. Gravity model of trade
   c. Triffin dilemma
   d. Comparative advantage

20. In economics, the _____ can be defined as the graph depicting the relationship between the price of a certain commodity, and the amount of it that consumers are willing and able to purchase at that given price. It is a graphic representation of a demand schedule. The _____ for all consumers together follows from the _____ of every individual consumer: the individual demands at each price are added together.
   a. Kuznets curve
   b. Cost curve
   c. Wage curve
   d. Demand curve

21. In economics, an _____ is any good or commodity, transported from one country to another country in a legitimate fashion, typically for use in trade. _____ goods or services are provided to foreign consumers by domestic producers. _____ is an important part of international trade.
   a. ACEA agreement
   b. AD-IA Model
   c. ACCRA Cost of Living Index
   d. Export

22. _____ in economics refers to metrics and measures of output from production processes, per unit of input. Labor _____, for example, is typically measured as a ratio of output per labor-hour, an input. _____ may be conceived of as a metrics of the technical or engineering efficiency of production.
   a. Production-possibility frontier
   b. Fordism
   c. Productivity
   d. Piece work

23. _____ describes a set of laws relating to domestic agriculture and imports of foreign agricultural products. Governments usually implement agricultural policies with the goal of achieving a specific outcome in the domestic agricultural product markets. Outcomes can involve, for example, a guaranteed supply level, price stability, product quality, product selection, land use or employment.
   a. ACCRA Cost of Living Index
   b. ACEA agreement
   c. Intercropping
   d. Agricultural Policy

24. _____ is subcontracting a process, such as product design or manufacturing, to a third-party company. The decision to outsource is often made in the interest of lowering cost or making better use of time and energy costs, redirecting or conserving energy directed at the competencies of a particular business, or to make more efficient use of land, labor, capital, (information) technology and resources. _____ became part of the business lexicon during the 1980s.
   a. Averch-Johnson effect
   b. Electronic business
   c. Outsourcing
   d. Additional Funds Needed

25. Competition law, known in the United States as _____ law, has three main elements:

- prohibiting agreements or practices that restrict free trading and competition between business entities. This includes in particular the repression of cartels.
- banning abusive behaviour by a firm dominating a market, or anti-competitive practices that tend to lead to such a dominant position. Practices controlled in this way may include predatory pricing, tying, price gouging, refusal to deal, and many others.
- supervising the mergers and acquisitions of large corporations, including some joint ventures. Transactions that are considered to threaten the competitive process can be prohibited altogether, or approved subject to 'remedies' such as an obligation to divest part of the merged business or to offer licences or access to facilities to enable other businesses to continue competing.

The substance and practice of competition law varies from jurisdiction to jurisdiction. Protecting the interests of consumers (consumer welfare) and ensuring that entrepreneurs have an opportunity to compete in the market economy are often treated as important objectives. Competition law is closely connected with law on deregulation of access to markets, state aids and subsidies, the privatisation of state owned assets and the establishment of independent sector regulators. In recent decades, competition law has been viewed as a way to provide better public services.

a. Intellectual property law
b. United Kingdom competition law
c. Antitrust
d. Anti-Inflation Act

26.

The _____ was the first United States Federal statute to limit cartels and monopolies. It falls under antitrust law.

The Act provides: 'Every contract, combination in the form of trust or otherwise, or conspiracy, in restraint of trade or commerce among the several States, or with foreign nations, is declared to be illegal'. The Act also provides: 'Every person who shall monopolize, or attempt to monopolize, or combine or conspire with any other person or persons, to monopolize any part of the trade or commerce among the several States, or with foreign nations, shall be deemed guilty of a felony [. . .]' The Act put responsibility upon government attorneys and district courts to pursue and investigate trusts, companies and organizations suspected of violating the Act. The Clayton Act extended the right to sue under the antitrust laws to 'any person who shall be injured in his business or property by reason of anything forbidden in the antitrust laws.' Under the Clayton Act, private parties may sue in U.S. district court and should they prevail, they may be awarded treble damages and the cost of suit, including reasonable attorney's fees.

a. Sherman Antitrust Act
b. 100-year flood
c. 130-30 fund
d. 1921 recession

27. _____ is a broad label that refers to any individuals or households that use goods and services generated within the economy. The concept of a _____ is used in different contexts, so that the usage and significance of the term may vary.

Chapter 16. The Labor Market: Demand, Supply, and Outsourcing

Typically when business people and economists talk of _____s they are talking about person as _____, an aggregated commodity item with little individuality other than that expressed in the buy/not-buy decision.

a. Consumer
b. 130-30 fund
c. 1921 recession
d. 100-year flood

28. In economics, _____ are the resources employed to produce goods and services. They facilitate production but do not become part of the product (as with raw materials) or significantly transformed by the production process (as with fuel used to power machinery.) To 19th century economists, the _____ were land (natural resources, gifts from nature), labor (the ability to work), and capital goods (human-made tools and equipment.)

a. Product Pipeline
b. Hicks-neutral technical change
c. Factors of production
d. Long-run

29. In economics, the marginal product or _____ is the extra output produced by one more unit of an input (for instance, the difference in output when a firm's labour is increased from five to six units.) Assuming that no other inputs to production change, the marginal product of a given input (X) can be expressed as:

$MP = \Delta Y/\Delta X$ = (the change of Y)/(the change of X.)

In neoclassical economics, this is the mathematical derivative of the production function....

a. Diseconomies of scale
b. Marginal physical product
c. Multifactor productivity
d. Productive capacity

30. In microeconomics, _____ is quite simply the conversion of inputs into outputs. It is an economic process that uses resources to create a good or service that is suitable for exchange. This can include manufacturing, storing, shipping, and packaging.

a. Red Guards
b. Solved
c. MET
d. Production

31. In economics, _____ is the process by which a firm determines the price and output level that returns the greatest profit. There are several approaches to this problem. The total revenue--total cost method relies on the fact that profit equals revenue minus cost, and the marginal revenue--marginal cost method is based on the fact that total profit in a perfectly competitive market reaches its maximum point where marginal revenue equals marginal cost.

a. Normal profit
b. Profit margin
c. Profit maximization
d. 100-year flood

Chapter 17. Union and Labor Market Monopoly Power

1. The _____ was one of the first federations of labor unions in the United States. It was founded in Columbus, Ohio in 1886 by Samuel Gompers as a reorganization of its predecessor, the Federation of Organized Trades and Labor Unions. Gompers became president of the AFL in 1886 and was reelected every year except one until his death on December 13, 1924.
   a. American Federation of Labor
   b. AD-IA Model
   c. ACCRA Cost of Living Index
   d. ACEA agreement

2. The _____ proposed by John L. Lewis in 1932, was a federation of unions that organized workers in industrial unions in the United States and Canada from 1935 to 1955. The Taft-Hartley Act of 1947 required union leaders to swear that they were not Communists. Many CIO leaders refused to obey that requirement, later found unconstitutional.
   a. Chinese correction
   b. Congress of Industrial Organizations
   c. Foreign direct investment
   d. Multinational corporation

3. _____ is a field of economics that studies the strategic behavior of firms, the structure of markets and their interactions. The study of _____ adds to the perfectly competitive model real-world frictions such as limited information, transaction cost, cost of adjusting prices, government actions, and barriers to entry by new firms into a market. It then considers how firms are organized and how they compete.
   a. Inflation
   b. Economic
   c. Economic ideology
   d. Industrial Organization

4. _____, often referred to by his initials _____, was the 32nd President of the United States. He was a central figure of the 20th century during a time of worldwide economic crisis and world war. Elected to four terms in office, he served from 1933 to 1945 and is the only U.S. president to have served more than two terms.
   a. Adolf Hitler
   b. Adolph Fischer
   c. Adam Smith
   d. Franklin Delano Roosevelt

5. A _____ is a group of people who share or are motivated by at least one common issue or interest, or work together on a specific project(s) to achieve a common objective. _____s are also characterised by attempts to share and exercise political and social power and to make decisions on a consensus-driven and egalitarian basis. _____s differ from cooperatives in that they are not necessarily focused upon an economic benefit or saving (but can be that as well.)
   a. 130-30 fund
   b. 1921 recession
   c. Collective
   d. 100-year flood

6. In organized labor, _____ is the method whereby workers organize together (usually in unions) to meet, converse, and negotiate upon the work conditions with their employers normally resulting in a written contract setting forth the wages, hours, and other conditions to be observed for a stipulated period.It is the practice in which union and company representatives meet to negotiate a new labor contract. In various national labor and employment law contexts, _____ takes on a more specific legal meaning and so, in a broad sense, however, it is the coming together of workers to negotiate their employment.

A collective agreement is a labor contract between an employer and one or more unions.

   a. Collective bargaining
   b. Strikebreaker
   c. Designated Suppliers Program
   d. Demarcation dispute

7. _____ refers to organizing a union in a manner that seeks to unify workers in a particular industry along the lines of the particular craft or trade that they work in by class or skill level. It contrasts with industrial unionism, in which all workers in the same industry are organized into the same union, regardless of differences in skill.

_____ is perhaps best exemplified by many of the construction unions that formed the backbone of the old American Federation of Labor (which later merged with the industrial unions of the Congress of Industrial Organizations to form the AFL-CIO.)

   a. 100-year flood
   c. 1921 recession
   b. 130-30 fund
   d. Craft unionism

8. A trade union or _____ is an organization of workers who have banded together to achieve common goals in key areas and working conditions. The trade union, through its leadership, bargains with the employer on behalf of union members (rank and file members) and negotiates labor contracts (Collective bargaining) with employers. This may include the negotiation of wages, work rules, complaint procedures, rules governing hiring, firing and promotion of workers, benefits, workplace safety and policies.
   a. Labor union
   c. Business valuation standards
   b. Demand-side technologies
   d. Basis of futures

9. The term '_____' refers to the concept of collecting information and attempting to spot a pattern in the information. In some fields of study, the term '_____' has more formally-defined meanings.

In project management _____ is a mathematical technique that uses historical results to predict future outcome.

   a. Quantile regression
   c. Probit model
   b. Trend analysis
   d. Coefficient of determination

10. A _____ or labor union is an organization of workers who have banded together to achieve common goals in key areas and working conditions. The _____, through its leadership, bargains with the employer on behalf of union members (rank and file members) and negotiates labor contracts (Collective bargaining) with employers. This may include the negotiation of wages, work rules, complaint procedures, rules governing hiring, firing and promotion of workers, benefits, workplace safety and policies.
   a. Consumer goods
   c. Guaranteed investment contracts
   b. Case-Shiller Home Price Indices
   d. Trade union

11. In microeconomics, _____ is the extra revenue that an additional unit of product will bring. It is the additional income from selling one more unit of a good; sometimes equal to price. It can also be described as the change in total revenue/change in number of units sold.
   a. Reservation price
   c. Market demand schedule
   b. Long term
   d. Marginal revenue

12. _____ is an equity (stock) exchange located at 11 Wall Street in lower Manhattan, New York, USA. It is the largest stock exchange in the world by dollar value of its listed companies' securities. As of October 2008, the combined capitalization of all domestic _____ listed companies was US$10.1 trillion.

a. 130-30 fund
b. 1921 recession
c. 100-year flood
d. New York Stock Exchange

13. The U.S. _____ is an independent agency of the United States government which holds primary responsibility for enforcing the federal securities laws and regulating the securities industry, the nation's stock and options exchanges, and other electronic securities markets. The SEC was created by section 4 of the Securities Exchange Act of 1934 (now codified as 15 U.S.C. Â§ 78d and commonly referred to as the 1934 Act.)
a. Securities and Exchange Commission
b. 130-30 fund
c. 100-year flood
d. 1921 recession

14. _____ are the inflation-indexed bonds issued by the U.S. Treasury. The principal is adjusted to the Consumer Price Index, the commonly used measure of inflation. The coupon rate is constant, but generates a different amount of interest when multiplied by the inflation-adjusted principal, thus protecting the holder against inflation.
a. 1921 recession
b. 130-30 fund
c. 100-year flood
d. Treasury Inflation-Protected Securities

15. In economics, _____ is how a natione;s total economy is distributed among its population. . _____ has always been a central concern of economic theory and economic policy. Classical economists such as Adam Smith, Thomas Malthus and David Ricardo were mainly concerned with factor _____, that is, the distribution of income between the main factors of production, land, labour and capital.
a. Income distribution
b. Eco commerce
c. Equipment trust certificate
d. Authorised capital

16. _____ are statutes enforced in twenty-two U.S. states, mostly in the southern or western U.S., allowed under provisions of the Taft-Hartley Act, which prohibit agreements between trade unions and employers making membership or payment of union dues or 'fees' a condition of employment, either before or after hiring.

Prior to the passage of the Taft-Hartley Act by Congress over President Harry S. Truman's veto in 1947, unions and employers covered by the National Labor Relations Act could lawfully agree to a 'closed shop,' in which employees at unionized workplaces are required to be members of the union as a condition of employment. Under the law in effect before the Taft-Hartley amendments, an employee who ceased being a member of the union for whatever reason, from failure to pay dues to expulsion from the union as an internal disciplinary punishment, could also be fired even if the employee did not violate any of the employer's rules.

a. Community property
b. Chief Financial Officers Act of 1990
c. Right-to-work laws
d. Fee simple

17. A _____ is an attempt by labor to convince others to stop doing business with a particular firm because that firm does business with another firm that is the subject of a strike and/or a primary boycott.

This type of action is illegal in many countries. In the U.S. it is banned by the interpretation of the Sherman Antitrust Act, by the Taft-Hartley Act, which amends the National Labor Relations Act of 1935, also known as the Wagner Act.

a. 1921 recession
b. Secondary boycott
c. 100-year flood
d. 130-30 fund

18. In economics, _____ refers to the ability of a person or a country to produce a particular good at a lower marginal cost and opportunity cost than another person or country. It is the ability to produce a product most efficiently given all the other products that could be produced. It can be contrasted with absolute advantage which refers to the ability of a person or a country to produce a particular good at a lower absolute cost than another.
   a. Gravity model of trade
   b. Hot money
   c. Triffin dilemma
   d. Comparative advantage

19. _____ is subcontracting a process, such as product design or manufacturing, to a third-party company. The decision to outsource is often made in the interest of lowering cost or making better use of time and energy costs, redirecting or conserving energy directed at the competencies of a particular business, or to make more efficient use of land, labor, capital, (information) technology and resources. _____ became part of the business lexicon during the 1980s.
   a. Additional Funds Needed
   b. Outsourcing
   c. Electronic business
   d. Averch-Johnson effect

20. The _____ is the audit, evaluation, and investigative arm of the United States Congress. It is located in the Legislative branch of the United States government.

The _____ was established as the General Accounting Office by the Budget and Accounting Act of 1921 (Pub.L.

   a. 130-30 fund
   b. Government Accountability Office
   c. 100-year flood
   d. 1921 recession

21. The _____ is an international organization that oversees the global financial system by following the macroeconomic policies of its member countries, in particular those with an impact on exchange rates and the balance of payments. It is an organization formed to stabilize international exchange rates and facilitate development. It also offers financial and technical assistance to its members, making it an international lender of last resort.
   a. ACEA agreement
   b. International Monetary Fund
   c. Office of Thrift Supervision
   d. ACCRA Cost of Living Index

22. The _____ is a labor union in the United States and Canada. Formed in 1903 by the merger of several local and regional locals of teamsters, the union now represents a diverse membership of blue-collar and professional workers in both the public and private sectors. The union had approximately 1.4 million members in 2007.
   a. ACEA agreement
   b. ACCRA Cost of Living Index
   c. International Brotherhood of Teamsters
   d. AD-IA Model

23. A municipality is an administrative entity composed of a clearly defined territory and its population and commonly denotes a city, town or a small grouping of them. A municipality is typically governed by a mayor and a city council or _____ council.

The notion of municipality includes townships but is not restricted to them.

a. 130-30 fund
b. 1921 recession
c. 100-year flood
d. Municipal

24. In finance, the _____s between two currencies specifies how much one currency is worth in terms of the other. It is the value of a foreign natione;s currency in terms of the home natione;s currency. For example an _____ of 102 Japanese yen to the United States dollar means that JPY 102 is worth the same as USD 1.

   a. ACCRA Cost of Living Index
   b. Interbank market
   c. ACEA agreement
   d. Exchange rate

25. _____ to the arrival of new individuals into a habitat or population. It is a biological concept and is important in population ecology, differentiated from emigration and migration.

   _____ is a modern phenomenon.

   a. ACCRA Cost of Living Index
   b. ACEA agreement
   c. Immigration
   d. AD-IA Model

26. In economics, an _____ is any good (e.g. a commodity) or service brought into one country from another country in a legitimate fashion, typically for use in trade. It is a good that is brought in from another country for sale. _____ goods or services are provided to domestic consumers by foreign producers. An _____ in the receiving country is an export to the sending country.

   a. Import
   b. Incoterms
   c. Economic integration
   d. Import quota

27. In economics, _____ refers to either

   1. a simplifying assumption made by the new classical school that markets always go to where the quantity supplied equals the quantity demanded; or
   2. the process of getting there via price adjustment.

A _____ price is the price of a good or service at which quantity supplied is equal to quantity demanded. Also called the equilibrium price.

In simple terms, this means that markets tend to move towards prices which balance the quantity supplied and the quantity demanded, such that the market will eventually be cleared of all surpluses and shortages (excess supply and demand.) The first version assumes that this process occurs instantaneously.

   a. Market portfolio
   b. Noise trader
   c. Market data
   d. Market clearing

28. _____ is the controlled distribution of resources and scarce goods or services. _____ controls the size of the ration, one's allotted portion of the resources being distributed on a particular day or at a particular time.

In economics, it is often common to use the word '_____' to refer to one of the roles that prices play in markets, while _____ is called 'non-price _____.' Using prices to ration means that those with the most money (or other assets) and who want a product the most are first to receive it.

Chapter 17. Union and Labor Market Monopoly Power

a. Rationing
c. 100-year flood

b. 1921 recession
d. 130-30 fund

29. A _____ is a person who works despite an ongoing strike. _____s are usually individuals who are not employed by the company prior to the trade union dispute, but rather hired prior to or during the strike to keep production or services going. '_____s' may also refer to be workers who cross picket lines to work.

a. Designated Suppliers Program
c. Division of labour

b. Work-life balance
d. Strikebreaker

30. _____ is a broad label that refers to any individuals or households that use goods and services generated within the economy. The concept of a _____ is used in different contexts, so that the usage and significance of the term may vary.

Typically when business people and economists talk of _____s they are talking about person as _____, an aggregated commodity item with little individuality other than that expressed in the buy/not-buy decision.

a. 100-year flood
c. 1921 recession

b. 130-30 fund
d. Consumer

31. The _____ is a United States government corporation created by the Glass-Steagall Act of 1933. It provides deposit insurance, which guarantees the safety of deposits in member banks, currently up to $250,000 per depositor per bank. Funds in non-interest bearing transaction accounts are fully insured, with no limit, under the temporary Transaction Account Guarantee Program.

a. Foreign direct investment
c. Great Leap Forward

b. Luxembourg Income Study
d. Federal Deposit Insurance Corporation

32. _____s is the social science that studies the production, distribution, and consumption of goods and services. The term _____s comes from the Ancient Greek oá¼°κονομῖα from oá¼¶κος (oikos, 'house') + vÏŒμος (nomos, 'custom' or 'law'), hence 'rules of the house(hold)'. Current _____ models developed out of the broader field of political economy in the late 19th century, owing to a desire to use an empirical approach more akin to the physical sciences.

a. Inflation
c. Energy economics

b. Economic
d. Opportunity cost

33. _____ is a pejorative term for the practice of hiring more workers than are needed to perform a given job complex and time-consuming merely to employ additional workers. The term 'make-work' is sometimes used as a synonym for _____.

The term '_____' is usually used by management to describe behaviors and rules sought by workers.

a. Featherbedding
c. Channel coordination

b. Cultural synergy
d. Foreign ownership

34. _____ in economics refers to metrics and measures of output from production processes, per unit of input. Labor _____, for example, is typically measured as a ratio of output per labor-hour, an input. _____ may be conceived of as a metrics of the technical or engineering efficiency of production.

a. Piece work
b. Production-possibility frontier
c. Fordism
d. Productivity

35. _____ was a survey conducted by the U.S. Department of Justice to gauge the prevalence of alcohol and illegal drug use among prior arrestees. It was a reformulation of the prior Drug Use Forecasting (DUF) program, focused on five drugs in particular: cocaine, marijuana, methamphetamine, opiates, and PCP.

Participants were randomly selected from arrest records in major metropolitan areas; because no personally identifying information is taken from each record chosen, the resulting data can be correlated to arrest rates, but not to the total population of persons charged.

a. ACEA agreement
b. ACCRA Cost of Living Index
c. AD-IA Model
d. Arrestee Drug Abuse Monitoring

36. Competition law, known in the United States as _____ law, has three main elements:

- prohibiting agreements or practices that restrict free trading and competition between business entities. This includes in particular the repression of cartels.
- banning abusive behaviour by a firm dominating a market, or anti-competitive practices that tend to lead to such a dominant position. Practices controlled in this way may include predatory pricing, tying, price gouging, refusal to deal, and many others.
- supervising the mergers and acquisitions of large corporations, including some joint ventures. Transactions that are considered to threaten the competitive process can be prohibited altogether, or approved subject to 'remedies' such as an obligation to divest part of the merged business or to offer licences or access to facilities to enable other businesses to continue competing.

The substance and practice of competition law varies from jurisdiction to jurisdiction. Protecting the interests of consumers (consumer welfare) and ensuring that entrepreneurs have an opportunity to compete in the market economy are often treated as important objectives. Competition law is closely connected with law on deregulation of access to markets, state aids and subsidies, the privatisation of state owned assets and the establishment of independent sector regulators. In recent decades, competition law has been viewed as a way to provide better public services.

a. United Kingdom competition law
b. Anti-Inflation Act
c. Intellectual property law
d. Antitrust

37.

The _____ was the first United States Federal statute to limit cartels and monopolies. It falls under antitrust law.

Chapter 17. Union and Labor Market Monopoly Power

The Act provides: 'Every contract, combination in the form of trust or otherwise, or conspiracy, in restraint of trade or commerce among the several States, or with foreign nations, is declared to be illegal'. The Act also provides: 'Every person who shall monopolize, or attempt to monopolize, or combine or conspire with any other person or persons, to monopolize any part of the trade or commerce among the several States, or with foreign nations, shall be deemed guilty of a felony [. . .]' The Act put responsibility upon government attorneys and district courts to pursue and investigate trusts, companies and organizations suspected of violating the Act. The Clayton Act extended the right to sue under the antitrust laws to 'any person who shall be injured in his business or property by reason of anything forbidden in the antitrust laws.' Under the Clayton Act, private parties may sue in U.S. district court and should they prevail, they may be awarded treble damages and the cost of suit, including reasonable attorney's fees.

a. 130-30 fund
b. 1921 recession
c. Sherman Antitrust Act
d. 100-year flood

38. _____ was a Scottish moral philosopher and a pioneer of political economy. One of the key figures of the Scottish Enlightenment, Smith is the author of The Theory of Moral Sentiments and An Inquiry into the Nature and Causes of the Wealth of Nations. The latter, usually abbreviated as The Wealth of Nations, is considered his magnum opus and the first modern work of economics.

a. Alan Greenspan
b. Adolph Fischer
c. Adolf Hitler
d. Adam Smith

39. In economics, a monopsony 'purchase') is a market form in which only one buyer faces many sellers. It is an example of imperfect competition, similar to a monopoly, in which only one seller faces many buyers. As the only purchaser of a good or service, the '_____' may dictate terms to its suppliers in the same manner that a monopolist controls the market for its buyers.

a. 1921 recession
b. Monopsonist
c. 130-30 fund
d. 100-year flood

40. In economics _____ is defined as the sum of private and external costs. Economic theorists ascribe individual decision-making to a calculation costs and benefits. Rational choice theory assumes that individuals only consider their own private costs when making decisions, not the costs that may be borne by others.

a. Cost-Volume-Profit Analysis
b. Social cost
c. Psychic cost
d. Khozraschyot

41. _____ or national income by type of income is a measure of national income or output based on the cost of factors of production, instead of market prices. This allows the effect of any subsidy or indirect tax to be removed from the final measure.

a. Gross regional domestic product
b. Corporate synergy
c. Lehman scale
d. Factor cost

42. In economics, a _____ 'purchase') is a market form in which only one buyer faces many sellers. It is an example of imperfect competition, similar to a monopoly, in which only one seller faces many buyers. As the only purchaser of a good or service, the 'monopsonist' may dictate terms to its suppliers in the same manner that a monopolist controls the market for its buyers.

Chapter 17. Union and Labor Market Monopoly Power

a. Monopsony
b. 130-30 fund
c. 100-year flood
d. 1921 recession

43. In a _____ there is both a monopoly (a single seller) and monopsony (a single buyer) in the same market.

In such market price and output will be determined by the non economic forces like bargaining power of both buyer and seller. A _____ model is often used in situations where the switching costs of both sides are prohibitively high.

a. Price takers
b. Bilateral monopoly
c. Revenue-cap regulation
d. Market concentration

44. In economics, a _____ exists when a specific individual or enterprise has sufficient control over a particular product or service to determine significantly the terms on which other individuals shall have access to it. Monopolies are thus characterized by a lack of economic competition for the good or service that they provide and a lack of viable substitute goods. The verb 'monopolize' refers to the process by which a firm gains persistently greater market share than what is expected under perfect competition.

a. 100-year flood
b. 1921 recession
c. Monopoly
d. 130-30 fund

45. _____, in law and economics, is a form of risk management primarily used to hedge against the risk of a contingent loss. _____ is defined as the equitable transfer of the risk of a loss, from one entity to another, in exchange for a premium, and can be thought of as a guaranteed small loss to prevent a large, possibly devastating loss. An insurer is a company selling the _____; an insured or policyholder is the person or entity buying the _____.

a. ACEA agreement
b. ACCRA Cost of Living Index
c. AD-IA Model
d. Insurance

Chapter 18. Income, Poverty, and Health Care

1. The _____ is an international organization that oversees the global financial system by following the macroeconomic policies of its member countries, in particular those with an impact on exchange rates and the balance of payments. It is an organization formed to stabilize international exchange rates and facilitate development. It also offers financial and technical assistance to its members, making it an international lender of last resort.
    a. International Monetary Fund
    b. Office of Thrift Supervision
    c. ACEA agreement
    d. ACCRA Cost of Living Index

2. In economics, the _____ is a graphical representation of the cumulative distribution function of a probability distribution; it is a graph showing the proportion of the distribution assumed by the bottom y% of the values. It is a curve that illustrates income distribution. It is often used to represent income distribution, where it shows for the bottom x% of households, what percentage y% of the total income they have.
    a. Kuznets curve
    b. Phillips curve
    c. Lorenz Curve
    d. Demand curve

3. In economics, _____ is how a natione;s total economy is distributed among its population. ._____ has always been a central concern of economic theory and economic policy. Classical economists such as Adam Smith, Thomas Malthus and David Ricardo were mainly concerned with factor _____, that is, the distribution of income between the main factors of production, land, labour and capital.
    a. Authorised capital
    b. Income distribution
    c. Equipment trust certificate
    d. Eco commerce

4. In mathematics, an _____ is a statement about the relative size or order of two objects, or about whether they are the same or not

    - The notation a < b means that a is less than b.
    - The notation a > b means that a is greater than b.
    - The notation a ≠ b means that a is not equal to b, but does not say that one is greater than the other or even that they can be compared in size.

    In each statement above, a is not equal to b. These relations are known as strict inequalities. The notation a < b may also be read as 'a is strictly less than b'.

    a. Inequality
    b. ACEA agreement
    c. ACCRA Cost of Living Index
    d. AD-IA Model

5. _____ describes a set of laws relating to domestic agriculture and imports of foreign agricultural products. Governments usually implement agricultural policies with the goal of achieving a specific outcome in the domestic agricultural product markets. Outcomes can involve, for example, a guaranteed supply level, price stability, product quality, product selection, land use or employment.
    a. ACEA agreement
    b. Intercropping
    c. ACCRA Cost of Living Index
    d. Agricultural Policy

6. _____ is an equity (stock) exchange located at 11 Wall Street in lower Manhattan, New York, USA. It is the largest stock exchange in the world by dollar value of its listed companies' securities. As of October 2008, the combined capitalization of all domestic _____ listed companies was US$10.1 trillion.

Chapter 18. Income, Poverty, and Health Care

a. 1921 recession
c. 100-year flood
b. 130-30 fund
d. New York Stock Exchange

7. _____ is a comparison of the wealth of various members or groups in a society. It differs from the distribution of income in a manner analogous to the difference between position and speed.

Wealth is a person's net worth, expressed as:

   wealth = assets - liabilities

The word 'wealth' is often confused with 'income'.

a. Wealth condensation
c. 130-30 fund
b. 100-year flood
d. Distribution of wealth

8. In algebra, a _____ is a function depending on n that associates a scalar, det(A), to an n×n square matrix A. The fundamental geometric meaning of a _____ is a scale factor for measure when A is regarded as a linear transformation. _____s are important both in calculus, where they enter the substitution rule for several variables, and in multilinear algebra.

For a fixed nonnegative integer n, there is a unique _____ function for the n×n matrices over any commutative ring R. In particular, this function exists when R is the field of real or complex numbers.

a. Determinant
c. 1921 recession
b. 100-year flood
d. 130-30 fund

9. In finance, the _____s between two currencies specifies how much one currency is worth in terms of the other. It is the value of a foreign natione;s currency in terms of the home natione;s currency. For example an _____ of 102 Japanese yen to the United States dollar means that JPY 102 is worth the same as USD 1.

a. ACEA agreement
c. Interbank market
b. ACCRA Cost of Living Index
d. Exchange rate

10. In economics, the _____ or marginal physical product is the extra output produced by one more unit of an input (for instance, the difference in output when a firm's labour is increased from five to six units.) Assuming that no other inputs to production change, the _____ of a given input (X) can be expressed as:

   _____ = $\Delta Y / \Delta X$ = (the change of Y)/(the change of X.)

-
  -
    - Pending approval by Thomas Sowell***

In neoclassical economics, this is the mathematical derivative of the production function.... Note that the 'product' (Y) is typically defined ignoring external costs and benefits.

Chapter 18. Income, Poverty, and Health Care

a. Factor prices
b. Labor problem
c. Productive capacity
d. Marginal product

11. In microeconomics, _____ is the extra revenue that an additional unit of product will bring. It is the additional income from selling one more unit of a good; sometimes equal to price. It can also be described as the change in total revenue/change in number of units sold.
   a. Market demand schedule
   b. Long term
   c. Reservation price
   d. Marginal revenue

12. The marginal revenue productivity theory of wages, also referred to as the _____ of labor, is the change in total revenue earned by a firm that results from employing one more unit of labor. It is a neoclassical model that determines, under some conditions, the optimal number of workers to employ at an exogenously determined market wage rate.

The _____ of a worker is equal to the product of the marginal product of labor (MP) and the marginal revenue (MR), given by MR×MP = _____.

   a. Marginal revenue productivity theory of wages
   b. Coal depletion
   c. Marginal revenue product
   d. Real prices and ideal prices

13. _____ in economics refers to metrics and measures of output from production processes, per unit of input. Labor _____, for example, is typically measured as a ratio of output per labor-hour, an input. _____ may be conceived of as a metrics of the technical or engineering efficiency of production.
   a. Piece work
   b. Fordism
   c. Production-possibility frontier
   d. Productivity

14. A trade union or _____ is an organization of workers who have banded together to achieve common goals in key areas and working conditions. The trade union, through its leadership, bargains with the employer on behalf of union members (rank and file members) and negotiates labor contracts (Collective bargaining) with employers. This may include the negotiation of wages, work rules, complaint procedures, rules governing hiring, firing and promotion of workers, benefits, workplace safety and policies.
   a. Demand-side technologies
   b. Basis of futures
   c. Business valuation standards
   d. Labor union

15. A _____ is a group of people who share or are motivated by at least one common issue or interest, or work together on a specific project(s) to achieve a common objective. _____s are also characterised by attempts to share and exercise political and social power and to make decisions on a consensus-driven and egalitarian basis. _____s differ from cooperatives in that they are not necessarily focused upon an economic benefit or saving (but can be that as well.)
   a. Collective
   b. 1921 recession
   c. 100-year flood
   d. 130-30 fund

16. _____ refers to the stock of skills and knowledge embodied in the ability to perform labor so as to produce economic value. It is the skills and knowledge gained by a worker through education and experience. Many early economic theories refer to it simply as labor, one of three factors of production, and consider it to be a fungible resource -- homogeneous and easily interchangeable. Other conceptions of labor dispense with these assumptions.

a. General equilibrium
b. Law of increasing costs
c. Price theory
d. Human capital

17. To _____ is to impose a financial charge or other levy upon a taxpayer by a state or the functional equivalent of a state.

_____es are also imposed by many subnational entities. _____es consist of direct _____ or indirect _____, and may be paid in money or as its labour equivalent (often but not always unpaid.)

a. 1921 recession
b. Tax
c. 130-30 fund
d. 100-year flood

18. To tax is to impose a financial charge or other levy upon a taxpayer by a state or the functional equivalent of a state.

_____ are also imposed by many subnational entities. _____ consist of direct tax or indirect tax, and may be paid in money or as its labour equivalent (often but not always unpaid.)

a. 130-30 fund
b. 1921 recession
c. 100-year flood
d. Taxes

19. A _____ or labor union is an organization of workers who have banded together to achieve common goals in key areas and working conditions. The _____, through its leadership, bargains with the employer on behalf of union members (rank and file members) and negotiates labor contracts (Collective bargaining) with employers. This may include the negotiation of wages, work rules, complaint procedures, rules governing hiring, firing and promotion of workers, benefits, workplace safety and policies.

a. Case-Shiller Home Price Indices
b. Guaranteed investment contracts
c. Consumer goods
d. Trade union

20. _____s is the social science that studies the production, distribution, and consumption of goods and services. The term _____s comes from the Ancient Greek οἰκονομῖα from οἶκος (oikos, 'house') + νόμος (nomos, 'custom' or 'law'), hence 'rules of the house(hold)'. Current _____ models developed out of the broader field of political economy in the late 19th century, owing to a desire to use an empirical approach more akin to the physical sciences.

a. Inflation
b. Energy economics
c. Economic
d. Opportunity cost

21. In economic theory, _____ is the competitive situation in any market where the conditions necessary for perfect competition are not satisfied. It is a market structure that does not meet the conditions of perfect competition.

Forms of _____ include:

- Monopoly, in which there is only one seller of a good.
- Oligopoly, in which there is a small number of sellers.
- Monopolistic competition, in which there are many sellers producing highly differentiated goods.
- Monopsony, in which there is only one buyer of a good.
- Oligopsony, in which there is a small number of buyers.

Chapter 18. Income, Poverty, and Health Care

There may also be _____ in markets due to buyers or sellers lacking information about prices and the goods being traded.

There may also be _____ due to a time lag in a market.

a. ACEA agreement
b. Imperfect Competition
c. AD-IA Model
d. ACCRA Cost of Living Index

22. _____ are the inflation-indexed bonds issued by the U.S. Treasury. The principal is adjusted to the Consumer Price Index, the commonly used measure of inflation. The coupon rate is constant, but generates a different amount of interest when multiplied by the inflation-adjusted principal, thus protecting the holder against inflation.

a. 1921 recession
b. 100-year flood
c. 130-30 fund
d. Treasury Inflation-Protected Securities

23. In economics, _____ refers to the ability of a person or a country to produce a particular good at a lower marginal cost and opportunity cost than another person or country. It is the ability to produce a product most efficiently given all the other products that could be produced. It can be contrasted with absolute advantage which refers to the ability of a person or a country to produce a particular good at a lower absolute cost than another.

a. Comparative advantage
b. Hot money
c. Triffin dilemma
d. Gravity model of trade

24. The U.S. _____ (EEOC) is a federal agency whose goal is ending employment discrimination. The _____ investigates discrimination complaints based on an individual's race, color, national origin, religion, sex, age, disability and retaliation for reporting and/or opposing a discriminatory practice. The Commission is also tasked with filing suits on behalf of alleged victim(s) of discrimination against employers and as an adjudicatory for claims of discrimination brought against federal agencies.

a. EEOC
b. ACEA agreement
c. ACCRA Cost of Living Index
d. AD-IA Model

25. _____ is the shortage of common things such as food, clothing, shelter and safe drinking water, all of which determine the quality of life. It may also include the lack of access to opportunities such as education and employment which aid the escape from _____ and/or allow one to enjoy the respect of fellow citizens. According to Mollie Orshansky who developed the _____ measurements used by the U.S. government, 'to be poor is to be deprived of those goods and services and pleasures which others around us take for granted.' Ongoing debates over causes, effects and best ways to measure _____, directly influence the design and implementation of _____-reduction programs and are therefore relevant to the fields of public administration and international development.

a. Poverty
b. Poverty map
c. Growth Elasticity of Poverty
d. Liberal welfare reforms

26. The _____ is an international financial institution that provides financial and technical assistance to developing countries for development programs (e.g. bridges, roads, schools, etc.) with the stated goal of reducing poverty.

140 *Chapter 18. Income, Poverty, and Health Care*

The _____ differs from the _____ Group, in that the _____ comprises only two institutions:

- International Bank for Reconstruction and Development (IBRD)
- International Development Association (IDA)

Whereas the latter incorporates these two in addition to three more:

- International Finance Corporation (IFC)
- Multilateral Investment Guarantee Agency (MIGA)
- International Centre for Settlement of Investment Disputes (ICSID)

John Maynard Keynes (right) represented the UK at the conference, and Harry Dexter White represented the US.

The _____ is one of two major financial institutions created as a result of the Bretton Woods Conference in 1944. The International Monetary Fund, a related but separate institution, is the second.

    a. Flow to Equity-Approach   b. Bank-State-Branch
    c. Financial costs of the 2003 Iraq War   d. World Bank

27. In economics, _____ refers to the ability of a party to produce a good or service using fewer real resources than another entity producing the same good or service..A party has an _____ when using the same input as another party, it can produce a greater output. Since _____ is determined by a simple comparison of labor productivities, it is possible for a a party to have no _____ in anything. It can be contrasted with the concept of comparative advantage which refers to the ability to produce a particular good at a lower opportunity cost.

    a. ACCRA Cost of Living Index   b. International economics
    c. Absolute advantage   d. Index number

28. _____ is a misspelled phrase from Latin 'pro capite' phrase meaning per head with pro meaning 'per' or 'for each' and capite meaning 'head.' Both words together equate to the phrase 'for each head.'

It is usually used in the field of statistics to indicate the average per person for any given concern, such as income, crime rate, etc.

It is also used in wills to indicate that each of the named beneficiaries should receive, by devise or bequest, equal shares of the estate. This is in contrast to a per stirpes division, in which each branch of the inheriting family inherits an equal share of the estate.

    a. Per capita   b. False positive rate
    c. Sargan test   d. Population statistics

29. _____ means how much each individual receives, in monetary terms, of the yearly income generated in the country. This is what each citizen is to receive if the yearly national income is divided equally among everyone. _____ is usually reported in units of currency per year.

Chapter 18. Income, Poverty, and Health Care

a. Family income
b. Real income
c. Lerman ratio
d. Per capita income

30. A _____ refers to any type debt instrument, such as a loan, bond, mortgage that does not have a fixed rate of interest over the life of the instrument. Such debt typically uses an index or other base rate for establishing the interest rate for each relevant period. One of the most common rates to use as the basis for applying interest rates is the London Inter-bank Offered Rate, or LIBOR
   a. Floating interest rate
   b. Moneylender
   c. Money market
   d. Disposal tax effect

31. The United States federal _____ is a refundable tax credit. For tax year 2008, a claimant with one qualifying child can receive a maximum credit of $2,917. For two or more qualifying children, the maximum credit is $4,824.
   a. Earned Income Tax Credit
   b. ACCRA Cost of Living Index
   c. AD-IA Model
   d. ACEA agreement

32. The _____ is the audit, evaluation, and investigative arm of the United States Congress. It is located in the Legislative branch of the United States government.

The _____ was established as the General Accounting Office by the Budget and Accounting Act of 1921 (Pub.L.

   a. 1921 recession
   b. 130-30 fund
   c. Government Accountability Office
   d. 100-year flood

33. An _____ is a tax levied on the financial income of people, corporations, or other legal entities. Various _____ systems exist, with varying degrees of tax incidence. Income taxation can be progressive, proportional, or regressive.
   a. ACCRA Cost of Living Index
   b. ACEA agreement
   c. AD-IA Model
   d. Income Tax

34. The term _____ describes two different concepts:

   - The first is a recognition of partial payment already made towards taxes due.
   - The second is a state benefit paid to workers through the tax system, which has the effect of increasing (rather than reducing) net income.

Within the Australian, Canadian, United Kingdom, and United States tax systems, a _____ is a recognition of partial payment already made towards taxes due. A similar concept exists (fr:Avoir fiscal) in the French tax system. This situation arises, for example, when standard rate tax has been deducted at source, but the tax-payer is subject to further taxation at a higher rate. It also applies in dividend imputation systems.

   a. 100-year flood
   b. 130-30 fund
   c. 1921 recession
   d. Tax Credit

Chapter 18. Income, Poverty, and Health Care

35. _____ is a broad label that refers to any individuals or households that use goods and services generated within the economy. The concept of a _____ is used in different contexts, so that the usage and significance of the term may vary.

Typically when business people and economists talk of _____s they are talking about person as _____, an aggregated commodity item with little individuality other than that expressed in the buy/not-buy decision.

- a. 100-year flood
- b. 130-30 fund
- c. 1921 recession
- d. Consumer

36. Economics:

- _____,the desire to own something and the ability to pay for it
- _____ curve,a graphic representation of a _____ schedule
- _____ deposit, the money in checking accounts
- _____ pull theory,the theory that inflation occurs when _____ for goods and services exceeds existing supplies
- _____ schedule,a table that lists the quantity of a good a person will buy it each different price
- _____ side economics,the school of economics at believes government spending and tax cuts open economy by raising _____

- a. McKesson ' Robbins scandal
- b. Variability
- c. Production
- d. Demand

37. _____, in law and economics, is a form of risk management primarily used to hedge against the risk of a contingent loss. _____ is defined as the equitable transfer of the risk of a loss, from one entity to another, in exchange for a premium, and can be thought of as a guaranteed small loss to prevent a large, possibly devastating loss. An insurer is a company selling the _____; an insured or policyholder is the person or entity buying the _____.

- a. AD-IA Model
- b. ACEA agreement
- c. ACCRA Cost of Living Index
- d. Insurance

38. Competition law, known in the United States as _____ law, has three main elements:

- prohibiting agreements or practices that restrict free trading and competition between business entities. This includes in particular the repression of cartels.
- banning abusive behaviour by a firm dominating a market, or anti-competitive practices that tend to lead to such a dominant position. Practices controlled in this way may include predatory pricing, tying, price gouging, refusal to deal, and many others.
- supervising the mergers and acquisitions of large corporations, including some joint ventures. Transactions that are considered to threaten the competitive process can be prohibited altogether, or approved subject to 'remedies' such as an obligation to divest part of the merged business or to offer licences or access to facilities to enable other businesses to continue competing.

Chapter 18. Income, Poverty, and Health Care

The substance and practice of competition law varies from jurisdiction to jurisdiction. Protecting the interests of consumers (consumer welfare) and ensuring that entrepreneurs have an opportunity to compete in the market economy are often treated as important objectives. Competition law is closely connected with law on deregulation of access to markets, state aids and subsidies, the privatisation of state owned assets and the establishment of independent sector regulators. In recent decades, competition law has been viewed as a way to provide better public services.

a. Intellectual property law
b. Anti-Inflation Act
c. United Kingdom competition law
d. Antitrust

39.

The _____ was the first United States Federal statute to limit cartels and monopolies. It falls under antitrust law.

The Act provides: 'Every contract, combination in the form of trust or otherwise, or conspiracy, in restraint of trade or commerce among the several States, or with foreign nations, is declared to be illegal'. The Act also provides: 'Every person who shall monopolize, or attempt to monopolize, or combine or conspire with any other person or persons, to monopolize any part of the trade or commerce among the several States, or with foreign nations, shall be deemed guilty of a felony [. . .]' The Act put responsibility upon government attorneys and district courts to pursue and investigate trusts, companies and organizations suspected of violating the Act. The Clayton Act extended the right to sue under the antitrust laws to 'any person who shall be injured in his business or property by reason of anything forbidden in the antitrust laws.' Under the Clayton Act, private parties may sue in U.S. district court and should they prevail, they may be awarded treble damages and the cost of suit, including reasonable attorney's fees.

a. 130-30 fund
b. 1921 recession
c. 100-year flood
d. Sherman Antitrust Act

40. In an insurance policy, the _____ or excess (UK term) is the portion of any claim that is not covered by the insurance provider. It is the amount of expenses that must be paid out of pocket before an insurer will cover any expenses. It is normally quoted as a fixed quantity and is a part of most policies covering losses to the policy holder.

a. Double indemnity
b. Deductible
c. Dual trigger insurance
d. PVNBP

41. _____ or government expenditure is classified by economists into three main types. Government purchases of goods and services for current use are classed as government consumption. Government purchases of goods and services intended to create future benefits, such as infrastructure investment or research spending, are classed as government investment.

a. 1921 recession
b. 100-year flood
c. 130-30 fund
d. Government spending

42. _____ is the prospect that a party insulated from risk may behave differently from the way it would behave if it were fully exposed to the risk. In insurance, _____ that occurs without conscious or malicious action is called morale hazard.

_____ is related to information asymmetry, a situation in which one party in a transaction has more information than another.

   a. Moral hazard
   c. 1921 recession
   b. 100-year flood
   d. 130-30 fund

43. _____ is a common concept in economics, and gives rise to derived concepts such as consumer debt. Generally _____ is defined by opposition to production. But the precise definition can vary because different schools of economists define production quite differently.

   a. Federal Reserve Bank Notes
   c. Cash or share options
   b. Foreclosure data providers
   d. Consumption

44. _____s are accounts maintained by retail financial institutions that pay interest but can not be used directly as money (for example, by writing a cheque.) These accounts let customers set aside a portion of their liquid assets while earning a monetary return.

_____s are offered by commercial banks, savings and loan associations, credit unions, building societies and mutual savings banks.

   a. Lombard Club
   c. Fair Finance Watch
   b. Savings account
   d. Fractional-reserve banking

Chapter 19. Environmental Economics

1. _____ was a survey conducted by the U.S. Department of Justice to gauge the prevalence of alcohol and illegal drug use among prior arrestees. It was a reformulation of the prior Drug Use Forecasting (DUF) program, focused on five drugs in particular: cocaine, marijuana, methamphetamine, opiates, and PCP.

Participants were randomly selected from arrest records in major metropolitan areas; because no personally identifying information is taken from each record chosen, the resulting data can be correlated to arrest rates, but not to the total population of persons charged.

   a. ACEA agreement
   b. AD-IA Model
   c. Arrestee Drug Abuse Monitoring
   d. ACCRA Cost of Living Index

2. _____ is a broad label that refers to any individuals or households that use goods and services generated within the economy. The concept of a _____ is used in different contexts, so that the usage and significance of the term may vary.

Typically when business people and economists talk of _____s they are talking about person as _____, an aggregated commodity item with little individuality other than that expressed in the buy/not-buy decision.

   a. Consumer
   b. 100-year flood
   c. 1921 recession
   d. 130-30 fund

3. _____ was a Scottish moral philosopher and a pioneer of political economy. One of the key figures of the Scottish Enlightenment, Smith is the author of The Theory of Moral Sentiments and An Inquiry into the Nature and Causes of the Wealth of Nations. The latter, usually abbreviated as The Wealth of Nations, is considered his magnum opus and the first modern work of economics.
   a. Adolf Hitler
   b. Alan Greenspan
   c. Adolph Fischer
   d. Adam Smith

4. _____ is the electronic delivery and presentation of financial statements, bills, invoices, and related information sent by a company to its customers. _____ is also known as other payment models based on consumer-to-business and business-to-business:

   - Electronic billingPP -- Electronic Bill Presentment ' Payment (typically focused on business-to-consumer billing and payment)
   - EIPP -- Electronic Invoice Presentment and Payment (typically focused on business-to-business billing and payment)

   a. ACCRA Cost of Living Index
   b. EInvoice
   c. ACEA agreement
   d. Electronic billing

5. In economics _____ is defined as the sum of private and external costs. Economic theorists ascribe individual decision-making to a calculation costs and benefits. Rational choice theory assumes that individuals only consider their own private costs when making decisions, not the costs that may be borne by others.
   a. Cost-Volume-Profit Analysis
   b. Khozraschyot
   c. Psychic cost
   d. Social cost

6. To _____ is to impose a financial charge or other levy upon a taxpayer by a state or the functional equivalent of a state.

_____es are also imposed by many subnational entities. _____es consist of direct _____ or indirect _____, and may be paid in money or as its labour equivalent (often but not always unpaid.)

 a. 1921 recession   b. 100-year flood
 c. 130-30 fund   d. Tax

7. To tax is to impose a financial charge or other levy upon a taxpayer by a state or the functional equivalent of a state.

_____ are also imposed by many subnational entities. _____ consist of direct tax or indirect tax, and may be paid in money or as its labour equivalent (often but not always unpaid.)

 a. 1921 recession   b. 100-year flood
 c. 130-30 fund   d. Taxes

8. In finance, the _____s between two currencies specifies how much one currency is worth in terms of the other. It is the value of a foreign natione;s currency in terms of the home natione;s currency. For example an _____ of 102 Japanese yen to the United States dollar means that JPY 102 is worth the same as USD 1.

 a. Interbank market   b. ACCRA Cost of Living Index
 c. ACEA agreement   d. Exchange rate

9. _____ describes a set of laws relating to domestic agriculture and imports of foreign agricultural products. Governments usually implement agricultural policies with the goal of achieving a specific outcome in the domestic agricultural product markets. Outcomes can involve, for example, a guaranteed supply level, price stability, product quality, product selection, land use or employment.

 a. Agricultural Policy   b. ACCRA Cost of Living Index
 c. ACEA agreement   d. Intercropping

10. In economics, a common-pool resource, alternatively termed a _____ resource, is a particular type of good consisting of a natural or human-made resource system, the size or characteristics of which makes it costly, but not impossible, to exclude potential beneficiaries from obtaining benefits from its use. Unlike pure public goods, common pool resources face problems of congestion or overuse, because they are subtractable. A common-pool resource typically consists of a core resource, which defines the stock variable, while providing a limited quantity of extractable fringe units, which defines the flow variable.

 a. Government monopoly   b. Price-cap regulation
 c. Common-pool resource   d. Common property

11. _____s is the social science that studies the production, distribution, and consumption of goods and services. The term _____s comes from the Ancient Greek oá¼°κονομῖα from oá¼¶κος (oikos, 'house') + vÏŒμος (nomos, 'custom' or 'law'), hence 'rules of the house(hold)'. Current _____ models developed out of the broader field of political economy in the late 19th century, owing to a desire to use an empirical approach more akin to the physical sciences.

 a. Economic   b. Inflation
 c. Energy economics   d. Opportunity cost

Chapter 19. Environmental Economics

12. In economics and related disciplines, a _____ is a cost incurred in making an economic exchange. For example, most people, when buying or selling a stock, must pay a commission to their broker; that commission is a _____ of doing the stock deal. Or consider buying a banana from a store; to purchase the banana, your costs will be not only the price of the banana itself, but also the energy and effort it requires to find out which of the various banana products you prefer, where to get them and at what price, the cost of traveling from your house to the store and back, the time waiting in line, and the effort of the paying itself; the costs above and beyond the cost of the banana are the _____s.

    a. Cost of poor quality
    b. Sliding scale fees
    c. Transaction cost
    d. Cost allocation

13. In economics, _____ refers to the ability of a person or a country to produce a particular good at a lower marginal cost and opportunity cost than another person or country. It is the ability to produce a product most efficiently given all the other products that could be produced. It can be contrasted with absolute advantage which refers to the ability of a person or a country to produce a particular good at a lower absolute cost than another.

    a. Hot money
    b. Triffin dilemma
    c. Comparative advantage
    d. Gravity model of trade

14. In economics, _____ is how a natione;s total economy is distributed among its population. _____ has always been a central concern of economic theory and economic policy. Classical economists such as Adam Smith, Thomas Malthus and David Ricardo were mainly concerned with factor _____, that is, the distribution of income between the main factors of production, land, labour and capital.

    a. Eco commerce
    b. Equipment trust certificate
    c. Authorised capital
    d. Income distribution

15. _____ involves processing used materials into new products in order to prevent waste of potentially useful materials, reduce the consumption of fresh raw materials, reduce energy usage, reduce air pollution (from incineration) and water pollution (from landfilling) by reducing the need for 'conventional' waste disposal, and lower greenhouse gas emissions as compared to virgin production. _____ is a key component of modern waste management and is the third component of the 'Reduce, Reuse, Recycle' waste hierarchy.

Recyclable materials include many kinds of glass, paper, metal, plastic, textiles, and electronics.

    a. Cash or share options
    b. History of minimum wage
    c. 2008 budget crisis
    d. Recycling

16. _____s (economically referred to as land or raw materials) occur naturally within environments that exist relatively undisturbed by mankind, in a natural form. A _____'s is often characterized by amounts of biodiversity existent in various ecosystems.

Mining, petroleum extraction, fishing, hunting, and forestry are generally considered natural-resource industries.

    a. 1921 recession
    b. 130-30 fund
    c. Natural resource
    d. 100-year flood

Chapter 20. Comparative Advantage and the Open Economy

1. The _____ consists of a number of economic theories which describe the nature of the firm, company including its existence, its behaviour, and its relationship with the market.

In simplified terms, the _____ aims to answer these questions:

1. Existence - why do firms emerge, why are not all transactions in the economy mediated over the market?
2. Boundaries - why the boundary between firms and the market is located exactly there? Which transactions are performed internally and which are negotiated on the market?
3. Organization - why are firms structured in such specific way? What is the interplay of formal and informal relationships?

Despite looking simple, these questions are not answered by the established economic theory, which usually views firms as given, and treats them as black boxes without any internal structure.

The First World War period saw a change of emphasis in economic theory away from industry-level analysis which mainly included analysing markets to analysis at the level of the firm, as it became increasingly clear that perfect competition was no longer an adequate model of how firms behaved. Economic theory till then had focussed on trying to understand markets alone and there had been little study on understanding why firms or organisations exist.

a. Policy Ineffectiveness Proposition
b. Technology gap
c. Theory of the firm
d. Khazzoom-Brookes postulate

2. The _____ is an international organization that oversees the global financial system by following the macroeconomic policies of its member countries, in particular those with an impact on exchange rates and the balance of payments. It is an organization formed to stabilize international exchange rates and facilitate development. It also offers financial and technical assistance to its members, making it an international lender of last resort.

a. International Monetary Fund
b. ACCRA Cost of Living Index
c. ACEA agreement
d. Office of Thrift Supervision

3. _____ is exchange of capital, goods, and services across international borders or territories. In most countries, it represents a significant share of gross domestic product (GDP.) While _____ has been present throughout much of history, its economic, social, and political importance has been on the rise in recent centuries.

a. Import license
b. Intra-industry trade
c. Incoterms
d. International trade

4. To _____ is to impose a financial charge or other levy upon a taxpayer by a state or the functional equivalent of a state.

_____es are also imposed by many subnational entities. _____es consist of direct _____ or indirect _____, and may be paid in money or as its labour equivalent (often but not always unpaid.)

a. 1921 recession
b. Tax
c. 130-30 fund
d. 100-year flood

5. To tax is to impose a financial charge or other levy upon a taxpayer by a state or the functional equivalent of a state.

Chapter 20. Comparative Advantage and the Open Economy

_____ are also imposed by many subnational entities. _____ consist of direct tax or indirect tax, and may be paid in money or as its labour equivalent (often but not always unpaid.)

- a. 100-year flood
- b. 130-30 fund
- c. 1921 recession
- d. Taxes

6. _____ was a survey conducted by the U.S. Department of Justice to gauge the prevalence of alcohol and illegal drug use among prior arrestees. It was a reformulation of the prior Drug Use Forecasting (DUF) program, focused on five drugs in particular: cocaine, marijuana, methamphetamine, opiates, and PCP.

Participants were randomly selected from arrest records in major metropolitan areas; because no personally identifying information is taken from each record chosen, the resulting data can be correlated to arrest rates, but not to the total population of persons charged.

- a. ACEA agreement
- b. ACCRA Cost of Living Index
- c. Arrestee Drug Abuse Monitoring
- d. AD-IA Model

7. _____ describes a set of laws relating to domestic agriculture and imports of foreign agricultural products. Governments usually implement agricultural policies with the goal of achieving a specific outcome in the domestic agricultural product markets. Outcomes can involve, for example, a guaranteed supply level, price stability, product quality, product selection, land use or employment.

- a. Intercropping
- b. ACCRA Cost of Living Index
- c. ACEA agreement
- d. Agricultural Policy

8. In economics, _____ refers to the ability of a person or a country to produce a particular good at a lower marginal cost and opportunity cost than another person or country. It is the ability to produce a product most efficiently given all the other products that could be produced. It can be contrasted with absolute advantage which refers to the ability of a person or a country to produce a particular good at a lower absolute cost than another.

- a. Comparative advantage
- b. Triffin dilemma
- c. Hot money
- d. Gravity model of trade

9. In economics, an _____ is any good or commodity, transported from one country to another country in a legitimate fashion, typically for use in trade. _____ goods or services are provided to foreign consumers by domestic producers. _____ is an important part of international trade.

- a. AD-IA Model
- b. ACEA agreement
- c. ACCRA Cost of Living Index
- d. Export

10. In economics, _____ refers to the ability of a party to produce a good or service using fewer real resources than another entity producing the same good or service..A party has an _____ when using the same input as another party, it can produce a greater output. Since _____ is determined by a simple comparison of labor productivities, it is possible for a a party to have no _____ in anything. It can be contrasted with the concept of comparative advantage which refers to the ability to produce a particular good at a lower opportunity cost.

- a. ACCRA Cost of Living Index
- b. International economics
- c. Index number
- d. Absolute advantage

11. The _____ is a term used for industries primarily concerned with the design or manufacture of clothing as well as the distribution and use of textiles.

Prior to the manufacturing processes were mechanized, textiles were produced in the home, and excess sold for extra money. Most cloth was made from either wool, cotton, or flax, depending on the era and location.

  a. 100-year flood
  b. Textile manufacture during the Industrial Revolution
  c. 130-30 fund
  d. Textile industry

12. _____ are legal property rights over creations of the mind, both artistic and commercial, and the corresponding fields of law. Under _____ law, owners are granted certain exclusive rights to a variety of intangible assets, such as musical, literary, and artistic works; ideas, discoveries and inventions; and words, phrases, symbols, and designs. Common types of _____ include copyrights, trademarks, patents, industrial design rights and trade secrets.

  a. Independent contractor
  b. Expedited Funds Availability Act
  c. Intellectual property
  d. Ease of Doing Business Index

13. The U.S. _____ (EEOC) is a federal agency whose goal is ending employment discrimination. The _____ investigates discrimination complaints based on an individual's race, color, national origin, religion, sex, age, disability and retaliation for reporting and/or opposing a discriminatory practice. The Commission is also tasked with filing suits on behalf of alleged victim(s) of discrimination against employers and as an adjudicatory for claims of discrimination brought against federal agencies.

  a. ACEA agreement
  b. AD-IA Model
  c. EEOC
  d. ACCRA Cost of Living Index

14. In economics, an _____ is any good (e.g. a commodity) or service brought into one country from another country in a legitimate fashion, typically for use in trade. It is a good that is brought in from another country for sale. _____ goods or services are provided to domestic consumers by foreign producers. An _____ in the receiving country is an export to the sending country.

  a. Incoterms
  b. Economic integration
  c. Import quota
  d. Import

15. The _____ is a labor union in the United States and Canada. Formed in 1903 by the merger of several local and regional locals of teamsters, the union now represents a diverse membership of blue-collar and professional workers in both the public and private sectors. The union had approximately 1.4 million members in 2007.

  a. ACEA agreement
  b. ACCRA Cost of Living Index
  c. AD-IA Model
  d. International Brotherhood of Teamsters

16. _____ is a comparative concept of the ability and performance of a firm, sub-sector or country to sell and supply goods and/or services in a given market. Although widely used in economics and business management, the usefulness of the concept, particularly in the context of national _____, is vigorously disputed by economists, such as Paul Krugman .

The term may also be applied to markets, where it is used to refer to the extent to which the market structure may be regarded as perfectly competitive.

Chapter 20. Comparative Advantage and the Open Economy

a. Quota share
b. Debt moratorium
c. Competitiveness
d. Countervailing duties

17. _____ is generally measured by standards such as real (i.e. inflation adjusted) income per person and poverty rate. Other measures such as access and quality of health care, income growth inequality and educational standards are also used. Examples are access to certain goods (such as number of refrigerators per 1000 people), or measures of health such as life expectancy.

a. Standard of living
b. Remuneration
c. 130-30 fund
d. 100-year flood

18. _____ is an equity (stock) exchange located at 11 Wall Street in lower Manhattan, New York, USA. It is the largest stock exchange in the world by dollar value of its listed companies' securities. As of October 2008, the combined capitalization of all domestic _____ listed companies was US$10.1 trillion.

a. 1921 recession
b. 130-30 fund
c. 100-year flood
d. New York Stock Exchange

19. In neoclassical economics and microeconomics, _____ describes the perfect being a market in which there are many small firms, all producing homogeneous goods. In the short term, such markets are productively inefficient as output will not occur where mc is equal to ac, but allocatively efficient, as output under _____ will always occur where mc is equal to mr, and therefore where mc equals ar. However, in the long term, such markets are both allocatively and productively efficient.

a. Law of supply
b. Co-operative economics
c. General equilibrium
d. Perfect competition

20. _____ is a type of trade policy that allows traders to act and transact without interference from government. Thus, the policy permits trading partners mutual gains from trade, with goods and services produced according to the theory of comparative advantage.

Under a _____ policy, prices are a reflection of true supply and demand, and are the sole determinant of resource allocation.

a. 100-year flood
b. 130-30 fund
c. 1921 recession
d. Free trade

21. In economics, market concentration is a function of the number of firms and their respective shares of the total production (alternatively, total capacity or total reserves) in a market. Alternative terms are _____ and Seller concentration.

Market concentration is related to the concept of industrial concentration, which concerns the distribution of production within an industry, as opposed to a market.

a. ACCRA Cost of Living Index
b. ACEA agreement
c. AD-IA Model
d. Industry concentration

22. The _____ is an economic reason for protectionism. The crux of the argument is that nascent industries often do not have the economies of scale that their older competitors from other countries may have, and thus need to be protected until they can attain similar economies of scale. It was first used by Alexander Hamilton in 1790 and later by Friedrich List, in 1841, to support protection for German manufacturing against British industry.
   a. AD-IA Model
   b. ACCRA Cost of Living Index
   c. ACEA agreement
   d. Infant industry argument

23. _____s is the social science that studies the production, distribution, and consumption of goods and services. The term _____s comes from the Ancient Greek oá¼°κονομῖα from oá¼¶κος (oikos, 'house') + vÏŒμος (nomos, 'custom' or 'law'), hence 'rules of the house(hold)'. Current _____ models developed out of the broader field of political economy in the late 19th century, owing to a desire to use an empirical approach more akin to the physical sciences.
   a. Inflation
   b. Economic
   c. Energy economics
   d. Opportunity cost

24. _____ is a branch of economics with three main subdisciplines international trade, monetary economics and international finance.

   - International trade studies goods-and-services flows across international boundaries from supply-and-demand factors, economic integration, and policy variables such as tariff rates and trade quotas.
   - International finance studies the flow of capital across international financial markets, and the effects of these movements on exchange rates.
   - International monetary economics and macroeconomics studies money and macro flows across countries.
   - Stanley W. Black (2008.) 'international monetary institutions,' The New Palgrave Dictionary of Economics. 2nd Edition.

   a. ACCRA Cost of Living Index
   b. Economic depreciation
   c. Index number
   d. International Economics

25. _____ was a predominant American integrated oil producing, transporting, refining, and marketing company. Established in 1870 as an Ohio Corporation, it was the largest oil refiner in the world and operated as a major company trust and was one of the world's first and largest multinational corporations until it was broken up by the United States Supreme Court in 1911. John D. Rockefeller was a founder, chairman and major shareholder, and the company made him a billionaire and eventually the richest man in history.
   a. 100-year flood
   b. 130-30 fund
   c. 1921 recession
   d. Standard Oil

26. An _____ is a type of protectionist trade restriction that sets a physical limit on the quantity of a good that can be imported into a country in a given period of time. Quotas, like other trade restrictions, are used to benefit the producers of a good in a domestic economy at the expense of all consumers of the good in that economy.

Critics say quotas often lead to corruption (bribes to get a quota allocation), smuggling (circumventing a quota), and higher prices for consumers.

   a. Economic integration
   b. Agreement on Agriculture
   c. International Monetary Systems
   d. Import quota

Chapter 20. Comparative Advantage and the Open Economy

27. The _____ was the outcome of the failure of negotiating governments to create the International Trade Organization (ITO.) GATT was formed in 1947 and lasted until 1994, when it was replaced by the World Trade Organization. The Bretton Woods Conference had introduced the idea for an organization to regulate trade as part of a larger plan for economic recovery after World War II.
   a. General Agreement on Tariffs and Trade
   b. General Agreement on Trade in Services
   c. GATT
   d. Dutch-Scandinavian Economic Pact

28. A _____ is a duty imposed on goods when they are moved across a political boundary. They are usually associated with protectionism, the economic policy of restraining trade between nations. For political reasons, _____s are usually imposed on imported goods, although they may also be imposed on exported goods.
   a. 1921 recession
   b. 130-30 fund
   c. 100-year flood
   d. Tariff

29. The _____ is an economic and political union of 27 member states, located primarily in Europe. It was established by the Treaty of Maastricht on 1 November 1993, upon the foundations of the pre-existing European Economic Community. With a population of almost 500 million, the _____ generates an estimated 30% share (US$18.4 trillion in 2008) of the nominal gross world product.
   a. European Court of Justice
   b. ACCRA Cost of Living Index
   c. ACEA agreement
   d. European Union

30. The _____ commenced in September 1986 and continued until April 1994. The round, based on the General Agreement on Tariffs and Trade (GATT) ministerial meeting in Geneva (1982), was launched in Punta del Este in Uruguay (hence the name), followed by negotiations in Montreal, Geneva, Brussels, Washington, D.C., and Tokyo, with the 20 agreements finally being signed in Marrakech - the Marrakesh Agreement. The Round transformed the GATT into the World Trade Organization.
   a. AD-IA Model
   b. Uruguay Round
   c. ACEA agreement
   d. ACCRA Cost of Living Index

31. The _____ is an important selective, mainly private, international organization designed by its founders to supervise and liberalize international trade. The organization officially commenced on 1 January 1995, under the Marrakesh Agreement, succeeding the 1947 General Agreement on Tariffs and Trade (GATT.)

The _____ deals with regulation of trade between participating countries; it provides a framework for negotiating and formalising trade agreements, and a dispute resolution process aimed at enforcing participants' adherence to _____ agreements which are signed by representatives of member governments and ratified by their parliaments.

   a. 2009 G-20 London summit protests
   b. Backus-Kehoe-Kydland consumption correlation puzzle
   c. World Trade Organization
   d. Bio-energy village

32. _____ in economics and business is the result of an exchange and from that trade we assign a numerical monetary value to a good, service or asset. If Alice trades Bob 4 apples for an orange, the _____ of an orange is 4 apples. Inversely, the _____ of an apple is 1/4 oranges.

Chapter 20. Comparative Advantage and the Open Economy

a. Price war
b. Premium pricing
c. Price book
d. Price

33. In economics, a _____ may be either a subsidy or a price control, both with the intended effect of keeping the market price of a good higher than the competitive equilibrium level.

In the case of a price control, a _____ is the minimum legal price a seller may charge, typically placed above equilibrium. It is the support of certain price levels at or above market values by the government.

a. Payment schedule
b. Labor intensity
c. Marginal profit
d. Price support

34. A _____ is an object whose consumption increases the utility of the consumer, for which the quantity demanded exceeds the quantity supplied at zero price. _____s are usually modeled as having diminishing marginal utility. The first individual purchase has high utility; the second has less.

a. Merit good
b. Pie method
c. Composite good
d. Good

Chapter 21. Exchange Rates and the Balance of Payments

1. In finance, the _____s between two currencies specifies how much one currency is worth in terms of the other. It is the value of a foreign natione;s currency in terms of the home natione;s currency. For example an _____ of 102 Japanese yen to the United States dollar means that JPY 102 is worth the same as USD 1.
   a. ACEA agreement
   b. ACCRA Cost of Living Index
   c. Interbank market
   d. Exchange rate

2. The _____ is an international organization that oversees the global financial system by following the macroeconomic policies of its member countries, in particular those with an impact on exchange rates and the balance of payments. It is an organization formed to stabilize international exchange rates and facilitate development. It also offers financial and technical assistance to its members, making it an international lender of last resort.
   a. ACEA agreement
   b. International Monetary Fund
   c. Office of Thrift Supervision
   d. ACCRA Cost of Living Index

3. In economics, _____ refers to the ability of a party to produce a good or service using fewer real resources than another entity producing the same good or service..A party has an _____ when using the same input as another party, it can produce a greater output. Since _____ is determined by a simple comparison of labor productivities, it is possible for a a party to have no _____ in anything. It can be contrasted with the concept of comparative advantage which refers to the ability to produce a particular good at a lower opportunity cost.
   a. Index number
   b. International economics
   c. ACCRA Cost of Living Index
   d. Absolute advantage

4. In economics, the _____ measures the payments that flow between any individual country and all other countries. It is used to summarize all international economic transactions for that country during a specific time period, usually a year. The _____ is determined by the country's exports and imports of goods, services, and financial capital, as well as financial transfers.
   a. Gross domestic product per barrel
   b. Skyscraper Index
   c. Gross world product
   d. Balance of payments

5. The _____ is the difference between the monetary value of exports and imports in an economy over a certain period of time. It is the relationship between a nation's imports and exports. A positive _____ is known as a trade surplus and consists of exporting more than is imported; a negative _____ is known as a trade deficit or, informally, a trade gap.
   a. Rational expectations
   b. SIMIC
   c. Marginal propensity to import
   d. Balance of trade

6. _____ is money accepted for exchange of goods in an economy. The prevalence of one money over another arises, usually, when a government designates through decrees that the government shall accept only particular notes and coins in payment for taxes. Typically, money of _____ consists of stamped coins and minted paper bills.
   a. Security thread
   b. Totnes pound
   c. Local currency
   d. Currency

7. _____ is a term used in accounting, economics and finance to spread the cost of an asset over the span of several years.

In simple words we can say that _____ is the reduction in the value of an asset due to usage, passage of time, wear and tear, technological outdating or obsolescence, depletion, inadequacy, rot, rust, decay or other such factors.

Chapter 21. Exchange Rates and the Balance of Payments

In accounting, _____ is a term used to describe any method of attributing the historical or purchase cost of an asset across its useful life, roughly corresponding to normal wear and tear.

a. Net income per employee
b. Salvage value
c. Depreciation
d. Historical cost

8. A _____ is the transfer of wealth from one party (such as a person or company) to another. A _____ is usually made in exchange for the provision of goods, services or both, or to fulfill a legal obligation.

The simplest and oldest form of _____ is barter, the exchange of one good or service for another.

a. Social gravity
b. Going concern
c. Soft count
d. Payment

9. In microeconomics, _____ is quite simply the conversion of inputs into outputs. It is an economic process that uses resources to create a good or service that is suitable for exchange. This can include manufacturing, storing, shipping, and packaging.

a. Production
b. MET
c. Red Guards
d. Solved

10. To _____ is to impose a financial charge or other levy upon a taxpayer by a state or the functional equivalent of a state.

_____es are also imposed by many subnational entities. _____es consist of direct _____ or indirect _____, and may be paid in money or as its labour equivalent (often but not always unpaid.)

a. 130-30 fund
b. 1921 recession
c. 100-year flood
d. Tax

11. To tax is to impose a financial charge or other levy upon a taxpayer by a state or the functional equivalent of a state.

_____ are also imposed by many subnational entities. _____ consist of direct tax or indirect tax, and may be paid in money or as its labour equivalent (often but not always unpaid.)

a. 130-30 fund
b. 1921 recession
c. 100-year flood
d. Taxes

12. In economics, the _____ is one of the two primary components of the balance of payments, the other being the capital account. It is the sum of the balance of trade (exports minus imports of goods and services), net factor income (such as interest and dividends) and net transfer payments (such as foreign aid.)

$$\text{Current account} = \text{Balance of trade} \\ + \text{Net factor income from abroad} \\ + \text{Net unilateral transfers from abroad}$$

Chapter 21. Exchange Rates and the Balance of Payments

The _____ balance is one of two major metrics of the nature of a country's foreign trade (the other being the net capital outflow.)

a. Current account
b. National Income and Product Accounts
c. Gross private domestic investment
d. Compensation of employees

13. In economics, an _____ is any good or commodity, transported from one country to another country in a legitimate fashion, typically for use in trade. _____ goods or services are provided to foreign consumers by domestic producers. _____ is an important part of international trade.

a. AD-IA Model
b. Export
c. ACCRA Cost of Living Index
d. ACEA agreement

14. In economics, an _____ is any good (e.g. a commodity) or service brought into one country from another country in a legitimate fashion, typically for use in trade. It is a good that is brought in from another country for sale. _____ goods or services are provided to domestic consumers by foreign producers. An _____ in the receiving country is an export to the sending country.

a. Import quota
b. Incoterms
c. Economic integration
d. Import

15. _____ is an equity (stock) exchange located at 11 Wall Street in lower Manhattan, New York, USA. It is the largest stock exchange in the world by dollar value of its listed companies' securities. As of October 2008, the combined capitalization of all domestic _____ listed companies was US$10.1 trillion.

a. 130-30 fund
b. 100-year flood
c. 1921 recession
d. New York Stock Exchange

16. In business and accounting, _____ are everything of value that is owned by a person or company. It is a claim on the property your income of a borrower. The balance sheet of a firm records the monetary value of the _____ owned by the firm.

a. ACEA agreement
b. Assets
c. Amortization schedule
d. ACCRA Cost of Living Index

17. In financial accounting, the _____ is one of the accounts in shareholders' equity. Sole proprietorships have a single _____ in the owner's equity. Partnerships maintain a _____ for each of the partners.

a. Net national product
b. Current account
c. Compensation of employees
d. Capital account

18. _____ is sometimes referred to as _____, actually it means Economic Monetary Union.

First ideas of an economic and monetary union in Europe were raised well before establishing the European Communities. For example, already in the League of Nations, Gustav Stresemann asked in 1929 for a European currency (Link) against the background of an increased economic division due to a number of new nation states in Europe after WWI.

Chapter 21. Exchange Rates and the Balance of Payments

a. Exchange rate mechanism
b. Euro Interbank Offered Rate
c. European Monetary System
d. European Monetary Union

19. An economic and _____ is a single market with a common currency. It is to be distinguished from a mere currency union, which does not involve a single market. This is the fifth stage of economic integration.
   a. Commercial invoice
   b. Customs union
   c. Free trade zone
   d. Monetary Union

20. In neoclassical economics and microeconomics, _____ describes the perfect being a market in which there are many small firms, all producing homogeneous goods. In the short term, such markets are productively inefficient as output will not occur where mc is equal to ac, but allocatively efficient, as output under _____ will always occur where mc is equal to mr, and therefore where mc equals ar. However, in the long term, such markets are both allocatively and productively efficient.
   a. Co-operative economics
   b. Law of supply
   c. General equilibrium
   d. Perfect competition

21. In economics, market concentration is a function of the number of firms and their respective shares of the total production (alternatively, total capacity or total reserves) in a market. Alternative terms are _____ and Seller concentration.

Market concentration is related to the concept of industrial concentration, which concerns the distribution of production within an industry, as opposed to a market.

   a. ACCRA Cost of Living Index
   b. AD-IA Model
   c. ACEA agreement
   d. Industry concentration

22. In economics, _____ is a rise in the general level of prices of goods and services in an economy over a period of time. When the general price level rises, each unit of currency buys fewer goods and services; consequently, _____ is also a decline in the real value of money--a loss of purchasing power in the medium of exchange which is also the monetary unit of account in the economy. A chief measure of general price-level _____ is the general _____ rate, which is the percentage change in a general price index (normally the Consumer Price Index) over time.
   a. Energy economics
   b. Opportunity cost
   c. Economic
   d. Inflation

23. _____ are potential claims on the freely usable currencies of International Monetary Fund members. _____s have the ISO 4217 currency code XDR.

_____s are defined in terms of a basket of major currencies used in international trade and finance.

   a. Quota share
   b. Bilateral Investment Treaty
   c. Special drawing rights
   d. Metzler paradox

24. The _____ is where currency trading takes place. It is where banks and other official institutions facilitate the buying and selling of foreign currencies. FX transactions typically involve one party purchasing a quantity of one currency in exchange for paying a quantity of another.

Chapter 21. Exchange Rates and the Balance of Payments

a. Covered interest arbitrage
c. Currency swap
b. Floating currency
d. Foreign exchange market

25. The U.S. _____ is a federal agency whose goal is ending employment discrimination. The _____ investigates discrimination complaints based on an individual's race, color, national origin, religion, sex, age, disability and retaliation for reporting and/or opposing a discriminatory practice. The Commission is also tasked with filing suits on behalf of alleged victim(s) of discrimination against employers and as an adjudicatory for claims of discrimination brought against federal agencies.
   a. ACEA agreement
   c. ACCRA Cost of Living Index
   b. AD-IA Model
   d. Equal Employment Opportunity Commission

26. _____ is a term used in accounting relating to the increase in value of an asset. In this sense it is the reverse of depreciation, which measures the fall in value of assets over their normal life-time.

   _____ is a rise of a currency in a floating exchange rate.

   a. AD-IA Model
   c. ACCRA Cost of Living Index
   b. ACEA agreement
   d. Appreciation

27. In economics, _____ is how a natione;s total economy is distributed among its population. ._____ has always been a central concern of economic theory and economic policy. Classical economists such as Adam Smith, Thomas Malthus and David Ricardo were mainly concerned with factor _____, that is, the distribution of income between the main factors of production, land, labour and capital.
   a. Eco commerce
   c. Authorised capital
   b. Income distribution
   d. Equipment trust certificate

28. Economics:

   - _____,the desire to own something and the ability to pay for it
   - _____ curve,a graphic representation of a _____ schedule
   - _____ deposit, the money in checking accounts
   - _____ pull theory,the theory that inflation occurs when _____ for goods and services exceeds existing supplies
   - _____ schedule,a table that lists the quantity of a good a person will buy it each different price
   - _____ side economics,the school of economics at believes government spending and tax cuts open economy by raising _____

   a. Variability
   c. Production
   b. McKesson ' Robbins scandal
   d. Demand

29. _____ is a term in economics, where demand for one good or service occurs as a result of demand for another. This may occur as the former is a part of production of the second. For example, demand for coal leads to _____ for mining, as coal must be mined for coal to be consumed.

a. Derived demand
b. Days Sales Outstanding
c. Leontief production function
d. Rate risk

30. The _____ proposed by John L. Lewis in 1932, was a federation of unions that organized workers in industrial unions in the United States and Canada from 1935 to 1955. The Taft-Hartley Act of 1947 required union leaders to swear that they were not Communists. Many CIO leaders refused to obey that requirement, later found unconstitutional.
    a. Multinational corporation
    b. Chinese correction
    c. Foreign direct investment
    d. Congress of Industrial Organizations

31. A _____ refers to any type debt instrument, such as a loan, bond, mortgage that does not have a fixed rate of interest over the life of the instrument. Such debt typically uses an index or other base rate for establishing the interest rate for each relevant period. One of the most common rates to use as the basis for applying interest rates is the London Inter-bank Offered Rate, or LIBOR
    a. Disposal tax effect
    b. Money market
    c. Moneylender
    d. Floating interest rate

32. The United States federal _____ is a refundable tax credit. For tax year 2008, a claimant with one qualifying child can receive a maximum credit of $2,917. For two or more qualifying children, the maximum credit is $4,824.
    a. ACEA agreement
    b. AD-IA Model
    c. ACCRA Cost of Living Index
    d. Earned Income Tax Credit

33. An _____ is a tax levied on the financial income of people, corporations, or other legal entities. Various _____ systems exist, with varying degrees of tax incidence. Income taxation can be progressive, proportional, or regressive.
    a. Income Tax
    b. ACCRA Cost of Living Index
    c. AD-IA Model
    d. ACEA agreement

34. _____ is a field of economics that studies the strategic behavior of firms, the structure of markets and their interactions. The study of _____ adds to the perfectly competitive model real-world frictions such as limited information, transaction cost, cost of adjusting prices, government actions, and barriers to entry by new firms into a market. It then considers how firms are organized and how they compete.
    a. Economic ideology
    b. Industrial Organization
    c. Inflation
    d. Economic

35. The term _____ describes two different concepts:

    - The first is a recognition of partial payment already made towards taxes due.
    - The second is a state benefit paid to workers through the tax system, which has the effect of increasing (rather than reducing) net income.

Within the Australian, Canadian, United Kingdom, and United States tax systems, a _____ is a recognition of partial payment already made towards taxes due. A similar concept exists (fr:Avoir fiscal) in the French tax system. This situation arises, for example, when standard rate tax has been deducted at source , but the tax-payer is subject to further taxation at a higher rate. It also applies in dividend imputation systems.

Chapter 21. Exchange Rates and the Balance of Payments

a. 100-year flood
b. 130-30 fund
c. 1921 recession
d. Tax Credit

36. _____s is the social science that studies the production, distribution, and consumption of goods and services. The term _____s comes from the Ancient Greek oá¼°κονομῖα from oá¼¶κος (oikos, 'house') + vÏŒμος (nomos, 'custom' or 'law'), hence 'rules of the house(hold)'. Current _____ models developed out of the broader field of political economy in the late 19th century, owing to a desire to use an empirical approach more akin to the physical sciences.
   a. Inflation
   b. Opportunity cost
   c. Energy economics
   d. Economic

37. _____ refers to an absence of excessive fluctuations in the macroeconomy. An economy with fairly constant output growth and low and stable inflation would be considered economically stable. An economy with frequent large recessions, a pronounced business cycle, very high or variable inflation, or frequent financial crises would be considered economically unstable.
   a. Income effect
   b. Export subsidy
   c. Export-led growth
   d. Economic stability

38. Preparing to rebuild the international economic system as World War II was still raging, 730 delegates from all 44 Allied nations gathered at the Mount Washington Hotel in Bretton Woods, New Hampshire, United States, for the United Nations Monetary and Financial Conference. The delegates deliberated upon and signed the _____ during the first three weeks of July 1944.

Setting up a system of rules, institutions, and procedures to regulate the international monetary system, the planners at Bretton Woods established the International Monetary Fund (IMF) and the International Bank for Reconstruction and Development (IBRD), which today is part of the World Bank Group.

   a. Heavy-Chemical Industry Drive
   b. Land reform
   c. Bretton Woods Agreements
   d. Dromography

39. A _____, sometimes called a pegged exchange rate, is a type of exchange rate regime wherein a currency's value is matched to the value of another single currency or to a basket of other currencies such as gold.

A _____ is usually used to stabilize the value of a currency, vis-a-vis the currency it is pegged to. This facilitates trade and investments between the two countries, and is especially useful for small economies where external trade forms a large part of their GDP.

   a. Law of supply
   b. Monetary economics
   c. Leading indicators
   d. Fixed exchange rate

40. The _____ is a monetary system in which a region's common medium of exchange are paper notes that are normally freely convertible into pre-set, fixed quantities of gold. The _____ is not currently used by any government, having been replaced completely by fiat currency. Gold certificates were used as paper currency in the United States from 1882 to 1933, these certificates were freely convertable into gold coins.

In the 1790s Britain suffered a massive shortage of silver coinage and ceased to mint larger silver coins.

Chapter 21. Exchange Rates and the Balance of Payments

a. 100-year flood
b. 130-30 fund
c. Gold standard
d. 1921 recession

41. In economics, the _____ of a good or of a service is the utility of the specific use to which an agent would put a given increase in that good or service, or of the specific use that would be abandoned in response to a given decrease. In other words, _____ is the utility of the marginal use -- which, on the assumption of economic rationality, would be the least urgent use of the good or service, from the best feasible combination of actions in which its use is included. Under the mainstream assumptions, the _____ of a good or service is the posited quantified change in utility obtained by increasing or by decreasing use of that good or service.

a. 1921 recession
b. 130-30 fund
c. 100-year flood
d. Marginal utility

42. In economics, _____ is a measure of the relative satisfaction from consumption of various goods and services. Given this measure, one may speak meaningfully of increasing or decreasing _____, and thereby explain economic behavior in terms of attempts to increase one's _____. For illustrative purposes, changes in _____ are sometimes expressed in units called utils.

a. Ordinal utility
b. Expected utility hypothesis
c. Utility
d. Utility function

43. _____ is the a method of technical and economic research of the systems for purpose to optimize a parity between system's consumer functions or properties and expenses to achieve those functions or properties.

This methodology for continuous perfection of production, industrial technologies, organizational structures was developed by Juryj Sobolev in 1948 at the 'Perm telephone factory'

- 1948 Juryj Sobolev - the first success in application of a method analysis at the 'Perm telephone factory' .
- 1949 - the first application for the invention as result of use of the new method.

Today in economically developed countries practically each enterprise or the company use methodology of the kind of functional-cost analysis as a practice of the quality management, most full satisfying to principles of standards of series ISO 9000.

- Interest of consumer not in products itself, but the advantage which it will receive from its usage.
- The consumer aspires to reduce his expenses
- Functions needed by consumer can be executed in the various ways, and, hence, with various efficiency and expenses. Among possible alternatives of realization of functions exist such in which the parity of quality and the price is the optimal for the consumer.

The goal of _____ is achievement of the highest consumer satisfaction of production at simultaneous decrease in all kinds of industrial expenses Classical _____ has three English synonyms - Value Engineering, Value Management, Value Analysis.

a. Monopoly wage
b. Staple financing
c. Willingness to pay
d. Function cost analysis

Chapter 21. Exchange Rates and the Balance of Payments

44. A _____ is a foreign exchange agreement between two parties to exchange principal and fixed rate interest payments on a loan in one currency for principal and fixed rate interest payments on an equal (regarding net present value) loan in another currency. _____s are motivated by comparative advantage. _____s were introduced by the World Bank in 1981 to obtain Swiss franks and German marks by exchanging cash flows with IBM.
   a. Foreign exchange spot trading
   b. Strong dollar policy
   c. Non-deliverable forward
   d. Currency swap

45. The _____ is an economic and political union of 27 member states, located primarily in Europe. It was established by the Treaty of Maastricht on 1 November 1993, upon the foundations of the pre-existing European Economic Community. With a population of almost 500 million, the _____ generates an estimated 30% share (US$18.4 trillion in 2008) of the nominal gross world product.
   a. ACEA agreement
   b. ACCRA Cost of Living Index
   c. European Court of Justice
   d. European Union

46. _____ in economics and business is the result of an exchange and from that trade we assign a numerical monetary value to a good, service or asset. If Alice trades Bob 4 apples for an orange, the _____ of an orange is 4 apples. Inversely, the _____ of an apple is 1/4 oranges.
   a. Price book
   b. Price war
   c. Premium pricing
   d. Price

47. In economics, a _____ may be either a subsidy or a price control, both with the intended effect of keeping the market price of a good higher than the competitive equilibrium level.

In the case of a price control, a _____ is the minimum legal price a seller may charge, typically placed above equilibrium. It is the support of certain price levels at or above market values by the government.

   a. Price support
   b. Payment schedule
   c. Labor intensity
   d. Marginal profit

Chapter 1
1. c	2. a	3. d	4. d	5. d	6. d	7. b	8. d	9. a	10. a
11. c	12. b	13. d	14. b	15. c	16. b	17. c	18. d	19. b	20. d
21. b	22. d	23. d	24. a	25. d	26. c	27. c	28. d	29. d	30. c
31. d	32. b	33. c	34. a	35. d					

Chapter 2
1. c	2. d	3. a	4. c	5. d	6. d	7. c	8. d	9. d	10. d
11. d	12. d	13. a	14. d	15. d	16. d	17. d	18. d	19. a	20. c
21. b	22. c	23. d	24. c	25. d	26. d	27. d	28. d	29. d	30. a
31. d	32. d	33. d	34. d						

Chapter 3
1. a	2. d	3. d	4. b	5. b	6. a	7. d	8. d	9. d	10. b
11. d	12. d	13. d	14. a	15. c	16. d	17. b	18. b	19. d	20. d
21. a	22. c	23. d	24. c	25. a	26. d	27. d	28. c	29. d	30. b
31. d	32. a	33. b	34. b	35. a	36. c	37. b	38. a	39. a	40. b
41. d									

Chapter 4
1. d	2. a	3. a	4. b	5. d	6. b	7. a	8. d	9. b	10. a
11. c	12. d	13. d	14. d	15. b	16. d	17. a	18. a	19. d	20. b
21. b	22. d	23. b	24. d	25. c					

Chapter 5
1. a	2. c	3. d	4. d	5. d	6. d	7. b	8. d	9. d	10. d
11. c	12. a	13. b	14. c	15. d	16. a	17. c	18. c	19. d	20. a
21. d	22. b	23. b	24. d	25. a	26. d	27. b	28. b	29. d	30. c
31. b	32. b	33. a	34. d	35. c	36. d	37. c	38. d	39. d	40. d
41. d	42. d	43. c	44. d	45. c	46. a	47. d	48. c	49. d	50. d
51. d	52. b	53. b	54. d	55. d	56. a	57. d	58. d	59. b	60. d
61. d	62. c								

Chapter 6
1. c	2. c	3. d	4. d	5. b	6. c	7. d	8. d	9. b	10. a
11. c	12. d	13. d	14. d	15. d	16. d	17. d	18. c	19. d	20. b
21. d	22. d	23. c	24. d	25. d	26. c	27. b	28. d	29. d	30. c
31. b	32. c								

Chapter 7
1. c	2. b	3. d	4. d	5. d	6. b	7. d	8. a	9. b	10. d
11. d	12. d	13. d	14. c	15. d	16. d	17. b	18. d	19. a	20. c
21. a	22. c	23. d	24. b	25. c	26. d	27. c	28. d		

ANSWER KEY

Chapter 8
1. c	2. a	3. c	4. d	5. d	6. d	7. d	8. d	9. d	10. d
11. d	12. b	13. b	14. a	15. d	16. b	17. d	18. a	19. c	20. d
21. d	22. d	23. d	24. d						

Chapter 9
1. d	2. d	3. d	4. d	5. d	6. d	7. d	8. a	9. d	10. a
11. c	12. a	13. a	14. d	15. b	16. d	17. b	18. d	19. d	20. d
21. d	22. d	23. d	24. d	25. d	26. d	27. d	28. a	29. d	30. d
31. d	32. c	33. a	34. d	35. d	36. d	37. c	38. d	39. d	40. c
41. d	42. d	43. d	44. d	45. d	46. d	47. d	48. d	49. b	50. d
51. d	52. d	53. d	54. c						

Chapter 10
1. b	2. d	3. b	4. d	5. d	6. d	7. d	8. d	9. c	10. d
11. b	12. d	13. d	14. d	15. d	16. d	17. d	18. b	19. b	20. d
21. d	22. d	23. d	24. d	25. d	26. d	27. d	28. d	29. d	30. d
31. b	32. b	33. d							

Chapter 11
1. d	2. a	3. d	4. d	5. a	6. d	7. d	8. d	9. d	10. a
11. d	12. b	13. d	14. d	15. b	16. d	17. c	18. d	19. a	20. b
21. d	22. a	23. d	24. a	25. d	26. d	27. a	28. a	29. d	30. c
31. d	32. d	33. d							

Chapter 12
1. d	2. a	3. d	4. d	5. d	6. d	7. d	8. d	9. a	10. b
11. d	12. d	13. b	14. d	15. d	16. d	17. b	18. d	19. a	20. d
21. b	22. a	23. d	24. d	25. d	26. d	27. d	28. a	29. d	30. b
31. c	32. a	33. a	34. d	35. b	36. d	37. a	38. c	39. d	40. c

Chapter 13
1. a	2. a	3. c	4. d	5. b	6. a	7. d	8. c	9. b	10. c
11. a	12. d	13. d	14. c	15. d	16. d	17. b	18. b	19. c	20. d
21. d	22. d	23. d	24. b	25. c	26. d	27. c	28. c	29. d	

Chapter 14
1. b	2. d	3. d	4. a	5. d	6. b	7. d	8. a	9. d	10. a
11. b	12. c	13. d	14. d	15. d	16. c	17. b	18. d	19. d	20. b
21. a	22. d	23. d	24. d	25. a	26. d	27. a	28. c	29. d	30. b
31. d	32. b	33. d	34. d	35. d	36. b	37. d	38. b	39. c	40. a
41. a	42. c	43. d	44. d	45. d					

Chapter 15

1. c	2. b	3. d	4. c	5. d	6. b	7. d	8. d	9. c	10. c
11. b	12. d	13. d	14. b	15. b	16. a	17. d	18. c	19. d	20. d
21. a	22. b	23. d	24. d	25. d	26. d	27. c	28. d	29. d	30. d
31. d	32. d	33. b	34. d	35. a	36. c	37. d	38. a	39. a	40. d
41. b	42. a	43. d	44. d	45. d	46. c	47. a	48. c		

Chapter 16

1. d	2. a	3. d	4. d	5. b	6. d	7. a	8. d	9. d	10. d
11. d	12. d	13. c	14. a	15. b	16. c	17. a	18. c	19. d	20. d
21. d	22. c	23. d	24. c	25. c	26. a	27. a	28. c	29. b	30. d
31. c									

Chapter 17

1. a	2. b	3. d	4. d	5. c	6. a	7. d	8. a	9. b	10. d
11. d	12. d	13. a	14. d	15. a	16. c	17. b	18. d	19. b	20. b
21. b	22. c	23. d	24. d	25. c	26. a	27. d	28. a	29. d	30. d
31. d	32. b	33. a	34. d	35. d	36. d	37. c	38. d	39. b	40. b
41. d	42. a	43. b	44. c	45. d					

Chapter 18

1. a	2. c	3. b	4. a	5. d	6. d	7. d	8. a	9. d	10. d
11. d	12. c	13. d	14. d	15. a	16. d	17. b	18. d	19. d	20. c
21. b	22. d	23. a	24. a	25. a	26. d	27. c	28. a	29. d	30. a
31. a	32. c	33. d	34. d	35. d	36. d	37. d	38. d	39. d	40. b
41. d	42. a	43. d	44. b						

Chapter 19

1. c	2. a	3. d	4. d	5. d	6. d	7. d	8. d	9. a	10. d
11. a	12. c	13. c	14. d	15. d	16. c				

Chapter 20

1. c	2. a	3. d	4. b	5. d	6. c	7. d	8. a	9. d	10. d
11. d	12. c	13. c	14. d	15. d	16. c	17. a	18. d	19. d	20. d
21. d	22. d	23. b	24. d	25. d	26. d	27. a	28. d	29. d	30. b
31. c	32. d	33. d	34. d						

Chapter 21

1. d	2. b	3. d	4. d	5. d	6. d	7. c	8. d	9. a	10. d
11. d	12. a	13. b	14. d	15. d	16. b	17. d	18. d	19. d	20. d
21. d	22. d	23. c	24. d	25. d	26. d	27. b	28. d	29. a	30. d
31. d	32. d	33. a	34. b	35. d	36. d	37. d	38. c	39. d	40. c
41. d	42. c	43. d	44. d	45. d	46. d	47. a